JAN 2 4 1990

TERRIBLE BEAUTY

A terrible beauty is born.
    —W. B. Yeats, "Easter 1916"

It is murder and death that make possible the terrible beautiful thing we call physical life. Life springs from death; life lives on death.
    —Padraic Pearse, "By Way of Comment"

Life out of death, life out of death eternally.
    —Maud Gonne, *A Servant of the Queen*

    —But it's no use, says he. Force, hatred, history, all that. That's not life for men and women, insult and hatred. And everybody knows that it's the very opposite of that that is really life.
    —What? says Alf.
    —Love, says Bloom. I mean the opposite of hatred.
        —James Joyce, *Ulysses*

TERRIBLE BEAUTY

Yeats, Joyce, Ireland,
and the Myth of the Devouring Female

Patrick J. Keane

University of Missouri Press
Columbia, 1988

Copyright © 1988 by
The Curators of the University of Missouri
University of Missouri Press, Columbia, Missouri 65211
Printed and bound in the United States of America
All rights reserved

Library of Congress Cataloging-in-Publication Data

Keane, Patrick J.
  Terrible beauty.

  Bibliography: p.
  Includes index.
  1. English literature—Irish authors—History and criticism. 2. Ireland in literature. 3. Women in literature. 4. Yeats, W. B. (William Butler), 1865-1939—Knowledge—Folklore, mythology. 5. Joyce, James, 1882-1941—Knowledge—Folklore, mythology. 6. Women—mythology. 7. Mythology, Celtic, in literature. 8. English literature—20th century—History and criticism. I. Title
  PR8755.K43   1988   820'.9.'89162   88-4792
  ISBN 0-8262-0686-7 (alk. paper)

∞™ This paper meets the minimum requirements of
the American National Standard for Permanence of Paper
for Printed Library Materials, Z39.48, 1984.

For permissions, see pp. 145-46

For Maura Keane Shortall
1905–1987

This book is dedicated to the memory of my aunt and godmother, Maura Shortall, whose conversation and correspondence over the years kept me aware of Irish history and of my Irish heritage. While she might not have been pleased with my emphasis, on *this* occasion, on Ireland as a Devouring Female, she would agree with the related emphasis on alternatives to physical force. Thus, while this book is not explicitly concerned with contemporary politics, it is also dedicated to those in Northern Ireland who, crossing sectarian lines and the divisive myths of Cathleen and King Billy, struggle nonviolently for peace with justice. I am thinking particularly of those in the Women's Peace Movement and of certain men and women in the SDLP, the Social Democratic Labour Party. The latter developed from a Catholic movement, and I should add that, given my own Catholic background, I am not unaware that there are more forms of violence than the gunman's. Yet, despite centuries of institutional violence and its legacy of bitterness and frustration, few Catholics in the North seek a solution through the gun and the bomb.

Reality is more complex than a stereotype, more complex even than an archetype; nor, as I stress at the conclusion of the Preface, were Yeats and Joyce simply enslaved or repelled by the image of the female as an enchantress who is really the "terrible mother." But my theme in this short book is Ireland as a Devourer. Varying a remark of Oscar Wilde, Yeats once said of the Irish "Cerberus" that it had "but two heads"—first Parnellite and anti-Parnellite, then pro-Treaty and anti-Treaty. Being (he continued) "sedentary and thoughtful," he had tried to achieve "a premature impossible peace between those two devouring heads" (Au 363). Catholic and Protestant, the mutually devouring heads in the contemporary North, have yet to learn that they are parts of a single body. But if peace is *still* "premature," is it "impossible"? Contrasting himself to his own muse and "terrible beauty," his Cathleen ni Houlihan incarnate, Yeats concluded this passage from "The Stirring of the Bones" by acknowledging the tragic fascination of revolutionary violence: "Maud Gonne was not sedentary." It is hardly necessary to add that hope for Northern Ireland lies not with the violent or with those who are "sedentary and thoughtful," but with those who are active and thoughtful. Of course, I hope that in pursuing my theme and in stressing the human cost of violence I have not conveyed any insensitivity to the reality of oppression.

Acknowledgments

In addition to my Aunt Maura, I'd like to mention two younger women: Elizabeth Costello, who saved me from several errors, some of a prose nature; and Annie Everson, who has read much of my work over the years and whose affectionate encouragement has meant much to me.

I'm also grateful to Robert Boyers, George M. Harper, William H. O'Donnell, and Mary M. Lago, who read the first complete draft, and to several Le Moyne colleagues who offered encouragement, help, or both. Along with the participants in the Myth and Politics seminar mentioned in the Preface, they include Jyotsna Singh, Jonathan Schonsheck, and, especially, David Lloyd, who directed me to valuable material on the sheela-na-gigs. I'm happy to acknowledge, once again, the support of the Faculty Research and Development Committee of Le Moyne College.

P.J.K.
March 1988
Syracuse, N.Y.

Contents

Acknowledgments, vi

Preface, ix

1. Cathleen ni Houlihan, 1

2. Priestesses of the Great Mother, 23

3. Devouring Ireland, 49

4. The Cries of the Perishing, 82

Epilogue, 100

Appendix: *Cathleen ni Houlihan*, 103

Notes, 113

Works Cited, 132

Index, 140

Permissions, 145

Abbreviations

References to the work of Yeats and Joyce are abbreviated and included parenthetically in the text. Standard editions and abbreviations used are as follows:

Yeats

Au   *   *Autobiographies*. London: Macmillan, 1955.
E&I   *   *Essays and Introductions*. London and New York: Macmillan, 1961.
Ex   *   *Explorations*. London: Macmillan, 1962; New York: Macmillan, 1963.
LY   *   *The Letters of W. B. Yeats*. Edited by Allan Wade. London: Rupert Hart-Davis, 1954; New York: Macmillan, 1955.
Mem   *   *Memoirs*. Edited by Denis Donoghue. London: Macmillan, 1972; New York: Macmillan, 1973.
Myth   *   *Mythologies*. London and New York: Macmillan, 1959.
UP1   *   *Uncollected Prose by W. B. Yeats*, vol. 1. Edited by John P. Frayne. London: Macmillan, 1970; New York: Columbia University Press, 1970.
V-B   *   *A Vision*. London: Macmillan, 1962.
VP   *   *The Variorum Edition of the Poems of W. B. Yeats*. Edited by Peter Allt and Russell K. Alspach. New York: Macmillan, 1957.
VPl   *   *The Variorum Edition of the Plays of W. B. Yeats*. Edited by Russell K. Alspach. London and New York: Macmillan, 1966.

Joyce

CW   *   *The Critical Writings of James Joyce*. Edited by Ellsworth Mason and Richard Ellmann. New York: Viking, 1959.
D   *   *Dubliners*. Edited by Robert Scholes in consultation with Richard Ellmann. New York: Viking, 1967.
FW   *   *Finnegans Wake*. New York: Viking; London: Faber and Faber, 1939.
GJ   *   *Giacomo Joyce*. Edited by Richard Ellmann. New York: Viking, 1968.
LJ   *   *Letters of James Joyce*, 3 vols. Vol. 1, edited by Stuart Gilbert. New York: Viking, 1957; reissued with corrections, 1965. Vols. 2–3, edited by Richard Ellmann. New York: Viking, 1966.
P   *   *A Portrait of the Artist as a Young Man*. Edited by Chester G. Anderson. New York: Viking, 1968.
SH   *   *Stephen Hero*. Edited by John J. Slocum and Herbert Cahoon. New York: New Directions, 1944, 1963.
U   *   *Ulysses: The Corrected Text*. Edited by Hans Walter Gabler, with Wolfhard Steppe and Claus Melchior. New York: Random House, 1986.

Preface

We look up at her
hunkered into her angle
under the eaves.

She bears the whole stone burden
on the small of her back and shoulders
and pinioned elbows,

the astute mouth, the gripping fingers
saying push, push hard,
push harder.

As the hips go high
her big tadpole forehead
is rounded out in sunlight.

And here beside her are two birds,
a rabbit's head, a ram's,
a mouth devouring heads.

    —Seamus Heaney[1]

    This book comes bearing more than vestigial traces of its genesis: a Le Moyne College Faculty Seminar on "Myth and Politics" directed by Professor Barron Boyd of the political science department. One of the participants, Professor Susan Bordo of the philosophy department, was working on a project examining contemporary ramifications of the myth of the Devouring Female. My own project—having to do with Yeats, Joyce, and the lethal political mythology of modern Ireland—underwent a gradual transmogrification: the subject remained the same, but my thematic focus became Ireland as Terrible Mother or, more specifically, Ireland as one of Susan's Devouring Females.

    More than serendipity was involved. After all, in both *A Portrait of the Artist as a Young Man* and *Ulysses*, Joyce's alter ego Stephen Dedalus refers bitterly to Ireland as "the old sow that eats her farrow." Furthermore, the figure at the center of Irish political mythology, Charles Stewart Parnell, is presented by both Yeats and Joyce as a scapegoat hero torn to pieces and devoured by a collective Ireland represented by female figures. There is also the negative aspect of "Ireland herself," Cathleen ni Houlihan, as presented in Yeats's 1902 play, the central document in the specifically political history of the Irish Literary Revival.

    Yeats's play has been treasured as *the* literary embodiment of Irish Nationalism, cherished almost as a "sacrament" or, as Con Markiewicz called it from her prison cell, "gospel." For Yeats—to complete this religious imagery—it was at once a labor of love and part of what he referred to in a letter to Lady Gregory as "the baptism of the gutter" (LY 339). Because it may provoke resistance, and because the remainder of the book rests heavily on *Joyce's* negative treatment of Yeats's Old Woman, I begin with a subversive, almost deconstructive, reading of *Cathleen ni Houlihan,* placing it in the context of Yeats's personal, artistic, and political life at the time and allying the central figure with what Erich Neumann calls "the negative elementary character" of the Great Mother.[2]

In the case of Yeats's Old Woman transformed into a young girl with "the walk of a queen," there are, of course, "positive" elements as well. But in her negative, destructive aspect, I shall be arguing, she bears comparison with three Celtic versions of the Terrible Mother: the "Leanhaun Shee," the Morrigu, and Sheela-na-gig.

The latter we have already encountered, visually and verbally. The grotesque devourer described by Heaney in part 1 of his poem "Sheelagh na Gig" is the Celtic goddess of creation and destruction, a Kali-like vulva-woman whose "blatant sexual nature relates to male fear-fantasies of the devouring mother."[3] In the introductory material to his compilation *Fairy and Folk Tales of Irish Peasantry* (1888) and in the theosophical magazine *Lucifer* (15 January 1889), Yeats described the Leanhaun Shee as a solitary fairy mistress who

> seeks the love of men. If they refuse, she is their slave; if they consent, they are hers. . . . Her lovers waste away, for she lives on their life. Most of the Gaelic poets, down to quite recent times, have had a Leanhaun Shee, for she gives inspiration to her slaves. She is the Gaelic Muse, this malignant fairy. Her lovers, the Gaelic poets, died young. She grew restless, and carried them away to other worlds, for death does not destroy her power.[4]

This inspiring but destructive Gaelic muse is associated, on the archetypal level, with the Terrible Mother; Robert Graves's lunar muse—Cerridwen, the Welsh White Goddess—is her closest equivalent. On the personal level, she was incarnate, for Yeats, in his own muse, Maud Gonne.

The Morrigu, one-eyed and with the head of a crow, is the Celtic goddess of war. It is she who, in Yeats's final play, *The Death of Cuchulain,* dances before the severed head of Ireland's, and Yeats's, principal hero. Presiding over the cycle of life and death, she boasts in the play's climactic line: "I arranged the dance." Like the Germanic Valkyries and other ancient demons of war and death, the Morrigu is identified with the crow or raven, "the dark bird of the dead." The Terrible Mother as Earth Mother, writes Neumann, is a "goddess of death," the "devourer of the dead bodies of mankind" described in the Egyptian Book of the Dead. In addition she is, "in her aspect as bird of the dead, vulture and raven. The vulture is the symbol of Nekhbet, one of the oldest mother goddesses of Egypt, who in her good aspect watches over the dead in the underworld but originally rends bodies in pieces like the corpse-devouring crow, a form of the Celtic enchantress-goddess Morrigan."[5]

A cognate creature is the sow: Joyce's old sow that eats her own farrow; the Welsh sow who, in the fourth branch of the *Mabinogi*, eats the putrefied flesh of the male hero; those "old Celtic boars and sows" referred to by Yeats in his note to "The Valley of the Black Pig"—all of them going back to ancient Egyptian and other Mediterranean versions of the Earth and Sky Goddess as an offspring-devouring sow.

There are other bestial devourers. In the scene featuring the most terrifying Terrible Mother in Joyce's work, Stephen Dedalus addresses the ghost of his own mother as "ghoul," "hyena," and "corpsechewer"; she is also a crab, her claws resembling those of the Terrible Mother as "crab-woman." Glancingly but revealingly, Yeats and Joyce both touch on the image of the Devouring Female as spider. Jung describes the initiatory labyrinth as a net with the Terrible Mother as a spider at its center. Once men advance beyond the initiatory stage in their relationship with the Great Mother, they become what Neumann calls "strugglers" in the web of "the spider," the ensnaring "witch character of the negative mother."[6] Yeats speaks, in "Solomon and the Witch," of "love" having "a spider's eye / To find out some appropriate pain" (VP 388); and Joyce repressed a connection between Molly Bloom and the female spider who destroys her mate after copulation. As Penelope, Molly is a weaver of webs. So are spiders, "and female spiders," as Joyce reminded himself in his working notes for the "Penelope" episode, "devour their mates after sexual intercourse"—though in this case it would have been the husband, Leopold Bloom, rather than the lover, Blazes Boylan, "who is eaten."[7] However ambiguous she is, Molly seems sufficiently "positive" to make us applaud Joyce's decision to delete the spider analogue. Yet even as she stands, or lies, in "Penelope," Molly has been described by at least one prominent if rather puritanical critic as a whorish, rapacious female who "would devour any man," a "great lust-lump" and "symbol of the immutable animality of womankind," an "eternally recurring version of Sheela-na-gig."[8]

n more than "mere images" (VP 373). Whatever her manifesta-
⸺w-headed, allied with spider, snake, hyena, or sow—the Devouring
Female is a subdivision of the Terrible Mother, the destructive aspect of the
Magna Mater. As Leanhaun Shee or White Goddess, she is the muse of the
poets she inspires and inevitably destroys, a Celtic enchantress who, in her
warrior role, is allied with the Morrigu. The coalescence is uniquely complete
in Yeats's Cathleen ni Houlihan: the Old Woman rejuvenated by the blood of
young men she lures into battle, and played onstage by Yeats's own femme
fatale and destructive Helen of Troy, Maud Gonne.

As comparative mythologists (Eliot called them the co-inventors of the "mythical method") and as writers equally immersed in the fin de siècle, Yeats and Joyce were fascinated by the irresistible, often fatal power of the Female. Much of Yeats's work is a series of variations on the relationship of poet and muse, and Joyce's obsession with the positive and negative aspects of the Female, a dominant theme in his published work, is even more strikingly evident in the prose sketchbook he kept locked up in his desk in Trieste: a reverie on a devouring seductress published twenty-seven years after his death as *Giacomo Joyce*. These Yeatsian and Joycean reveries, whether languid or excited, can seem as dated as the Decadence. But the dread and fascination attending the archetype are restricted neither to primordial Devourers nor to the Consuming Woman of the fin de siècle. William Safire reported in 1987 that readers of his "On Language" column, challenged to come up with a female equivalent of *womanizer*, voted overwhelmingly for *man-eater*.⁹

From the Hindu goddess Kali and the Kali-like Celtic goddess Sheela-na-gig to Salome, destroyer of the Baptist and darling of the Decadence, the Fatal Woman is a decapitator, the priestess of man's severed head. In his fin-de-siècle volume *The Wind Among the Reeds* (1899) and in the late dance plays written almost forty years afterward, Yeats presents us with the head-huntress as young queen. His commentary on *The King of the Great Clock Tower*, the first version of *A Full Moon in March*, reveals Yeats's sources in the fin de siècle, in Gaelic legend, and in the archaic rituals he had studied, in the nineties, in the two-volume edition of Frazer's *The Golden Bough*:

The dance with the severed head suggests the central idea of Wilde's Salome. Wilde took it from Heine who has somewhere described Salome in hell throwing into the air the head of John the Baptist.¹⁰ Heine may have found it in some Jewish religious legend for it is part of the old ritual of the year: the mother goddess and the slain god. In the first edition of *The Secret Rose* there is a story based on some old Gaelic legend. A certain man swears to sing the praise of a certain woman, his head is cut off and the head sings. A poem of mine . . . was the song of the head. (VP 840; VPl 1010)

The story in *The Secret Rose* was "The Binding of the Hair," and the untitled poem, which appears in *The Wind Among the Reeds* as "He gives his Beloved certain Rhymes," has the heart "Building" poetry of "sorrowful loveliness / Out of the battles of old times." The poet's labor is in sharp contrast to his muse's provocative languor. To make "all men's hearts . . . burn and beat," the beloved "need but lift a pearl-pale hand, / And bind up your long hair and sigh," for even the sea and stars (in the poem's final line) "Live but to light your passing feet" (VP 158). The beloved's "feet" are of more than "passing" interest in Yeats's poetry of the nineties—feet are associated not only with masochistic submission to his muse but also with that muse's identification with Ireland. For Maud Gonne was both a leading revolutionary and the very embodiment of Cathleen ni Houlihan.

In *The Wind Among the Reeds*, "He gives his Beloved certain Rhymes" is followed (two poems later) by a more celebrated lyric, "The Cap and Bells," which ends by evoking the young queen's hair, "And"—the final line again—"the quiet of love in her feet." In his American reading and lecture tour of 1920, Yeats persistently described "The Cap and Bells" as "the way to win a lady," while "He Wishes for the Cloths of Heaven" was the way to "lose" one.[11] The final lines of the latter ("I have spread my dreams under your feet; / Tread softly because you tread on my dreams") suggest why the "*quiet* of love in her feet" was a consummation devoutly to be wished—even, apparently, at the price exacted in "The Cap and Bells," in which a jester "dies" in yielding up his very being to the aloof young queen he abjectly and hopelessly adores. But "quiet" and "softly" notwithstanding, those feet do "tread." Wilde's Salome, "a princess who has little white doves for feet," is a headhuntress and devourer, "hungry for thy body" as she tells her victim. Salome's biblical sister, Judith, is ostensibly a heroine; yet the "haughty disdain with which the murderess pushes the bleeding head of her victim away with her foot" recalled, for a critic scrutinizing a sculpture of Judith and Holofernes, the ferocity of "one of those maenads who, in a similar fashion, used their white feet to batter the decapitated head of the divine Orpheus."[12]

If he was not engaging in either massive repression or sardonic irony in describing "The Cap and Bells" (discussed at length below) as the way to win a woman, Yeats must have believed that Maud Gonne was to be won only through total sacrifice. Instead of the masochistic petition that his domina tread softly on *his* dreams, he would defer to *hers*—dreams not of him, as he was all too painfully aware, but of Ireland.

In the same year and in the same periodical in which "The Cap and Bells" first appeared (*The National Observer*, 1894), Yeats published a story,

"Kathleen-ny-Houlihan," featuring a poem said to be Maud's favorite among her worshiper's lyrics. Given the fin-de-siècle foot-fetishism just described, the central stanza, despite the pivotal "But," suggests as much similarity as contrast between stormy "angers" (compare Keats's "Or if thy mistress some rich anger shows") and the "quiet feet" of personified Ireland:

The wind has bundled up the clouds high over Knocknarea,
And thrown the thunder on the stones for all that Maeve can say.
Angers that are like noisy clouds have set our hearts abeat;
But we have all bent low and low and kissed the quiet feet
Of Cathleen, the daughter of Houlihan.[13]

The Cathleen ni Houlihan to whom *Yeats* bends low, to whom indeed he must prostrate himself if he is to "kiss" her "quiet feet," seems less Ireland than Maud Gonne, a muse whose feet necessarily concerned a poet who had spread his dreams under them. Conceived eight years later, *Cathleen ni Houlihan* is the only other work by Yeats that so much as mentions Cathleen by name. Written for and featuring Maud Gonne in the title role, the play is, whatever its patriotic aspects, a poet's offering to his muse, a "Gaelic Muse" or Leanhaun Shee in the flesh. Like the jester of "The Cap and Bells," Yeats here offered Maud his genius in a form, finally, acceptable to her.

But how could Yeats have made the play into a form fully acceptable to *himself*? Despite his pride in having for once deeply moved a popular audience, he was filled with the misgivings that attained their most memorable form in the famous question asked in a poem completed just three months before his own death: "Did that play of mine send out / Certain men the English shot?" (VP 632). Nothing is more characteristic of Yeatsian dialectic than to have things both ways, to take away with the left hand what is given with the right. In *Cathleen ni Houlihan*, I believe, a poet and playwright committed to art rather than Nationalist propaganda managed to insinuate, beneath the sympathetic and patriotic appeal of the Old Woman portrayed by his beloved, the terrible truth of the sacrifice she was demanding: a call of country requiring a total sacrifice understood and rejected not only by Yeats but also by James Joyce and his fictional surrogate, Stephen Dedalus.

Working through the fin-de-siècle variations on the archetype of the Terrible Mother as blood-exacting goddess and tracking Joyce's parodies of Cathleen ni Houlihan in *Dubliners* and, particularly, *Ulysses*, have persuaded me that my original project, "Myth and Politics in the Ireland of Yeats and Joyce," and Susan Bordo's, on the myth of the Devouring Female, were, if not the same project, certainly mutually illuminating areas of investigation.

Preface

Three final prefatory points, or caveats, must be registered.

First, despite my thematic emphasis in this book, there is much to be said about the *positive* treatment of the Female in Yeats and Joyce. As I have stressed in *Yeats's Interactions with Tradition* (1987), the poet, though hardly a "feminist," expanded his imaginative, emotional, and intellectual range in old age by writing two moving poetic sequences from the perspective of women, the Crazy Jane poems and the relatively neglected *A Woman Young and Old*. Joyce reconciled the conflicting fin-de-siècle stereotypes of Whore and Virgin in the radiant image of the bird-girl in the crucial passage of *Portrait*; his *Ulysses* ends with the life-affirming "Yes" of Molly Bloom, which, while it has not won over every feminist critic, is certainly not negative; and the opening word of *Finnegans Wake*, "riverrun," evokes Anna Liffey, Dublin's river and the *Wake's* female archetype. *Finnegans Wake*, like *Ulysses*, also *ends* with a woman speaking; indeed, the book's disjointed, interruptive style has been recently described as that of a "feminine voice," a revelation of Joyce's awareness of an "un-Cartesian . . . discourse that lies outside male use of language."[14] Though fully aware that Joyce "created female monsters who may have fulfilled his need to feel betrayed or hounded or reconfirmed his suspicions of the pervasive power of the church," the author of the most thorough and best-balanced feminist study of Joyce concludes by stressing his exposure—in the earlier, "realistic" work—of the *conditions* that often *made* women domineering, and his reclaiming—in the later works, with Molly and Anna Livia Plurabelle—of "the sovereignty and power of the goddess as an image of woman, an alternate tradition offered by ancient Irish culture." Bonnie Kime Scott even finds, in the *Wake's* Issy, the "intellectual woman."[15]

The second point involves the reaction of feminist critics to the images of the Female, "positive" and "negative," in the work not only of Yeats and Joyce but of male authors in general. There was, to begin with, an inevitable and productive reaction to such male-founded archetypes as the Jungian *anima* and the "great mother" of Jung's disciple Neumann: these emphases were replaced either by female-founded archetypal images for woman or by a realistic refocusing on individual women characters. A synthesis is achieved in studies that confront rather than simply deplore the residual power of such archetypes as the Woman as Creator or Destroyer, as Nature or Muse. In a crucial 1975 essay defining the varieties of feminist literary criticism, Annette Kolodny warned against the sort of overreaction that would utterly dispose of "the images of Nature-as-Woman or Woman-as-Muse," images that "once held their own kinds of truths and worked forcefully within" a cultural milieu shared by men and women: "as such they will always be with us—an inheritance from our past, not to be annihilated or forgotten, but, with a new consciousness of their less attractive implications, to be transcended, superseded, or even subsumed into something else."[16]

These are guidelines not just for intelligent feminist criticism but for intelligent criticism, period. In what follows, I have tried to communicate a consciousness of the "less attractive implications" of both "Woman-as-Muse" and Woman-as-Mother Ireland, the old woman who, transformed into the young girl with the walk of a queen, lures men to their graves.

Of course, and this is the third and final caveat, to expose such "myths" is not necessarily to demythologize them. Though we can hope that they will be transcended, superseded, or even subsumed into something else, they remain an inheritance from the past. In Ireland, a country with a past longer and more embittered than almost any other, the myth continues to be lethal, continues to devour. The figure at the heart of the Irish myth remains Cathleen ni Houlihan, the embodiment of murderous innocence, heroine of the attractive and destructive romance of what Yeats called "Romantic Ireland." "Romantic Ireland," wrote Denis Donoghue in his 1986 collection *We Irish*, "is a myth rather than a fiction, a distinction that may be verified by thinking of modern Irish history as a drama at once romantic and revolutionary. I do not need to prove that people have acted upon the genre or category of desires which we call Romantic Ireland." Donoghue himself is unsympathetic to the position of Conor Cruise O'Brien, with whom he shares a transatlantic prestige and visibility exceeding that of any of their fellow Irish intellectuals. In a 1976 University College Dublin speech keying on Yeats's famous phrase from "September 1913," O'Brien, "disgusted by the consequences" of the myth of Romantic Ireland, had admonished his student listeners to "transcend it." This seems reasonable enough, but, for Donoghue, O'Brien is *too* reasonable, a demythologizer who leaves behind not only Irish myth but also Irish reality. The "secular, humanist" vision of O'Brien, Donoghue complains, "offers us a life without passion," amounting to an invitation not to transcend but to "disown" the Irish past. And that is impossible. As Donoghue puts it elsewhere in the book, "The past is another country; yes, but in Ireland it is the same country." Even if we agree with O'Brien, can we refute Donoghue? Or history?[17]

Indeed, as of this writing (March 1988), the myth is likely to become even more potent, an abstraction blooded by continuing injustice. With the Thatcher government's recent jeopardizing of the 1985 Anglo-Irish accord—

its dismaying failure to publish results of the official investigation of the members of the Royal Ulster Constabulary alleged to have pursued in 1982–1983 a shoot-to-kill policy, and, in February, the shocking parole and reinstatement of the one British soldier convicted of murder while on duty in Northern Ireland—the confrontation between Cathleen ni Houlihan and her Protestant counterpart, King Billy, seems destined to enter an even more ominous phase.[18]

1

Cathleen ni Houlihan

There is a sinking away of national feeling which is very simple in its origin. You cannot keep the idea of a nation alive where there are no national institutions to reverence, no national success to admire, without a model of it in the mind of the people. You can call it "Kathleen-ni-Houlihan" or the "Shan Van Vocht" in a mood of simple feeling, and love that image, but for the general purposes of life you must have a complex mass of images, making up a model like an architect's model. The Young Ireland poets created this with certain images rather simple in their conception that filled the mind of the young, . . . sensible images for the affections, vivid enough to follow men on to the scaffold. As was necessary, the ethical ideas were very simple, needing neither study nor unusual gifts for the understanding of them. Our own movement began by trying to do the same thing in a more profound and enduring way. . . . [But] the Irish people were not educated enough to accept as an image of Ireland anything more profound, more true of human nature as a whole, than the schoolboy thought of Young Ireland.
—W. B. Yeats[1]

He can't be intelligently political: he dreams of what the Shan Van Vocht said in ninety-eight. If you want to interest him in Ireland you've got to call the unfortunate island Kathleen ni Hoolihan and pretend she's a little old woman. It saves thinking. It saves working. It saves everything except imagination.
—George Bernard Shaw[2]

One has only to remember Yeats's Cathleen Ni Houlihan to realize that, for good or ill, the goddess is still with us in one avatar or another. . . . Historically it was to become increasingly difficult to distinguish between Church and Nation in the folk mind. The wheel had come full circle, and the two personifications, erstwhile mistrustful of each other, could be reconciled as one. Indeed so successful was the identification of one with the other that in the years before 1916 Eoin Mac Neill, Celtic Scholar and Commander-in-Chief of the Volunteers, also a devout Catholic, had to organize a special course of lectures to impress on the rank-and-file that Éire, or mother Ireland, or Cathleen Ní Houlihan, or whatever, was a pagan deity and that devotion lavished on her was idolatry. He could have spared himself the trouble; in whatever avatar, she was with us yet. Not only did she have her poets; she had her blood- sacrifice as well.

She has been demanding more of the same ever since.
—Maire Cruise O'Brien[3]

In October 1902, AE (George Russell) wrote to Yeats arranging for him to meet "the first spectre of the new generation." The specter haunting Dublin was twenty-year-old James Joyce. "I have suffered from him," wrote an annoyed but impressed Russell, "and I would like you to suffer." When Yeats accepted the challenge and agreed to meet the arrogant young genius, Russell told Joyce the poet "would be at the Antient Concert Rooms every night," where, Richard Ellmann tells us, he was "helping to rehearse *Cathleen ni Houlihan* and some other plays."[4] Joyce—who had, in "The Day of the Rabblement" (1901), criticized the Irish Literary Theatre for having "surrendered to the popular will" by catering to the "bulk and lungs" of an undiscriminating audience, "the rabblement of the most belated race in Europe"—preferred to meet elsewhere. In Yeats's famous account of the interview, he reports that Joyce, having read him some of his prose epiphanies,

began to explain all his objections to everything I had ever done. Why had I concerned myself with politics, with folklore, with the historical setting of events . . . ? I had been doing some little plays for our Irish theatre, and had founded them all on emotions or stories that I had got out of folklore. He objected to these particularly and told me that I was deteriorating.[5]

One target of Joyce's haughty dismissal was evidently *Cathleen ni Houlihan*, a "little play" concerned with politics and folklore and historically set in 1798. The play had been performed first in April 1902 and was published in *Samhain* in October—when Yeats and Joyce met, and when the play was again in rehearsal.

The setting for that rehearsal, the Antient Concert Rooms, is also the setting for Joyce's first parody of the play, "A Mother" (1905). The "Kathleen" of that story is, like the servant girl of "Two Gallants" and like other women in *Dubliners*, at once a character and an allegorical depiction of Ireland. The very name of the young singer and reciter of patriotic pieces, a name taken "advantage of" by her domineering mother when "the Irish Revival began to be appreciable" (D 137), allies her with Cathleen ni Houlihan, the most celebrated of the many female names for Ireland and especially current in the wake of the popular success of Yeats's play. Indeed, the allusion to *Cathleen ni Houlihan*, reinforced by the fact that the concert-manager is named "Holohan," is sustained throughout "A Mother," which Ben Collins has examined as an "exquisite" and "trenchant" burlesque of Yeats's "fervently patriotic play."⁶ There is more than burlesque of *Cathleen ni Houlihan* in *Dubliners*. When, speaking of the dead Michael Furey, Gretta Conroy tells her husband, "I think he died for me," a "vague terror seized Gabriel" ("The Dead," D 220). "As well it might," remarks Hugh Kenner,

> since Gretta had inadvertently quoted from the play which Joyce thought lay on the Irish imagination like frost: from *Cathleen ni Houlihan* [in which the Old Woman says of a man she "knew one time," now hanged]: "He died for love of me: many a man has died for love of me." "I think he died for me": Gretta Conroy does not know that she has echoed the words of sinister old Cathleen.⁷

Not only is Yeats's Cathleen detectable throughout *Dubliners*; *Ulysses* is replete with parodic allusions that are far more explicit. And Yeats's Old Woman, transformed in the curtain line to a young girl with "the walk of a queen," even appears in *Finnegans Wake*. "Who are you? The cat's mother. . . . What do you lack? The look of a queen" (FW 223). I agree with Kenner that Joyce brooded over "that metamorphosis" at the climax of Yeats's play and that "those words of Yeats were still ringing in his head" when he wrote this passage of the *Wake*. "The look of a queen, that is what Joyce rejects," Kenner rightly notes. Joyce "sees the old woman who beckons young men to go off and die, and not marry, and he will let no fine talk deflect attention from that."⁸ In *Autumn Journal*, published the same year as *Finnegans Wake*, Louis MacNeice described Cathleen ni Houlihan as "both a bore and a bitch," a "Mother or sweetheart" who inspires fantasies and "longings which / Are under a fatal tariff." But it is in *Finnegans Wake* itself that Cathleen ni Houlihan is most fully demythologized. She appears as "Kate Strong," a scavenger and widow wheeling a "dungcart" to her "filthdump"; her cottage—resembling the Yeatsian "foul rag-and-bone shop" with its "mound of refuse or the sweepings of a street, / Old kettles, old bottles, and a broken can, / Old iron, old bones, old rags" presided over by "that raving slut / Who keeps the till"—is full of "droppings of biddies, stinkend pushies, moggies' duggies, rotten witchawubbles, festery rubbages and beggars' bullets, if not worse" (FW 79–80).⁹

It is true that, for all his demythologizing, Joyce never fully escapes the myth of Cathleen and Romantic Ireland. As Denis Donoghue has observed, "A full account of Joyce's work in the deconstruction of Romantic Ireland would . . . eventually begin to deconstruct itself, and would find Joyce baptized by desire, as deeply as by revulsion, in the naivete he would officially expose."[10] Nevertheless, I would still contend, with Kenner, that Joyce's parodic echoings of *Cathleen ni Houlihan* constitute a significant motif in his work, one revealing his deep-seated revulsion from violent Nationalism and from Ireland herself as a devouring female: an aspect of the archetypal Terrible Mother fusing, as Kathleen and Mrs. Kearney do in "A Mother," Church and State, Roman Catholicism and Ireland. Furthermore, I shall argue, Yeats himself was haunted by the play, not only because of the bloodshed to which it eventually led but also because he must have wondered at times—despite his protestation that he was expressing, solely "for my own pleasure," personal "emotions about this country" (Ex 199)—about the motivation that compelled him, on this single occasion, to also cater to Joyce's "rabblement," a Nationalist audience less interested in art than in propaganda.

As in his cruelly accurate pun in *Finnegans Wake* about Yeats's "cultic twalette," Joyce pounces on a part of the truth in his satirical poem "The Holy Office," published in the same year "A Mother" was completed. There Yeats is "him that hies him to appease / His giddy dames' frivolities." Yeats's attendant ladies were Annie Horniman, the theater's financial patroness; Lady Gregory, who helped Yeats with the peasant dialect in *Cathleen ni Houlihan*;[11] and Maud Gonne, the poet's beloved, for whom he wrote the play and who played the title role. Together, Joyce claims in "The Holy Office," they "console" Yeats

> when he whinges
> With gold-embroidered Celtic fringes. (CW 149)

While none of the three ladies in question dominated Yeats artistically, he *did* offer up his genius to Maud Gonne when he wrote *Cathleen ni Houlihan*, an appeasement whose "Celtic fringes" were more than decorative. When he created the role of "Ireland herself" for "the most beautiful woman in Ireland, the inspiration of the whole revolutionary movement," Yeats appeared to temporarily ally himself with a *political* "fringe," with the extreme views of Maud Gonne and her Daughters of Erin, a Nationalist group founded by Maud and pledged "to combat in every way English influence . . . and to work for the cause of Irish Independence."[12] Both that manifesto and the description of Maud just quoted are from Máire nic Shiublaigh, a Daughter of Erin who went on to become one of Dublin's principal actresses and who based her own later interpretation of Cathleen ni Houlihan on the performance of Maud Gonne, "the very personification of the figure she portrayed on the stage."[13]

Cathleen ni Houlihan

Having decided that she must play a part in Yeats's "theatrical world or lose him for his country and herself," Maud had in 1902 "agreed to act in a play he would write for her on the condition that he give her Daughters of Erin the right to produce it."[14] The play was *Cathleen ni Houlihan*, and once it was put onstage, Erin was destined to be changed, changed utterly. There is no way to synopsize *Cathleen ni Houlihan* without coloring it with my thesis. Given that, and the play's brevity, it has seemed best to place it before the reader in its entirety (see the Appendix). It is set "close to Killala, in 1798," the "Year of the French," the year of the Great Rebellion in which Wolfe Tone and Lord Edward Fitzgerald lost their lives. Yeats and Maud Gonne had devoted considerable time and energy to organizing the centennial celebrations of the '98 rising; thus, when he wrote the play, four years later, it was inevitable that Maud Gonne should play the title role: that of Cathleen ni Houlihan, "Ireland herself."

Cathleen ni Houlihan seems transparent enough. It has been universally read, and seen, as a "fervently patriotic play," a "simple statement of faith," according to one critic, in which the "queenly spirit of Ireland," "in the cause of Irish independence," lures away the young man about to be married. Registering the characteristically Yeatsian contempt for materialistic comfort and money-grubbing, another student of the play concludes: "a narrow domesticity is vanquished by commitment to the cause of national independence."[15] Such judgments seem abundantly supported both by the play itself and by Yeats's comments at the time. In his response to questions submitted to him in May 1902 by *The United Irishman*, Yeats began by declaring, "My subject is Ireland and its struggle for independence." Into the house, consumed by dreams of prosperity and plans for both sons, comes the disruptive catalyst, the personification of Ireland herself as Cathleen ni Houlihan, and, Yeats continued, "the bridegroom leaves his bride, and all the hopes come to nothing. It is the perpetual struggle of the cause of Ireland and every other ideal cause against private hopes and dreams, against all that we mean when we say the world" (in VPl 234).

No poet, least of all Yeats, will want to endorse that world which is too much with us, getting and spending. Like every audience, like every reader, of the play, we respond to the siren call of the Old Woman and to the larger impulse of generosity that prompts Michael to commit himself to her cause. There are, to be sure, "private hopes and dreams" that cannot be reduced to materialistic and selfish complacency, and Michael's allurement by the spirit of Ireland comes at the highest of all prices. But Yeats handles these aspects of the situation delicately. "The little play," notes John Rees Moore, "hinted at the sorrow but showed none of the pain of self-sacrifice."[16] And yet—for with Yeats as with Wallace Stevens, there is always "an and yet, and yet"—those hintings at the sorrows of sacrifice extend to more than the martyrdom of Michael Gillane.

Yeats concluded his *United Irishman* interview with an important revelation of the play's thematic and emotional center: "I have put into the mouth of Kathleen Ni Houlihan verses about those who have died or are about to die for her, and those verses are the key of the rest." Those fatal songs or "verses" were again emphasized in Yeats's 1903 dedication of volumes 1 and 2 of *Plays for an Irish Theatre* to Lady Gregory:

> One night I had a dream almost as distinct as a vision, of a cottage where there was well-being and firelight and talk of a marriage, and into the midst of that cottage there came an old woman in a long cloak. She was Ireland herself, that Cathleen ni Houlihan for whom so many songs have been sung and about whom so many stories have been told and for whose sake so many have gone to their death. (VPl 232)

We shall return to the play's origin in "a dream almost as distinct as a vision." Cathleen's songs of death and dying, "the key of the rest," first appeared in print in *The United Irishman*, quoted by Yeats as epitomizing "the call of country" in contrast to "the call of the heart, the heart seeking its own desire."[17] He cited the verses, suggested to him "by some old Gaelic folksong" about "yellow-haired Donough," who will no longer be found "ploughing his field" or "building his barn on the hill" because he is

>   dead,
> With a hempen-rope for a neck-cloth,
>   And a white cloth on his head. (VPl 234)

He also quoted Cathleen's final songs of triumphant sacrifice. There shall be "wakes," "graves," and "buryings . . . to-morrow," but we are "not" to "make a great keening," because the martyrs

>   shall be remembered for ever;
> They shall be alive for ever;
> They shall be speaking for ever,
> The people shall hear them for ever. (VPl 235)

There can be no doubt that this is "the call of country"; but this call, when the country is Ireland, is invariably fatal, and Cathleen ni Houlihan, as "Ireland herself," is necessarily a femme fatale.

When one's nation is personified as beloved, mother, and Muse—Dana, Éire, Erin, Fótla, Banba, Dark Rosaleen, the Shan Van Vocht, Cathleen ni Houlihan—she is a necessarily ambiguous figure: a Triple Goddess at once creative and destructive, benevolent and malign, nurturing and devouring. When, in "Easter 1916," Yeats asked, "What if excess of love / Bewildered them till they died?," he was echoing Padraic Pearse, who frequently quoted the line attributed to St. Colmcille: "If I die it shall be for the excess of love I bear the Gael."[18] But the "excess of love" in Yeats's political poems is directed to Ireland specifically *as a woman*. Could we call back Ireland's dead heroes, we'd "cry 'Some woman's yellow hair / Has maddened every mother's son': / They weighed so lightly what they gave." That was in "September 1913"; in "Easter 1916," Ireland as beloved and as mother merges with the Yeatsian choral voice itself. The question as to when "sacrifice" will suffice is

> Heaven's part, our part
> To murmur name upon name
> As a *mother* names her child
> When sleep at last has come
> On limbs that had run wild.

The realist in Yeats recoils from this euphemism for the price paid by the heroes of the Rising. "No, no, not night but death"—perhaps "needless death after all," a sacrifice to a dream. But "enough / To know they dreamed and are dead," even if they were bewildered to the very end by that "excess of love." The crucial lines for my reading of *Cathleen ni Houlihan* come between the songs quoted two paragraphs earlier. There, too, there can be no mistake about the totality of the sacrifice demanded; yet the Old Woman claims that there will be abundant recompense. "It is a hard service they take that help me," says Yeats's Old Woman. "Many that are red-cheeked now will be pale cheeked. . . . They that have red cheeks will have pale cheeks for my sake, and for all that, they will think they are well paid." The "virtue" of Yeats's play, according to Elizabeth Cullingford, is that even after hearing the Old Woman say this, "the listener is convinced that Michael's sacrifice is not the kind that makes a stone of the heart, but a generous response to an irresistibly poetic appeal."[19] That is largely true. But, as Elizabeth Cullingford knows better than most, events proved that that irresistible appeal was more than "poetic" and that those who listened to it found themselves making a sacrifice in reality no less "generous" than the one Michael makes within the nonlethal confines of a stage play. Furthermore, "too long a sacrifice," no matter how generous, can, and *did*, "make a stone of the heart" (VP 394) in the case of the Irish revolutionaries of 1916, many of them lured specifically by the Old Woman of Yeats's play.

What lured *Yeats*, of course, was not only patriotism but love. In writing *Cathleen ni Houlihan* he was succumbing, not to Nationalist demands for a propagandistic theater, and not only to his own Nationalist "emotions," but to his desire to please, and appease, his muse. Yeats resisted, from start to finish, the Nationalist insistence that the Irish theater devote itself to the overt rousing of patriotic emotions. In the name of love, he may have violated his own priorities in the unique case of *Cathleen ni Houlihan*.

Of course, he explicitly denied that. Writing in 1905, he recalled being asked, at the inquiry preceding the granting of a patent to the Abbey Theatre, if "*Cathleen ni Houlihan* was not written to affect opinion." "Certainly it was not," he wrote. He had not asked himself how it would "strike" others, even though, a moment earlier in this *Samhain: 1905* essay, he had acknowledged that one of the burdens of the Irish writer is that he "must calculate the effect of his words before he writes them, whom they are to excite and to what end" (Ex 199, 198). That may be, as Yeats insists, an aesthetically illegitimate burden, an irrelevant impediment to pure self-expression; but can he really have given no thought to the play's likely impact, no thought about whom it would "excite and to what end"? Even if we grant that Yeats wrote the play to please himself rather than to rouse others, to express his own "emotions about this country" (Ex 199), they were only, as he says, "certain" of those emotions—emotions that were considerably more complicated than the emotions of the beautiful activist whose ardor the play seems to embody.

Yet, beneath its crowd-stirring appeal to patriotism, *Cathleen ni Houlihan* reveals the divided feelings of a complex man; even here Yeatsian art and ambivalence persist. That conclusion is based not only on the play's contexts (Yeats's relationship to Maud Gonne and his struggle to preserve the theater from mere propaganda) but also on the play itself and the connections Yeats established, perhaps not altogether consciously, between Cathleen and the Terrible Mother in three of that archetype's Celtic manifestations: Sheela-na-gig, the Leanhaun Shee, and the Celtic goddess of war, the Morrigu.

* * *

Like Padraic Pearse, whom he knew to have "a cult of Cuchulain"

("When Pearse summoned Cuchulain to his side / What stalked through the Post Office?"), Yeats was more drawn to the principal hero of Irish mythology than to Ireland personified as Cathleen.[20] He wrote several poems and a cycle of five plays centering on Cuchulain but only a single short story, a single poem, and a single play dealing with, or so much as mentioning, Cathleen ni Houlihan—and at least two of these were written for, and about, Maud Gonne. Though the play expressed his own commitment to Ireland's "struggle for independence" (*The United Irishman*, 5 May 1902), it embodied an appeal to violent revolution: a dream that was not his, but hers. Stephen Gwynn, one of the many moved and shaken by the opening performance, "went home asking myself if such plays should be produced unless one was prepared for people to go out to shoot and be shot."[21] It was a question that haunted Yeats all his life, one he asked publicly in that great poem "The Man and The Echo," written shortly before his own death:

Did that play of mine send out
Certain men the English shot?

If it was in part rhetorical, the question was neither insincere nor melodramatically self-aggrandizing. Yeats knew that his play *had* sent out men the English shot. In fact, the connection between *Cathleen ni Houlihan* and the blood sacrifice out of which Ireland arose as a nation is even more immediate than a case of myth becoming reality, though it is that as well. On the very day the Rising began, Easter Monday 1916, *Cathleen ni Houlihan* was on the Abbey program. Some of the members of the company, arriving at the theater to play "before the painted scene," found themselves enacting the drama of blood sacrifice not on the stage but in the streets of Dublin. But if Yeats was troubled, he was also proud of his own indirect but potent role in the national drama. In 1938, the same year he asked his anguished question about his own responsibility, Yeats also called on the nation to join him in praising once again those who came from "pit and gallery / Or from the painted scene" to fight and die "in the Post Office / Or round the City Hall"—such players-become-martyrs as the actor Séan Connolly, "the first man shot that day" (VP 608).

That is the third and much the best of the "Three Songs to the One Burden," a poem that ends by reminding us that "Patrick Pearse had said / That in every generation / Must Ireland's blood be shed." What is "genuine" in a poet like Yeats is not always identical with what is most humane. But no sensitive reader will confuse the rant and eugenic fantasies of these "Songs" with the true voice of poetry, the honest self-questioning of "The Man and the Echo." Still, when it came to *Cathleen ni Houlihan*, Yeats was characteristically divided. In this case, he was torn between pride and guilt: pride in having created the Irish Literary Revival's most effective contribution to Irish Nationalism, guilt over what the play had cost—eventually, in human blood; at the time, I believe, in terms of personal compromise. Even as he relished his ability to quiet the hostile Abbey mob during the 1907 *Playboy* riots by reminding them that they were being appealed to by "the author of *Cathleen ni Houlihan*," Yeats can only have been troubled by his realization that the audience howling down Synge's masterpiece was the same Nationalist mob, the Joycean "rabblement," he had brought to its feet five years earlier in thunderous approval.

One of the most enthusiastic applauders, Arthur Griffith, who three years later was to found Sinn Fein, had concluded his *United Irishman* review of *Cathleen ni Houlihan* by observing that the only thing that could strengthen "the National spirit" more than "the creation of an Irish theatre" would be "a victory on the battlefield."[22] As the work at the vital center of Irish mythology and of the Irish Nationalist movement, both theatrical and revolutionary, *Cathleen ni Houlihan*, "a thinly disguised call to arms,"[23] brought the battlefield very close indeed to the painted stage; it also brought Cathleen herself close to the Morrigu, the war-goddess and carrion-crow who feasts on the battle-dead.

In *A Vision*, Yeats has his persona Michael Robartes invoke the "dear predatory birds" of war (V-B 52), an invocation vulgarized when it was repeated in the raging prose of *On the Boiler* (1939). But Yeats's penchant, early and late, for apocalyptic violence should not blind us to his even more characteristic reticences. The "Angers that . . . have set our hearts abeat" in Maud Gonne's favorite poem beat more in the heart of the anything-but-"quiet" Maud than in that of Yeats, a person of "more skeptical intelligence," whose "virtues [were] the definition of the analytic mind" as opposed to Maud: "You, that have not lived in thought but deed, / [and so] Can have the purity of a natural force."[24] Even when, in the 1896 poem "The Valley of the Black Pig," he employed an Irish peasant myth popularly interpreted as prophetic of Ireland's final victory over her English oppressors, Yeats (as we shall see) ended in quiescent submission rather than by invoking an Irish Armageddon. His allegiances always included distinctions. In "To Ireland in the Coming Times," he wished to be accounted "True brother of a company / That sang to *sweeten* Ireland's wrong"—not necessarily to rectify it. It was a distinction perhaps lost on Arthur Griffith when, in attacking Synge's "un-Irish" *The Shadow of the Glen* and Yeats's 1903 defense of it, he exhorted "our greatest poet" to recover the Nationalism he had expressed in "To Ireland in the Coming Times."[25] Not that even that poem was invulnerable to Nationalist ire. When, on one occasion during the *Playboy* riots four years later, Yeats led into the Abbey Theatre members of the Dublin Metropolitan Police, outraged Nationalists rewrote for him his own celebrated lines:

Know that I would accounted be
True brother of the DMP . . .[26]

But he could still appeal to the rioters as "the author of *Cathleen ni Houlihan,*" a play that Griffith had hailed critically and to which some claim he contributed creatively. Griffith is reliably reported to have been transfixed at the final curtain, and there is even a rumor that he suggested the play's final line.[27]

Despite Griffith's political association, and infatuation, with Maud Gonne at the time, it is a rumor hard to credit. The play *is* that final thrilling line. Griffith *may* have made a suggestion; as his epigraph to the 1902 London edition of the play reveals, Yeats was recalling lines from James Clarence Mangan's "Kathaleen-ny-Houlahan":

Think her not a ghastly hag, too hideous to be seen,
Call her not unseemly names, our matchless Kathaleen;
Young she is, and fair she is, and would be crownéd queen.

Yeats, like Mangan, may also be recalling the transformation of the hideous old woman of the Celtic tale *Baile in Scail, the Phantom's Frenzy,* into "the most lovely girl imaginable, . . . the deified 'Sovereignty' of Ireland."[28]

In any case, the transformation of the Old Woman to a girl with "the walk of a queen" seems quintessential Yeats: at once an intervention of the supernatural into mortal life and the inevitable tribute to his own matchless Maud Gonne, who, with her superb carriage and great stature, certainly had the walk of a queen, indeed of a goddess. She played the role "very magnificently," wrote Yeats, "and her great height made Cathleen seem a divine being fallen into our mortal infirmity." Further, though "the most beautiful woman of her time," displaying no vanity, she " 'made up' centuries old" to play the role with utter "sincerity."[29] Stephen Gwynn has paid tribute to the double effect of this magnificence beneath decrepitude. At the play's end,

Maud's Cathleen rose, "still bent and weighed down with years or centuries; but for one instant, before she went out at the half-door, she drew herself up to her superb height; change was manifest; *patuit dea*."[30]

Yeats had given the theatergoers an Old Woman who elicited sympathy and gradually roused the blood; at the moment of incipient transformation, Maud Gonne, under Yeats's direction,[31] presented them, for an instant, with a woman for whom they would be willing to die, to give "all." The men in the audience knew what beauty, mythological and actual, was concealed by Maud Gonne's makeup and rags. Thus "Patriotism was invested with all the excitement of a sexual seduction so safely decent that not even the most respectable guardian of the Irish image could impute sinister or scandalous motives to it."[32]

But if the play was morally safe, it was hardly so politically. The company of *Cathleen ni Houlihan* was evicted from St. Teresa's Hall after a week by authorities aware of precisely what it was that the queenly spirit of Ireland was luring men into. Notwithstanding Yeats's insistence that the play was *not* "propaganda," it was in fact "the chiefest success ever of nationalist propaganda."[33]

Not even the most ardent Fenian could have asked for more. Certainly Griffith was pleased by a play that perfectly suited his priorities. Though never so frank as Maud Gonne in her demand for art as propaganda, Griffith did demand, as the Nationalist Davin does in Joyce's *Portrait*, that Ireland come "first," poetry "after" (P 203). Griffith may not have "suggested" Yeats's final line, but when, in that *United Irishman* article on *The Shadow of the Glen*, he took issue with Yeats, he reminded the poet of words he might well have contributed to *Cathleen ni Houlihan*. Defending Synge against Nationalist attacks in a *Samhain* article, Yeats had defined a "good Nationalist" as "one who is ready to give up a great deal that he may preserve to his country whatever part of her possessions he is best fitted to guard" (Ex 118). That was not good enough for Griffith: "He who is prepared to give up a good deal for his country is no doubt a good man, but unless he be prepared to give up all, we do not deem him a Nationalist." Griffith is echoing the very words Yeats put in the mouth of the Old Woman: "he must give me himself, he must give me all."

Yeats *had* given "all," not to Ireland, but to the woman who spoke those lines in *Cathleen ni Houlihan*. In terms of Nationalist politics, he would not do so again. In the *Samhain* article, Yeats responded to such attacks on the Irish National Theatre as those of Griffith and Maud Gonne, attacks made by those he called, in the next and last in the *Samhain: 1903* series, "friends, who live too deep in the labour of politics to give the thought to these things that we have given" (Ex 122). He was, Yeats wrote, capable of giving Nationalist thoughts "dramatic expression," and he was able to make *Cathleen ni Houlihan* out of "a very vivid dream" he had one night. But if he had been externally compelled to "write nothing but drama with an obvious patriotic intention . . . I would have lost, in a short time, the power to write movingly upon any theme. I could have aroused opinion; but I could not have touched the heart" (Ex 116). And he concluded the *Samhain: 1903* series by declaring, "One can serve one's country alone out of the abundance of one's own heart," writing with the aesthetic equivalent of the "sincerity and precision" of genuine revolutionaries, who would never "make a mob drunk with a passion they could not share" (Ex 123).

Maud could play Cathleen with the utter "sincerity" Yeats praised. But he himself, as his *Samhain* articles alone reveal, was too double-minded a man, too sincere and precise in his own way, to fully share the passion with which he made the mob drunk when he gave it *Cathleen ni Houlihan*. His subsequent reservations in the matter are abundantly clear, even before the famous question in "The Man and the Echo." "What if *excess* of love / *Bewildered* them till they died?" he asked of the martyred leaders of the Easter Rising, many of them inspired by that play of his that sent out men to be shot by the English—as well as the woman jailed by them. In her letters from prison, Con Markiewicz described Yeats's play as "a sort of gospel" for herself and her sister, Eva.[34]

Con and Eva, the "dear shadows" of Yeats's 1927 elegy, learned only in the grave "All the folly of a fight / With a common wrong or right." In life, they had, like Maud herself, grown "skeleton gaunt," an "image" of their fanatical "politics" (VP 475). Meditating on the Troubles, Yeats, as he admits, often fingered the chain of responsibility, wondering which links if any were "forged in my workshop." The one undeniable link was "that play," which proved less link than dynamite, its fuse sizzling in the patriotic mind. Lady Gregory, who herself played the lead part in three performances in March 1919, reports that even that most cosmopolitan of Irishmen, George Bernard Shaw, had been swept away by earlier performances of *Cathleen ni Houlihan*: "When I see that play I feel it might lead a man to do something foolish."[35] In *writing* the play, Yeats himself had been led—by his love for Maud Gonne—to do something that may have been "foolish." If so, it was just the sort of thing a "jester" *would* do for the "all"-demanding "queen" he adored.

I am alluding, again, to "The Cap and Bells," a Maud Gonne poem that had come to him in a dream, "more a vision than a dream" (VP 808). Yeats makes a similar claim of only two other works, the 1908 poem "His Dream" (VP 253n) and *Cathleen ni Houlihan*. "One night I had a dream almost as distinct as a vision," he began his description of the play's genesis (VPl 232). There is no reason to doubt him; indeed, his account suggests that the play is a variation on the *aisling*, a form of Gaelic dream-poem in which a visionary woman representing Ireland speaks of the day when she shall be rescued from her misery by help from beyond the seas. In Yeats's variation, the dreamt-of woman who is Ireland herself is to be liberated by the French landing at Killala. As Devourer, of course, she would be a parody of the visionary woman of the traditional *aisling*; and the play itself would be a sort of tragic counterpart of that great *comic* parody of the *aisling*, Brian Merriman's *The Midnight Court*. Whether or not *Cathleen ni Houlihan* is a parody of the Gaelic dream-poem, we should not let visionary dreams put us off the genetic track. For the psychological motivation behind the writing of the play, as it was behind the "dream"-poem "The Cap and Bells," remains Yeats's love of Maud Gonne.

What else but love could explain the paradox? In 1902 Yeats was struggling, as he would most of his life, against the Nationalists intent on reducing the theater he had founded into a bully pulpit for patriotism; for they knew as well as he that drama is "the most immediately powerful form of literature." How ironic, then, that he should be the man to write the play that, more than any other, fired the patriotic imagination of a people, thrilling them but also achieving at a stroke what he himself condemned in the *Samhain* series as the effect wrought by the life-denying "generalisations" and "partisan fictions" of Nationalist newspapers, whose sole aim was "to move men in squads, to keep them in uniform, with their faces to the right enemy, and enough hate in their hearts to make the muskets go off" (Ex 119, 120).

This is the single-minded, narrow, rabid Nationalism most memorably embodied in Joyce's crude and violent Citizen, the one-eyed Fenian of "Cyclops," who may not only represent Homer's Polyphemus but also stand as the male equivalent of Ireland's one-eyed Morrigu. Double-minded Yeats was as opposed as Joyce to this crude Cyclopean vision, described recently by Andrew Parkin as the "unintelligent, blinkered sort of nationalism Yeats and others had to combat in Ireland."[36] Joyce's answer to it and all it stood for, given Stephen in both *Portrait* and *Ulysses*, was "*Non serviam*!" Yeats, who elected to work in and for Ireland rather than escape to the Continent, was suspended between the Joycean *non serviam* and the positions of Padraic

Pearse ("patriotism needs service . . . 'I serve'") and of Maud Gonne, who described herself accurately in the title of her autobiography: *A Servant of the Queen*. Not of Victoria, of course, but of the "queen" envisioned at the beginning and end of Maud Gonne's book, the "queen" whose transformation is reported in the most famous line in modern Irish literature.[37]

But that transformation takes place offstage. Consider the *onstage* transformation required of Maud Gonne in Yeats's play. Again I quote Stephen Gwynn's memorable description of the impact of those first three performances in St. Teresa's Hall in April 1902: "Above all, Miss Gonne's impersonation had stirred the audience as I have never seen another audience stirred. At the height of her beauty, she transformed herself there into one of the half-mad old crones whom we were accustomed to see by Irish roadsides." That other, incipient, transformation that Gwynn described as "manifest; *patuit dea*" summons up the Goddess at her most magnificent. But *this*, the transformation of Maud Gonne, at the height of her beauty, into a half-mad old Irish crone evokes the Crone of Death, the dark, destructive side of the Great Mother. The Old Woman elicits our sympathy, yet she really *is* Mangan's "ghastly hag, too hideous to be seen." More specifically, she is a composite incarnation of the all-demanding Leanhaun Shee and of the one-eyed goddess who drives men to battle. And Maud Gonne is an appropriate embodiment of both manifestations: at once Yeats's Muse and *belle dame sans merci*, and an ardent Nationalist in whose "mysterious eye," as Yeats recorded with mingled fascination and dread, British journalists saw "the shadow of battles yet to come."[38]

In short, the Old Woman played by Maud Gonne is not only a supernatural enchantress but also a war goddess and devourer. In the play, young Patrick connects her with stories the local clairvoyant (Winnie of the Crossroads) has told of "the strange woman that goes through the country whatever time there's war or trouble coming." She had looked at Michael as she passed the cottage window, and it is he who, despite his premonition ("I'd sooner a stranger not to come to the house the night before my wedding"), opens the door, standing aside to make way for her. (As we know from Coleridge's *Christabel*, witches cannot cross a threshold by their own power.) Though aged, there is "no quiet in my heart," she tells the Gillanes; and the commotion in the town is "the noise I used to hear when my friends came to visit me." The friends on this occasion consist of the French force under General Humbert and accompanied by Wolfe Tone: the latest in the long line of those struggling to eject the "strangers in the house" and restore to the Old

Woman the "four beautiful green fields" (the original provinces of Ulster, Connacht, Munster, and Leinster) taken from her by the occupying English.

She "for whose sake so many have gone to their death" sings of those "who have died for love of me . . . some that died hundreds of years ago and . . . some that will die to-morrow." Michael's parents think to offer the famished Old Woman milk and oaten cake, even some money; but of course less than all cannot satisfy their visitor: "It is not food or drink that I want . . . It is not silver I want. . . . If any one would give me help he must give me himself, he must give me all." What she demands is a blood-offering; she sings of "the dead that shall be to-morrow," of the "red-cheeked" who shall be "pale-cheeked." Caught up in what Yeats would later call the "delirium of the brave" (that woman-inspired "excess of love" that has "maddened every mother's son" when the Mother is Ireland), Michael has forgotten his wedding: "What clothes will I be wearing to-morrow?" When Patrick and Michael's fiancée, along with a crowd of neighbors, burst in with the news that the French are landing at Killala, the clothes slip from Michael's arm and he looks at his fiancée "like a stranger." She puts her arms about him, and he is about to yield when the Old Woman's voice is heard outside, singing again that her martyr-heroes will be remembered "for ever." Michael breaks free and leads the neighbors after her. The Old Woman, in Patrick's report, has disappeared, replaced by "a young girl, and she had the walk of a queen."

Writing of *Cathleen ni Houlihan* in his memorial essay on Yeats, the poet's friend L. A. G. Strong observed that the play "convinces from the first word to the last, and mounts to a curtain which shook the heart of Ireland and sends a thrill up an audience's spine today."[39] He was writing in 1939, thirty-seven years after Maud Gonne had first electrified the audience. By then it was long since clear that Yeats's mythmaking had sent out men to be shot and that, during the "Troubles," the resultant "terrible beauty" had begun (in Sean O'Casey's phrase) "to lose her good looks."[40] Whatever his own responsibility, Yeats suggests even in the play that *ultimate* responsibility lies with Cathleen ni Houlihan in her destructive aspect as Dark and Terrible Mother. For her sake, Michael *will* be dressed "to-morrow" in his best garments, not his wedding suit but his grave clothes; and he will lie, not in the bed of mortal love, but in the devouring womb of the grave, of the hungry earth-mother who consumes her own children and exacts their blood. The old crone who is "Ireland herself" becomes "a young girl" because she has been rejuvenated by the prospect of fresh blood, by an infusion from those who, seduced from their marriage beds, die for love of her. It is not milk or bread or silver she wants, but blood. For her sake, the red-cheeked will be "pale-cheeked," like Keats's knight at arms on "whose cheeks a fading rose / Fast withereth" and who sees in his dream the past victims of the enchantress, "Pale warriors, death pale were they all."[41] Ireland's martyrs will be pale-cheeked for Cathleen ni Houlihan is a vampire, a blood-drinking goddess of death and of war who perpetually demands total sacrifice of her warrior sons and lovers.

Joyce's friend, C. P. Curran, writing in the anticlimactic years following the "Troubles," described "Kathleen ni Houlihan [as] a vampire hag of Beare, . . . we lie in mortmain. The words of dead men, the reliques of a bogus tradition, hold us in fetters."[42] Glossing his reference to "Clooth-na-Bare" in the line following those I quoted from the poem in his short story "Kathleen-ny-Houlihan," Yeats wrote: "Doubtless Clooth-na-Bare should be Cailleac Beare, which would mean the Old Woman Beare, . . . a very famous person, perhaps the Mother of the Gods herself" (Myth 79). As blood-exacting queen, Cathleen ni Houlihan assumes the negative aspect of the Great Mother, a Celtic Kali (Kali as the death-goddess Kalika is remembered in Ireland as Caillech or "old Woman")[43] representing "the insatiable hunger of the many fecund and life-giving goddesses, whose energies must be constantly replenished and reinvigorated by blood sacrifice."[44]

It will not seem so strange now to associate Cathleen ni Houlihan with the blood-bedabbled queens of *The King of the Great Clock Tower* and *A Full Moon in March* (1934, 1935) and with the Morrigu in *The Death of Cuchulain* (1939). Not only is the connecting link that embodiment of terrible beauty and Yeats's Gaelic Muse incarnate, Maud Gonne; beyond that, the fatal women of these four plays, prefigured by the "young queen" of "The Cap and Bells" (1894), are all embodiments of the negative or "Terrible" aspect of the archetypal Great Mother.

*   *   *

"That woman, the Great Mother imaging, / Cut out his heart." Yeats's most direct poetic reference to the Great Mother occurs, appropriately, in his most myth-clotted poem, "Parnell's Funeral." My general subject is the intersection of Irish myth and politics in the work of Yeats and Joyce, and the central figure in Irish political mythology, not only for Yeats and Joyce, is Charles Stewart Parnell, the hero under whose star much of modern Irish literature was written. But male heroes must, in mythology, struggle against the Great Mother. As indicated earlier, this study of Devouring Ireland as a blood-exacting queen (Yeats) or farrow-eating sow (Joyce) is concerned with what Erich Neumann calls, in the title of the eleventh chapter of his seminal Jungian analysis of the archetype, the "negative elementary character" of the Great Mother.[45] Though this local emphasis on the negative, on Jung's Terrible Mother, should not blind us to the positive treatment of the Female image in the work of both writers, this short study focuses on the negative elementary character—or *alimentary,* since my specific theme is that of the Devouring Female.

The myth of the Great Mother, in both her positive and negative aspects, functions on three levels: transcultural, cultural, and personal. On the first level, the universal, the negative character of the Feminine has its origin in inner experience, a primordial human fear that Neumann interprets—both in *The Great Mother* and in his earlier *Origins and History of Consciousness*—in terms of "masculine" human consciousness confronting the unconscious, generally if not exclusively symbolized as "maternal and feminine." Neumann's synopsis will recall for readers of Yeats and Joyce the cyclical myth of their shared mentor, Blake, especially as developed in his gnomic and terrifying ballad "The Mental Traveller," with its movement from Tirzah to Vala to cruel Rahab, from the Female as Necessity to Nature-as-Temptress to Nature-as-Destroyer, and back again in an eternal recurrence. It also coincides with the mythic pattern—the male's struggle to maturity—underlying Joyce's *Portrait, Ulysses,* and *Finnegans Wake.* But here is Neumann in *The Great Mother*:

> The phases in the development of consciousness appear then as embryonic containment in the mother, as childlike dependence on the mother, as the relation of the beloved son to the Great Mother, and finally as the heroic struggle of the male hero against the Great Mother. . . . The dialectical relation of consciousness to the unconscious takes the symbolic, mythological form of a struggle between the Maternal-Feminine and the male child. . . .
>
> The symbolism of the Terrible Mother . . . expresses itself in fantastic and chimerical images that do not originate in the outside world. . . . In the myths and tales of all peoples, ages, and countries—and even in the nightmares of our own nights—witches and vampires, ghouls and spectres, assail us, all terrifyingly alike. . . . Death and destruction, danger and distress, hunger and nakedness, appear as helplessness in the presence of the Dark and Terrible Mother.
>
> Thus the womb of the earth becomes the deadly devouring maw of the underworld, . . . the devouring womb of the grave and of death, of darkness without light, of nothingness. For this woman who generates life and all living things on earth is the same who takes them back into herself. . . . Disease, hunger, hardship, war above all, are her helpers, and among all peoples the goddesses of war and the hunt express

man's experience of life as a female exacting blood. This Terrible Mother is the hungry earth, which devours its own children and fattens on their corpses; . . . the flesh-eating sarcophagus voraciously licking up the blood seed of men.[46]

The Terrible Mother can still be experienced in perhaps her most archaic form in the tiny but frightening clay figurines found in temple sites of the "very earliest Indian culture," the fourth millennium B.C. And it is in India, notes Neumann, that "the experience of the Terrible Mother has been given its most grandiose form as Kali," described by Heinrich Zimmer in "The Indian World Mother," as "dark, all-devouring time, the bone-wreathed Lady of the place of skulls." At Kali's annual autumn festivals hundreds of animals were sacrificed in "the bloodiest temple on earth." As bestower of life, Kali claims "the life blood of all creatures," and since she "desires only the blood of the offerings," the form of sacrifice is "beheading"—not only because "blood drains quickly from the beheaded beasts" but also because "the head signifies the whole, the total sacrifice."[47] She represents what David Kinsley calls "the other face of the divine feminine in Hinduism," that "insatiable hunger" of the goddess, "whose energies must be constantly replenished and reinvigorated by blood sacrifice." On the archetypal level, Cathleen ni Houlihan, the Old Woman reinvigorated by the blood sacrifice of her red-cheeked martyr-heroes, is simply a less grotesque version of the vampire Hag of Beare and of the Kali-like Celtic goddess of creation and destruction, the all-devouring Sheela-na-gig. Nor is there anything strange in that; after all, as Lorna Reynolds and Maire Cruise O'Brien have recently reminded us, "Ireland had once participated in that bronze-age culture in which the dominant divinity had been female, the great, all-powerful Mother Goddess" who played a "quintessential part" in the structure of pre-Christian Irish society.[48]

Archetypal images of the Terrible Mother resonate in the unconscious, and fantasies of the devouring, insatiable female, as Susan Bordo points out, are more readily evoked in certain cultural contexts than others, among them "periods when women are . . . asserting themselves politically and socially." Twentieth-century "anxiety over women's uncontrollable hungers," experienced by women themselves in the form of eating disorders such as anorexia nervosa and bulimia, has its male expression, Bordo argues, in images such as those described by Christopher Lasch, who wrote of "the apparently aggressive overtures of sexually liberated women" that "convey to many males the same message—that women are voracious, insatiable" and "call up early fantasies" of a "possessive, suffocating, devouring and castrating mother."

Peter Gay has focused on this mixture of cultural misogyny and primordial terror as especially predominant in the wake of the nineteenth-century feminist movement; the theme of female oral insatiability, as Bordo notes, is common in the artistic and literary images of that era—a virtual "flood" (as Gay calls it) of visual and literary images of "sharp-teethed, devouring" Sphinxes and Salomes, "biting, tearing, murderous women." "No century," claims Gay, "depicted woman as vampire, as castrator, as killer, so consistently, so programmatically, and so nakedly as the nineteenth."[49]

In researching *Idols of Perversity*, which richly documents the nineteenth-century theme of devouring, Bram Dijkstra encountered "a veritable iconography of misogyny," an iconography fleshed out in its violent form in five chapters devoted to the fin-de-siècle version of the all-devouring, beheading Goddess. Synopsizing those chapters, Allesandra Comini stresses "the emergence of the Consuming Woman myth, from clinging vine, poison flower, siren, snake, sphinx and vampire to the most dreadful specter of them all—the priestesses of man's severed head, Judith and Salome."[50] Here the fin-de-siècle Decadence—the world of Mallarmé and Huysmans, Oscar Wilde and Aubrey Beardsley—meets the primordial world of Sheela-na-gig, of Heaney's "mouth devouring heads," and of Kali, the Devourer and Beheader of Indian Tantric texts who, "dressed in blood red, standing in a boat floating on a sea of blood," raises "the skull full of seething blood to her lips."[51]

Influenced by Blake's negative as well as his positive depictions of the Female, fascinated by comparative mythology, and immersed in the fin de siècle, Yeats and Joyce could hardly escape such archetypes: archetypes that in fact reach their height, or their depth, in Yeats's lunar queens kissing severed heads and in the sexual humiliation of masochistic Bloom in the hallucinatory "Circe" episode of *Ulysses*. And, of course, to the cultural influence of late-nineteenth-century Decadent Romanticism must be added both the Irish context and personal temperament and experience. Both Yeats and Joyce—as well as that other and even more obsessive acolyte of the Goddess in her terrible aspect, Robert Graves—tended to submit themselves to dominant women; and all three, as writers in the Irish tradition, knew well that fairy mistress the Leanhaun Shee. This malignant, vampirish phantom "gives inspiration to those she persecutes," wrote Yeats; "to her have belonged the greatest of the Irish poets, from Oisin down to the last century."[52] In his earliest poems, even before he had met that statuesque embodiment of the femme fatale and Gaelic Muse, Maud Gonne, Yeats was writing dramatic poems (*The Island of Statues, The Two Titans, The Seeker*) that are part of the Romantic agony of submission to the merciless belles dames, the fatal enchantresses and devouring earth- and sea-mothers of Celtic Romanticism.

Whether those archetypes dwell in the Collective, the cultural, or the individual Unconscious, artists resonate with those that tally with personal experience. Graves's White Goddess, for example, is experience mythologized and myth made personal. On the mythographic level, he notes, the Sacred King is "the Moon-goddess's divine victim," and "every Muse-poet must, in a sense, die for the Goddess whom he adores, just as the King died." Thus, on an individual level, "being in love does not, and should not, blind the poet to the cruel side of woman's nature—and many Muse-poems are written in helpless attestation of this by men whose love is no longer returned." It seems accurate to say that Graves has, in describing the White Goddess, woven "an always personal emotion . . . into a general pattern of myth and symbol." I am quoting Yeats (Au 151), whose equivalent of Graves's Laura Riding was the considerably more alluring Maud Gonne, and who, like Graves, submitted himself to a sometimes barbaric Muse, a femme fatale with lunar affiliations.[53]

* * *

In the chapters that follow, we will encounter a procession of fatal women—Yeatsian and Joycean, psychological, mythological, and political. This dark motif of the destroying and devouring Female is almost concealed by lyrical beauty in Yeats's early dream-poem "The Cap and Bells." After examining that ballad, I will leap ahead, chronologically though not thematically, to his most overt priestesses of man's severed head, the lunar queens of *The King of the Great Clock Tower* and its revision, *A Full Moon in March*, and to Yeats's final play, *The Death of Cuchulain*. Set in the context of these late, troubling mythological plays, *Cathleen ni Houlihan*, for all its allegorical transparence and direct political appeal, may be seen as no less bloody a myth drama.

Next, pivoting on the last of Yeats's Maud Gonne poems, "A Bronze Head," and that fin-de-siècle idol of perversity long buried in Joyce's Trieste sketchbook, I turn to Joyce's depictions of devoured Parnell and Ireland as Devouring Female in *Portrait* and *Ulysses*. My central text is in fact *Ulysses*, with emphasis placed on Joyce's three principal evocations of the Terrible Mother: Stephen's own mother, that "crazy queen . . . the holy Roman catholic and apostolic church," and devouring Ireland herself as parodies of Yeats's

Cathleen ni Houlihan. Finally, I devote—for reasons more-than-porcine and more-than-rondural—a section to "The Valley of the Black Pig," the mythological-political poem immediately following "The Cap and Bells" in Yeats's fin-de-siècle volume, *The Wind Among the Reeds*. For there the fatal maw of "the old sow that eats her farrow" is evaded by Yeats, his coat trailing what Joyce ridiculed as "gold-embroidered Celtic fringes," but nevertheless "Joycean" in his decision to fly by the nets of violent Irish Nationalism.

2

Priestesses of the Great Mother

When "The Cap and Bells," written in 1893 and first published in 1894, appeared in *The Wind Among the Reeds*, it was accompanied by a note Yeats repeated in all subsequent editions of his poems. Though it conceals as much as it reveals, the note confirms the poem's profound significance for Yeats:

> I dreamed this story exactly as I have written it, and dreamed another long dream after it, trying to make out its meaning, and whether I was to write it in prose or verse. The first dream was more a vision than a dream, for it was beautiful and coherent, and gave me the sense of illumination and exaltation that one gets from visions, while the second dream was confused and meaningless. The poem has always meant a great deal to me, though as is the way with symbolic poems, it has not always meant quite the same thing. Blake would have said, "The authors are in eternity," and I am quite sure they can only be questioned in dreams.—1899.

Yeats's double dream, the first "more a vision than a dream," recalls the celebrated note accompanying "Kubla Khan," subtitled by Coleridge "a Vision in a Dream." In a "profound sleep," which Coleridge confessed in a manuscript note was an opium-induced reverie, "images rose up before him as *things*, with a parallel production of the correspondent expressions, without any sensation or consciousness of effort." Awakening, he wrote down "the lines that are here preserved," continuing until allegedly interrupted by the notorious "person on business from Porlock." He had since, he concluded, "frequently" tried "to finish for himself what had been originally, as it were, given to him," but in vain.[1]

"Kubla Khan," far from being the "fragment" Coleridge and others have labeled it, is as "beautiful and coherent" as Yeats's vision and correspondent expression in "The Cap and Bells." Though he was being characteristically defensive, Coleridge was more accurate when he described the poem as a "psychological curiosity." So it is, with its mingling of the sublime and daemonic, its "damsel with a dulcimer" and its "woman wailing for her demon lover" beneath "a waning moon." "The Cap and Bells," featuring a "young queen" who is both aloof and passionate, gentle and terrifying, is also a psychological curiosity; and Yeats, in his note of Coleridgean evasiveness, offers no help to the curious. He had himself tried, in a "second dream," to make out the "meaning" of the first—what had been "originally, as it were, given to him." But his efforts, like Coleridge's, were in vain; that second dream "was confused and meaningless." Thus, while the poem "always meant a great deal" to him, it had not always "meant quite the same thing." That, he says, is "the way with symbolic poems," and he waves off further curiosity on the subject by referring himself and his readers to higher authority: those "authors . . . in eternity," of whom Blake claimed to be only the secretary, and who, Yeats adds in his single certainty in the note ("I am quite sure"), can "only be questioned in dreams."[2]

If Yeats is more than usually elusive and evasive here he had good reason, considering the "story" at once revealed and concealed in this particular "symbolic poem." It opens with the suddenness shared by dream and ballad:

The jester walked in the garden:
The garden had fallen still;
He bade his soul rise upward
And stand on her window-sill.

In a chivalric scenario reminiscent of Keats's "La Belle Dame sans Merci" and of Victorian poems by Rossetti and Morris, a lovelorn jester, walking in a garden "fallen" still, bids his soul "rise upward" to the sill of his beloved. In evening twilight, "When owls began to call," the soul "rose in a straight blue garment," a virginal color matched by the "pale night-gown" in which the "young queen" also "rose." But she "would not listen" to the soul "grown wise-tongued by thinking / Of a quiet and light footfall." Unresponsive, she decisively "drew in the heavy casement / And pushed the latches down."

Next, in predawn twilight "When the owls called out no more," he petitions her with his "heart," which does more than "stand" on her windowsill. In an appropriately "red and quivering garment / It sang to her through the door." As the disappearance of the wise owls confirms, heart's characteristic attribute is throbbing emotion; whereas soul has grown wise-tongued by thinking, heart has "grown sweet-tongued by dreaming"—dreaming of "a flutter of flower-like hair." But again, the queen is unmoved; indeed, her dismissal of the heart is even more painful because so casual: "she took up her fan from the table / And waved it off on the air."

The crisis of the poem follows. With soul and heart, thought and dream, both rejected by the haughty young queen, the jester sends her "what is most essential and individual in him,"[3] at once the sign of his occupation and of his manhood:

'I have cap and bells,' he pondered,
'I will send them to her and die';
And when the morning whitened
He left them where she went by.

She laid them upon her bosom,
Under a cloud of her hair,
And her red lips sang them a love-song
Till stars grew out of the air.

All day, from "morning" to night ("till stars grew out of the air"), the queen sings to a sacrificial offering she at last finds acceptable because it is total. Now, and only now, she opens her door and window, allowing the heart and soul in, to her right hand the red one, to her left the blue, to set up their "chattering wise and sweet." But this neat symmetry, this acceptance and reintegration of the previously rejected heart and soul, seems too little too late. The jester, having given up his "cap" (from *caput*, head), is *kaput*, dead, a Fool *être capot*, out of tricks. That it is his "*cap and bells,*" and that he chose to "give them to her *and die,*" symbolically fuses decapitation with self-castration. There is the suggestion that the severed parts, through the glory conferred by the queen's transmembering song, may become (varying Belinda's or Berenice's lock) a *male* constellation. But the organic root, prepared for by the way heart and soul had "grown," is not forgotten or utterly transcended: "stars *grew* out of the air."

This "caps," in a sense, the jester's posthumous progress. In life he had thought of her "footfall" and dreamed of her "hair"; in death his sacrificial offering is placed by the queen "upon her bosom, / Under a cloud of her hair," while "her red lips" sang them a "love-song."[4] Despite his note, Yeats did not publish "The Cap and Bells" "exactly" as he had dreamed it; and what his first drafts reveal even more clearly than the published text is the poem's underlying myth of the Destructive Goddess. The critical moment in which the queen lays the cap and bells "upon her bosom" was originally more morbidly erotic:

She took them into her chamber
Her breast began to heave.

Though Yeats was right to delete these lines (they would, as Brenda Webster says, have "disturbed the ethereal surface of the poem"),[5] they offer us a revealing glimpse—without having to query those "authors in eternity"—into the poem's human, all-too-human origins, the Dionysian disturbances under that Apollonian surface. For beneath what Webster calls the poem's "dance-like patterns suggestive of life and beauty" lurks the terrible beauty of quite another dance, that of Salome, and beyond her, the Beheading Goddess herself, she who decapitates, as Heinrich Zimmer notes, because "the head signifies the whole, the total sacrifice."[6]

The "young queen," her breast heaving in grief but even more in triumph (which Yeats must have realized and which partially explains the repressive deletion), takes the cap and bells "into her chamber," into what Keats called the Goddess's "sovereign shrine." When she lays them upon her "bosom, / Under a cloud of her hair," they may be said to be (in the final line of the "Ode on Melancholy") "among her cloudy trophies hung." I bring up Keats's ode because its final allusion is to lines of a Shakespeare sonnet ("Thou art the grave where buried love doth live, / Hung with the trophies of my lovers gone") Yeats also seems to be echoing in "The Cap and Bells." That Shakespearean sonnet, 31, begins, "Thy bosom is endeared with all hearts, / ... / And there reigns love and all love's loving parts," a pattern of genital innuendo that persists to the final line, in which the full-bosomed beloved "hast all the all of me."

"The Cap and Bells" is easy prey to reductive psychoanalyzing (I have at least refrained from going on about windows and doors); but even after such analysis it remains "beautiful and coherent," retaining much of the "sense of illumination and exaltation" Yeats experienced in his original dream or vision. But, once again, "an always personal emotion [has been] woven into a general pattern of myth and symbol." On the personal level of the Yeatsian drama of poet and muse, the aloof queen to whom the lowly jester gives "all" is Maud Gonne, she who "took / All till my youth was gone / With scarce a pitying look" (VP 315). On the level of generalized myth and symbol, the "young queen" whose "red lips" sang a "love-song" to those loving parts she lays on her bosom prefigures the "queens" of Yeats's late dance plays, those post-Decadent Salomes who press their lips to the lips of severed heads. She is, in short, the precursor of Yeats's later, more graphic, incarnations of that "Gaelic Muse" and "malignant fairy," the Leanhaun Shee, the fatal enchantress who inspires and destroys her adoring acolytes.

On the most profound mythographic level, the self-castrating jester seems suspended between what Neumann describes in *The Origins and History of Consciousness* as the first two stages in "the youthful lover's relation to the Great Mother." The jester surrenders to fate, the earliest stage in this relation, but, in offering his gift, seems to harbor some hope that he, like nature, "will be reborn through the Great Mother, out of the fullness of her grace"— though, as Neumann goes on to say, "with no activity or merit on his part," since it is precisely his suicidal act of symbolic self-castration that inspires the queen's possibly regenerative love song, sung "Till stars grew out of the air." The Great Mother devours her star-children; perhaps she can create, or re-create, them as well.[7] And of course "grew" has vegetative resonance. Is the jester a self-castrated Attis to the young queen's Magna Mater, Cybele? Having read the 1890 two-volume edition of *The Golden Bough*, Yeats knew that, driven by his jealous mother, Attis castrated himself, died, and then returned to life (transformed into a pine tree) in response to Cybele's intense mourning.[8]

Struggle and flight characterize the transition to Neumann's next stage, and the "primary expression of flight" is, precisely, "self-castration and suicide." Unlike the typical mythic "strugglers" (Narcissus, Pentheus, Hippolytus), Yeats's jester neither defies his Goddess nor refuses to love her; far from it. Yet he too yields up

the very thing the Terrible Mother wants, namely, the offering of the phallus, though the offering is made in a negative sense. The youths who flee in terror and madness from the demands of the Great Mother betray, in the act of self-castration, their abiding fixation to the central symbol of the Great Mother cult, the phallus; and this they offer up to her, albeit with denial in their consciousness and a protesting ego.[9]

By the time he wrote "The Cap and Bells" and its attendant note, Yeats, having read Frazer, knew all about castration, symbolic or otherwise, in the Great Mother cults. He employed that theme in his poem, albeit with the "denial in [his] consciousness" implicit in his emphasis on the poem's origin in a visionary dream and in his referral of the curious, himself included, to sources rather more obscure than Frazer—authors safely distant in eternity.

The truth, of course, had to do with a woman—closer to home but, in 1893 at least, no more accessible than eternity. Yeats's love for Maud Gonne was as seemingly hopeless as the jester's love for the young queen. I have already argued that—in another ambivalent sacrificial offering—Yeats gave Maud Gonne *his* "cap and bells," his genius, in the form of the play *Cathleen ni Houlihan*, the only other work (with the exception of "His Dream") that Yeats says came to him in "a dream almost as distinct as a vision" (VPl 232). But since I have also argued that there is a "negative" element in the offering, and that it takes the form of a covert, perhaps subconscious, identification of Cathleen with the blood-exacting Terrible Mother, with the Leanhaun Shee, and with the Morrigu, I want to support that claim by examining the last and grimmest of the Maud Gonne poems, "A Bronze Head," and the late Yeatsian dancers dancing before severed heads: those "queens" who look back not only to the "young queen" whose red lips sing to the dismembered parts of the jester but also to Cathleen ni Houlihan herself, the Old Woman transformed into a young girl with "the walk of a queen."

The motif handled so decorously in "The Cap and Bells" is later treated, in two of Yeats's dance plays, with a savagery only partially mitigated by their mode, which is not realistic but symbolic and mythological. Once again we have a confrontation of lowly fool and aloof queen, and once again a drama of poet and Gaelic Muse, of Yeats and Maud Gonne.[10] But in these 1934–1935 plays, *The King of the Great Clock Tower* and *A Full Moon in March*, the cap and bells are literally severed heads; Oscar Wilde's *Salome* has at last borne its fully ripened, and not very palatable, Yeatsian fruit. Ezra Pound hated the first of these plays, and Yeats himself did not think much of the second, essentially a reworking of the first (LY 830, 843). Only the most indiscriminate, or most forgiving, Yeatsian would disagree. But while Yeats did not like them he was evidently compelled to write—and rewrite—them.

In *The King of the Great Clock Tower*, the severed head the Queen dances before is that of a man "called / A stroller and a fool"; that is his own report, though he is more imperious when it comes to what he calls himself: "I am a poet," a "sacred man" (VPl 995, 996). In keeping with his audacious prophecy, his head, though severed, sings. The myth is of course Orphic, and Yeats is not the only modern poet to play with it. In Robert Graves's "Eurydice," Orpheus asks, "Is ours a fate can ever be forsworn / Though my lopped head sing to the yet unborn?" The "oracular head" in the White Goddess poem "Darien" is to be associated with this prophetic head of Orpheus, which recalls for Graves as well the singing head of the decapitated Welsh god Bran. But if there is an element here and in Yeats's late dance plays of sadomasochistic savagery parading as mythology, Yeats seems more guilty than Graves.[11] He is also more Celtic. Discussing the Celtic pagans, Anne Ross focuses on the cult of the severed human head, the "tête coupée"; the Celts' central symbol and "persistent theme," the severed head epitomizes "the most typical and universal of their religious attitudes."[12]

Priestesses of the Great Mother

The climax of *The King of the Great Clock Tower* comes when, at the end of the severed head's song, the Queen resumes her dance, pressing, at the last stroke of the gong, "her lips to the lips of the head" (VPl 1003). Far from abandoning this material, Yeats reworked it in *A Full Moon in March*, in the interests of what he called, in the preface to the latter play, "greater intensity." The reworking accomplished that; and the play certainly fulfills Yeats's description of it as a drama of "blood symbolism" (LY 830).

This time the fool of the play is even more bestial, a Swineherd who appears at the palace. His head too is quickly severed. The Queen had retired behind an inner curtain; when it parts she is discovered in an iconic pose, holding the severed head above her own. Hitherto she has been inhumanly pure—"Cruel as the winter of virginity" (VPl 982) in Yeats's echo of Mallarmé's Salome, delighted by the horror of her "own virginity," that "White night of ice and of the cruel snow."[13] Now she is blood-spattered: "Her hands are red. There are red blotches upon her dress" (VPl 987). Though these stage directions go on to say that the blood is "not realistically presented: red gloves, some patterns of red cloth" (987), the Queen resembles Moreau's Salome in the watercolor entitled *The Apparition*, or Otto Friedrich's "Salome," not to mention the Goddess herself in her "hideous aspect (*ghora-rupa*), as Kali, the dark one, [who] raises the skull full of seething blood to her lips; her devotional image shows her dressed in blood red."[14] In Yeats's play, the Queen's dance, "alluring and refusing," turns into "a dance of adoration," quickening until, as the drum-taps approach their "climax," she "presses her lips to the lips of the head." Her body "shivers" and she "sinks slowly down, holding the head to her breast," thus completing not only the play's thematic motif of "desecration and the lover's night" but also Yeats's more intimate motif of the femme fatale as a castrating and destroying woman (VPl 988–89).

Severed heads and the archetype of the female destroyer return, in majestic rather than decadent form, in Yeats's final play, *The Death of Cuchulain*. In this play, "strange and the most moving I have written for some years" (LY 922), Cuchulain—the Irish Achilles and Yeats's central hero—is about to die. Like Robert Graves's crucified god in *King Jesus* with the three Marys gathered at the foot of his cross, Cuchulain is surrounded by the three women who have figured centrally in his life: Eithne, his mistress; Aoife, the warrior-queen who bore his only son; and Emer, his wife. As John Rees Moore notes in *Masks of Love and Death*, "Cuchulain is the darling and the victim of the adoration he inspires."[15] Though she does not appear onstage, another fatal female, Cuchulain's enemy Queen Maeve, figures centrally as the plotter of his destruction. The play's dominant female, however, is the Morrigu, the primordial war goddess of Celtic mythology. Her triadic nature links her with the original Triple Goddess whose fullest manifestation is Kali, she who arranges the dance of life and death in Indian mythology; the Morrigu is also the Terrible Mother "in her aspect as bird of the dead, vulture and raven, . . . the corpse-devouring crow."[16]

An "Old Man," looking like "something out of mythology," introduced the audience to *The Death of Cuchulain* by "promis[ing] a dance": "Emer must dance, there must be severed heads—I am old, I belong to mythology—severed heads for her to dance before" (VPl 1051, 1052). Emer *will* dance—before the seven dark parallelograms representing the severed heads of the six who mortally wounded the hero and of Cuchulain himself, before whose "head" she "moves as if in adoration or triumph" (1062). She stops only when she hears "in the silence a few faint bird notes" heralding Cuchulain's metamorphosis in the underworld, a transformation he had prophesied:

> There floats out there
> The shape that I shall take when I am dead,
> My soul's first shape, a soft feathery shape,
> And is not that a strange shape for the soul
> Of a great fighting-man? . . .
> I say it is about to sing. (1060–61)

This transformation culminates in the strange and beautiful poem "Cuchulain Comforted," which Yeats dictated to his wife on his own deathbed and in which the dead hero is merged, or about to be merged, with his polar opposites, convicted cowards all: "They had changed their throats and had the throats of birds."

In the poem, the solitary warrior is, in death, folded into the single party of humanity, participating in a ghostly sewing bee that reconciles isolation and community, the "masculine" and the "feminine." The action of the play, however, is presided over by the war goddess. Though she yields the stage to Emer, it was the Morrigu who placed the head of Cuchulain on the ground, and it is she, the one-eyed "woman who is headed like a crow" (VPl 1054), who, Kali-like, determines the whole pattern of the hero's life and death, his destruction and reincarnation. As she says herself in the play's climactic line: "I arranged the dance" (VPl 1061).

*   *   *

In the last and most somberly impressive of the Maud Gonne poems, the 1938 "A Bronze Head," Yeats's muse, now as decrepit as the Old Woman she had portrayed thirty-six years earlier, seems to metamorphose into the Morrigu herself.

"A Bronze Head" is in some ways a darker reexamination of the relationship explored in "Among School Children" between unity and division, the One and the Many, underlying substance and its various manifestations.[17] The crucial philosophic question and speculation in the later poem is restricted to Maud Gonne:

> who can tell
> Which of her forms has shown her substance right?
> Or maybe substance can be composite . . . .

This would be no less at home in the poem in which the Yeatsian old man walks through the long schoolroom "questioning," dreaming of a "Ledaean body," Maud's, and of what came before and after: the beloved as "child" and in her "present" form, a devourer feeding on the insubstantial, her image "Hollow of cheek as though it drank the wind / And took a mess of shadows for its meat."

That is the image, though even further time-ravaged, sculpted in the plaster of Lawrence Campbell's bronze-painted bust of Maud Gonne in the Municipal Gallery. But not even the titular sculpture could permanently fix the protean image of his beloved for Yeats. In "A Bronze Head," Maud Gonne is an artifact. But she is also something "Human, superhuman, a bird's round eye, / Everything else withered and mummy-dead," a riveting image to which Yeats will return in the final stanza. Maud is also a "great tomb-haunter" sweeping the "distant sky" and terrified by her "own emptiness," though she was "once" a "form all full / As though with magnanimity of light." "Yet" she is also "a most gentle woman." And there is more. As the poet first saw her, she was an unmanageable filly—"even at the starting post, all sleek and new, / I saw the wildness in her"—and a vulnerable human creature, her animal wildness transferred by empathy to the protective poet-lover, who "had grown wild / And wandered murmuring everywhere, 'My child, my child!'" Finally, returning to the "bird's round eye" of the opening stanza, Yeats describes her in her anything but vulnerable aspect:

Or else I thought her supernatural;
As though a sterner eye looked through her eye
On this foul world in its decline and fall . . . .

Bronze head, bird, woman, child, horse, transparent eyeball; full and empty, dark and light, human and superhuman, natural and supernatural: the "extreme of life and death" indeed. Dispensing round his magnanimity of images, Yeats echoes but goes well beyond the tragic loss of the "rich" cornucopia bartered by Maud—"the loveliest woman born / Out of the mouth of Plenty's horn"—"For an old bellows full of angry wind" in "A Prayer for my Daughter," and even beyond the triads of "Among School Children"—though there too Maud had been evoked as child, beautiful woman, and aged crone, even as bird (a Ledaean "daughter of the swan") and animal (a wind-drinking chameleon).

The compelling image of Maud in "Among School Children"—"hollow of cheek" as though it "drank the wind / And took a mess of shadows for its meat"—though graphically Dantesque, derives its devouring imagery from Shakespeare, specifically from *Hamlet* and *King Lear*. "How fares our cousin Hamlet?" "Excellent, i' faith, of the chameleon's dish; I eat the air, promise crammed. You cannot feed capons so." (Nor can you feed the kites and croaking raven an avenging Hamlet would "fatten" on the "offal" of the king he here banters with.)[18] "A Bronze Head" is a more richly Shakespearean poem. From *King Lear* Yeats borrows the "*Hysterica passio*" of Maud's inner "emptiness" (line 7) as well as the rare word "Propinquity" (line 18), the closeness disclaimed by Lear when (1.1.113-20) he casts *his* "child," Cordelia, from him, making his "sometime daughter" as alien to him as "he that makes his generations *messes* / To gorge his appetite"—a devouring image Yeats had earlier applied, having changed the devourer's gender and fare, to the aged image of Maud Gonne, which, in addition to drinking wind, "took a *mess* of shadows for its *meat*."

In "A Bronze Head," Yeats's final image is even more severely metonymic than head or hollow cheek: that of a "sterner eye" looking through Maud's eye on "this foul world in its decline and fall." The cold and lofty eye cast here, its perspective as apocalyptically nihilistic as the finale of *Lear*,[19] seems Yeatsian in its politics and eugenic obsession, gazing down as it does at a foul "sty" into which the "Ancestral pearls" of Anglo-Irish tradition have been "pitched" and leaving Maud, Yeats, and us wondering "what was left for massacre to save." But that eye, more than Yeatsian, is of the very substance of Maud Gonne.

When Yeats wonders which of Maud's "forms" has shown her "substance right," he is echoing, in the poem's central Shakespearean allusion, the opening question in sonnet 53, where Shakespeare wonders about the beloved's Platonic essence and its relationship to her accidental attributes, her external appearances:

What is your substance, whereof are you made,
That millions of strange shadows on you tend?

Yet that underlying "substance" prevails beneath her various manifestations: "And you in every blessed shape we know." The same seems true of the multiplicitous Maud, whose essential being, or "substance," persists beneath her protean "forms." Though in "No Second Troy" she filled her poet's days with misery and would have "hurled the little streets upon the great," his violent Helen cannot be blamed: "Why, what could she have *done, being* what she *is*? / Was there another Troy for her to burn?" There is the quintessential Maud Gonne, unable to act except in accordance with her inner being, "what she is." And what she is is a destroyer.

"Among School Children" ends by asking if the tree is leaf, blossom, or bole. It is of course all three since we can no more break down the organic unity of the "great-rooted blossomer" than we can "know the dancer from the dance," or isolate Maud as child from Maud as "Ledaean body," or from her "present image" as hollow-cheeked but still voracious crone. Yet it is as tomb-haunting crone with a "bird's round eye" that Yeats compels us to envisage Maud Gonne in "A Bronze Head"—compels us by ending his poem on a repetition and intensification of that "present image." The birdlike "sterner eye" looking through Maud's eye—that "mysterious eye" that, British journalists felt, "contained the shadow of battles yet to come" (Mem 60)—seems ultimately that of the Morrigu, the one-eyed "woman with the head of a crow."[20] That Celtic goddess of war, the Terrible Mother as demoniac bird of the dead who haunts corpse-strewn battlefields, presides, here as in *The Death of Cuchulain*, over a dance of death in which nothing is left in Ireland even "for massacre to save."

The Old Woman of *Cathleen ni Houlihan* has come full circle. Even then she was a mythological femme fatale, a warrior-Muse for whose sake men die in battle. Now the woman who played her is made to wonder whether there is anything in post-revolutionary Ireland *worth* saving, no matter how much blood were to be shed. By 1938—when Yeats was wondering in another poem if that play of his sent out certain men the English shot—even the Morrigu may have had enough. Or so it seemed, for not even Yeats—a man almost telepathically attuned to portents of violence—could have predicted its re-eruption in Northern Ireland thirty-one years later.

*   *   *

The union of Maud Gonne with Ireland—that is, Maud as savior of a still salvageable Ireland—was performed by Yeats himself when he wrote *Cathleen ni Houlihan*. In Joyce, many women are peripherally, or even explicitly, associated with Ireland and Irish Nationalism. Whether victims or victimizers, pathetic or potentially destructive, or both, they are "negative" images.[21] The women who are celebrated, the positive lineage, are the major women in Joyce's work: Gretta Conroy of "The Dead," Bertha Rowan of *Exiles*, the birdlike girl of *Portrait*, Molly Bloom of *Ulysses*, and—the culmination of their vitality, variety, and amplitude—Anna Livia Plurabelle of *Finnegans Wake*.

At the crossroads, containing so many "forms" that she is a precursor of both positive and negative aspects of the female archetype, is a woman as protean as the Maud Gonne of "A Bronze Head" and as "devouring" as Yeats's various fatal "queens." The lady in question is the temptress and betrayer so lushly depicted in Joyce's unpublished Trieste sketchbook. Though she has nothing overt to do with Ireland, she has deep and labyrinthine connections with the mother of Stephen Dedalus, herself intimately associated with those two Terrible Mothers and "crazy queens," Ireland and the Church. We might approach the lady of the unpublished sketchbook by way of three women in another manuscript not published during Joyce's lifetime, *Stephen Hero*.

The refusal of Stephen Dedalus to pray for his mother at the hour of her death, a refusal that haunts him throughout most of *Ulysses*, was prefigured by his refusal, first in *Stephen Hero* and then in *A Portrait of the Artist as a Young Man*, to concede to her wishes and perform his Easter duty. In *Stephen Hero* (section XXI, 131–35), the refusal is particularly brutal. But his ridicule of the Irish peasant piety his devout mother shares confirms, along with a streak of cruelty in Stephen, his rejection of Catholicism as intimately related to his rejection of his country. Also rejected in *Stephen Hero*, and for similar reasons, is Emma Clery. Toward the end of the novel, Stephen gives all his coins to "the woman in the black straw hat."[22] Explicitly taking his cue from the embrace of the outcast female avatar in Yeats's "The Adoration of the Magi" (SH 192), Stephen turns to this prostitute having finally turned *from* Emma, the coquettish "virgin" who, despite her "incorrigible eyes" and seductive body "so compact of pleasure," remains a flirtatious but chaste daughter of the Church he has rejected and of the country he must escape. A Nationalist, she urges him to "learn Irish too," which he "lyingly" pursues in the hope of attaining *her* (SH 192, 187, 66, 46, 55).

The coins Stephen gives the prostitute were those he had fingered moments earlier as "the warmth of [Emma's] body seemed to flow into his": an act signaling his half-conscious realization that the price for admission to that warm body—as Lynch later confirms—is "marriage" (189, 192). But Stephen is not about to be tied down. Though he later proposes "one night... alone together," he has in fact rejected Emma and what he now seems to think she represents, those "foolish and grotesque virginities" he associates with his mother's Catholicism and with Ireland herself: all "nets" Blakean and Daedalian Stephen will "fly by" (SH 198, 193; P 203).

The images of virgin and whore—the Joycean double woman inspired by Mariolatry on the one hand, lust on the other—are finally, in Hegel's triple equivoque, *aufgehoben* in the central female icon of *A Portrait of the Artist as a Young Man*: the "darkplumaged" bird-girl whose aesthetic beauty reconciles flesh and spirit and who bears Ireland's "sign" on that flesh in the form of a trace of "emerald" seaweed (P 171). A far more problematic and protean double woman—one who would certainly rank high among Dijkstra's "idols of perversity"—remained buried in Joyce's manuscripts for more than half a century. She is the subject of the sixteen-page sheaf of "prose sketches" Joyce told Ezra Pound in 1917 he had "locked up in my desk in Trieste" (LJ 1:101). First discussed by Richard Ellmann in his 1959 biography and finally published a decade later as *Giacomo Joyce*,[23] this sketchbook reveals a woman—based on a Jewish student, Amalia Popper, to whom Joyce was attracted in Trieste—who assumes almost all forms of the Triple Goddess. As bird, filly, basilisk-eyed devourer; virgin, Virgin Mother, lover; whore, corpse, and lamia, Joyce's mysterious young temptress out-Mauds the Maud of "A Bronze Head," who is also bird, filly, child, gentle woman, dark tomb-haunter, and stern-eyed Morrigu. Like Maud, this protean femme fatale is an inspiring and destructive muse, in large part—of course, and as usual—a projection of her worshiper's own desire and terror. Like Maud, too, the "unfaithful" young lady committed the ultimate crime of preferring another. Her rejection of infatuated Giacomo, like Maud's of Yeats, is transformative. Yeats wrote of "her that took / All till my youth was gone" (VP 315). Joyce's spurned lover also bids farewell to the dreamy dreams of youth; he hears, in his imagination, the Dutch composer Sweelinck's "variations for the clavichord on an old air: *youth has no end.... The end is here*" (GJ 16).

The young lady had been a gentle "filly foal," a fragile "sparrow," a creature, like the changeling of Yeats's "Song of Wandering Aengus," "shimmering with silvery scales" (GJ 3, 7). She is also the potential victim of a rape weirdly transacted when, in the description of an operation she requires, the surgeon's knife becomes the sexual instrument of a "libidinous God." Following that operation, but as the result of her changed attitude toward *him, she* is changed utterly. Giacomo becomes the victim of a predatory aggressor, her iconic animals no longer gentle but venomous and devouring.

She also becomes a dead thing, a fin-de-siècle perversion of organic life. The grass-green embroidery of her opera gown now suggests Whitman's "hair of graves," her body itself becomes an "odourless flower"; corpselike, she emerges in a dream from "whirling wreaths of grey vapour," her face "grey and grave," her hair "dank matted," and when she kisses him, "her sighing comes through" (GJ 12, 13, 14).

Joyce's fusion of the fin-de-siècle Decadence with the archetype of the Terrible Mother is revealed in the astonishing degree to which these horrors anticipate the appearance of the ghost of Stephen's mother in *Ulysses*, especially the climactic visitation in "Circe," where, "emaciated," she rises through the brothel floor, "in leper grey with a wreath of faded orange-blossoms," her worn face "green with gravemould," her hair "scant and lank," breathing upon her terror-stricken son "an ashen breath." Even the "end of youth" is reenacted when Stephen shrinks from her, his features drawn "grey and old" (U 473, 475). To some extent, the bestiality of Stephen's mother—"ghoul," "hyena," "corpsechewer"—is also anticipated in the descriptions of the lady in *Giacomo Joyce*, who is a basilisk, an assaulting lamia, "a cold nightsnake" (15).

James Joyce received word that his mother was dying on Good Friday (10 April 1903). It is the Good Friday Passion chant that Stephen hums as he gives his coins to the woman with the black straw hat in *Stephen Hero*, and Giacomo's first sketch of his beloved is set on the same portentous day. Her identification with suffering Mother and Virgin is, however, obliterated by her eventual "betrayal." When she tells her idolater that she has chosen another, she becomes a daughter of Jerusalem who darts at Giacomo (now the afflicted "son of man") a "jet of liquorish venom," a betrayal completed by her reenactment of the Jews' preference of Barabbas to the condemned Christ: "*Non hunc sed Barabbam!*" (GJ 14–16).

Above all, she is a serpentine devourer. Milton had spoken in "Lycidas" of "blind mouths"; this lady's eyes are also mouths, but bright and sharp-visioned. Like those of Wilde's Salome ("a basilisk" born "from the seed of a serpent"), they are eyes at once venomous and devouring, capable of poisoning any man they look upon, able to drink Giacomo's thoughts as well as his soul, which is absorbed into her as a "liquid and abundant seed" (14). She is even a devouring female Satan, luring her victim into adultery: "coiling approach of starborn flesh . . . soft sucking lips. . . . A starry snake has kissed me: a cold nightsnake. I am lost!—Nora!—" (15). In "Circe," Stephen's exclamation at the climactic moment of his encounter with the ghoulish ghost of his mother is "*Nothung!*," an invocation of the sword with which Wagner's Siegfried slew the giant snake Fafner. Here, Joyce's own Nora Barnacle is invoked to save her manchild from a demonic and devouring nightsnake.

The nightsnake of *Giacomo Joyce* reappears as the devouring mother, the nightmare in "Circe." But her multitudinous manifestations may also qualify her as a precursor of Molly Bloom and Anna Livia Plurabelle—both inconstant, but emblematic not of death but of the protean fluidity of life. Of all these images of the female we might ask, as Yeats does of his protean Maud Gonne, "Which of her forms has shown her substance right?" Though we would have to answer, as Yeats does in "Among School Children," all of them, the lady of *Giacomo Joyce* incarnates primarily Neumann's "negative elementary character." Indeed, whereas Molly Bloom begins (U 56) with No (her sleepy "Mn") and ends (U 644) with her celebrated affirmation of life ("Yes I said yes I will Yes"), this lady, whose first word is "yes," ends on the No of rejection and betrayal: "*Non hunc sed Barabbam.*"

Vicki Mahaffey, from whom I borrow this positive-negative contrast, perceptively discusses the way in which Joyce "distributes" this lady's various characteristics not only between "the two most powerful figures of death and life in *Ulysses*, May Dedalus and Molly Bloom," but "almost equally" among that novel's "virgins, whores, mothers, wives, and daughters."[24] Still, even if she is as ambiguous as Keats's Lamia (woman or snake?), this lady is also Joyce's fullest early experiment with woman as Devouring Female. As such, she is the direct precursor not only of that "corpsechewer," Stephen's ghostly mother, but also of the negative and dismembering woman of *A Portrait of the Artist as a Young Man*, Stephen's aunt and nurse, Dante Riordan. If the lady of *Giacomo Joyce* is at the end a devouring snake, Mrs. Riordan is from the outset an avenging bird, threatening that if little Stephen does not "apologize" for some unspecified offense, "the eagles will come and pull out his eyes" (P 8). She is also a "corpsechewer," the harridan who, in the famous Christmas Dinner scene, reenacts the dismemberment and devouring of Joyce's political Messiah, Ireland's uncrowned "dead king," Charles Stewart Parnell.

*   *   *

The subjects of mythology and politics in an Irish context inevitably summon up the spirit of Parnell, half man, half myth. Every millennial myth requires a deliverer and redeemer. In the single figure of Parnell, Ireland found her Mosaic Deliverer and Christian Messiah; and it was Ireland herself that destroyed him, indeed "devoured" him—or so goes the myth.

The charismatic Protestant leader of the Irish Parliamentary party in the House of Commons, an adroit tactician who was the only man who could "keep those cats in the one bag," Charles Stewart Parnell brought Ireland to what many thought was the very verge of home rule. Then, at the height of his power, tragedy struck: on Christmas Eve 1889, he was cited as corespondent in Capt. William O'Shea's divorce trial against his wife, Katherine. Parnell was abandoned by Gladstone and the British Liberal party, violently attacked as a public sinner by the Catholic Church in Ireland, and—in the legendary scene on 6 December 1890 in Committee Room 15—"betrayed" by a majority of his own party, including his former lieutenant, Tim Healy: a rejection confirmed when Parnell was repudiated by the Irish electorate. After a strenuous ten-month campaign to regain his power base and his control of the party, Parnell died, exhausted, on 6 October 1891. When his coffin was lowered into the grave in the largest funeral in Irish history, thousands witnessed strange lights in the sky, and a star or meteor was reported to have fallen, visible in broad daylight. "The most glorious meteor sailed across the clear sky of the heavens and fell suddenly," wrote Yeats's friend Katherine Tynan. "He had omens and portents to the end."[25]

The myth had begun.[26] And so had the mythologizing literature. A precocious nine-year-old Joyce delighted his Parnellite father with "Et Tu, Healy," a poem that has not survived (though it may have served as the model for "The Death of Parnell," the turgidly sincere poem recited by Mr. Hynes at the end of "Ivy Day in the Committee Room"). Yeats, twenty-six at the time of Parnell's death, published in *United Ireland* a no less turgid poem that, though he never reprinted it, *has* survived. Whatever its faults, however, "Mourn— And Then Onward!" (VP 737-38) is valuable for its comparison of Parnell to Moses ("His memory now is a tall pillar, burning / Before us in the gloom!"), a persistent association that reached its peak in Lady Gregory's 1911 play *The Deliverer*. The fall of Parnell, especially his sacrificial "betrayal" at the hands of his own people, was to be a lifelong theme of Ireland's two most powerful writers, a theme expressed most bitterly by Yeats in "To a Shade" (1913) and "Parnell's Funeral" (1934) and by Joyce in "The Shade of Parnell" (1912) and the satiric poem that most succinctly epitomizes the betrayal motif, "Gas from a Burner" (also 1912):

But I owe a duty to Ireland;
I hold her honour in my hand,
This lovely land that always sent
Her writers and artists to banishment
And in a spirit of Irish fun
Betrayed her own leaders, one by one.
'Twas Irish humour, wet and dry,
Flung quicklime into Parnell's eye.[27]

Nor was literary treatment of the Parnell myth the exclusive property of Yeats and Joyce. Herbert Howarth was accurate in subtitling his study of six major modern Irish writers *Literature under Parnell's Star,* that star said to have fallen as the Chief was lowered into the earth of Joyce's lovely but traitorous land.[28]

Parnell's biographer, the late dean of Irish historians F. S. L. Lyons, described in 1977 the predicament he faced in responding to the "literary resonances of that famous name," to what "the writers made of him" after his death:

It is the predicament of a student trained to deal with what passes for historical reality who has not only to adjust himself to the existence of something loosely defined as myth, but has to recognize also that myth can itself be a kind of historical reality.[29]

Like Howarth, whose theme is the writers' development and modification of the Parnell story, Lyons stresses the "protean" nature of the myth, its capacity to change "according to the needs of the individuals who used it, and according to the exigencies of the situations with which they had to grapple";[30] a capacity, it might be added, common to all political myths.

In his acceptance speech on receiving the 1923 Nobel Prize for Literature, Yeats, responding to the "Troubles" Ireland had just endured, focused on the fall of Parnell as the genesis not only of the Irish Renaissance but also of subsequent Irish history:

The modern literature of Ireland, and indeed all that stir of thought which prepared for the Anglo-Irish war, began when Parnell fell from power in 1891. A disillusioned and embittered Ireland turned from parliamentary politics; an event was conceived; and the race began, as I think, to be troubled by that event's long gestation. (Au 559)

In short, as Yeats's self-referential birth imagery reveals, the terrible beauty born in 1916 was also inevitably an event vexed to nightmare by the rocking cradle of Parnell's fall. It is true that the seeds of the Irish Renaissance predated Parnell's rise and fall, and Lyons insists that a "hiatus" occurred between Parnell's death and the full impact of the myth.[31] But Parnell's fall *was* the catalyst in what Yeats called the "turn from parliamentary politics" and the "gestation" of the Rising. For Conor Cruise O'Brien the pivotal moment was 26 November 1890, when a majority of Parnell's party, responding to Gladstone's letter announcing that he could no longer work with Parnell, called for the fatal meeting:

It was a decision heavy with consequences, not only for Parnell, but for people then unborn. *For this was the decision that discredited constitutional democratic politics, and began the revival of enthusiasm among the young for the idea of armed revolution.* When Parnell died, the Gaelic Athletic Association in Cork elected as their patron in his place, not any constitutional politician—even among those who had stood by Parnell—but James Stephens, the founder of the Irish Republican Brotherhood. And it was the Irish Republican Brotherhood which was to decide, and time, the Rising of Easter Week 1916. As Parnell's most vindictive enemy, Tim Healy, had said: "We have the voters, but Parnell has their sons."[32]

Thus, Yeats's synopsis in his Nobel Address to the Swedish Academy reflects both kinds of Lyons's "historical reality."

Furthermore, in the Ireland "troubled" by the gestation of what became the Easter Rising and the subsequent Troubles (the Anglo-Irish War followed by the even more rending Irish Civil War), Yeats played a role aesthetically analogous to that of Parnell. In his resistance to the attempt by one-eyed Nationalists to reduce art to propaganda, Yeats emulated the hauteur with which that reserved aristocrat of fire and ice, of passion under control, had earlier faced down the mob. Dedicated to a cultural transformation that would lead to their shared goal, independent nationhood for Ireland, Yeats adopted in his dealings with the Nationalists a mask of arrogance similar to Parnell's, and with the same mixed results.

Nevertheless, it was precisely that arrogant pride, the Achilles' heel that actually brought Parnell down, that thrilled Yeats and Joyce. Though Parnell saw himself immediately after O'Shea's disclosure as a mythic scapegoat likely to be betrayed and devoured, he couched his appeal to his countrymen as a demand. In his manifesto to the Irish people, a document published shortly before a majority of his party rejected him under pressure from Gladstone's Liberals, the Chief demanded that he not be thrown to "the English wolves now howling for my destruction." Writing two decades later, in the Italian article "L'ombra di Parnell," Joyce sardonically commented of Parnell's fellow Irishmen: "It redounds to their honour that they did not throw him to the English wolves; they tore him to pieces themselves" (CW 196).

The dismembering and devouring of Parnell as a sacrificial hero-god proved to be an image of considerable resonance in the work of Yeats and Joyce. (In *The Deliverer*, Lady Gregory also had her Moses-Parnell thrown to the pack—in her case, cats!) Yeats reports that a phrase of Goethe's was much quoted in the newspapers during the Parnell controversy: "The Irish seem to me like a pack of hounds, always dragging down some noble stag" (Au 316). The point, one repeated in Joyce's Italian article, is that it was not the "English wolves" but the Irish pack that had inevitably brought down Parnell. The equation of Goethe's noble stag with Parnell is also echoed in "The Holy Office," when Joyce—solitary, indifferent, and "self-doomed"—declares his independence from the writers of the Irish Renaissance itself. Instead, he stands "Firm as the mountain ridges where / I flash my antlers on the air." The same image, repeated in the 1904 "A Portrait of the Artist," also appears in *Stephen Hero*: "There was his ground and he flung them disdain from flashing antlers" (CW 152, SH 35).

Though the "self-doomed" adds Romantic resonance, this is little more than youthful bravado. The crucial mythopoeic point, however, is that the noble stag *was* destroyed by that Irish pack. Clearly echoing Goethe's phrase, Yeats has a collective Ireland "dragg[ing] this quarry down" in "Parnell's Funeral." In the context of our theme and of the Parnell myth as handled by Yeats and Joyce, the Great Mother as destroyer and devourer appears in a variety of guises, manifestations as "protean" as the myth of Parnell and of the female archetype itself. The manifestations include a priestess-archer, a heart-devouring collective Ireland, a pair of vindictive harridans, a farrow-eating sow, and a lady quick to change sides.

"Parnell's Funeral" associates a private Yeatsian vision with the meteorological phenomena attending Parnell's burial, both fleshed out by mythopoeic material furnished by Frazer and Blake and later elucidated by a scholar of ancient Mediterranean religions:

A woman, and an arrow on a string;
A pierced boy, image of a star laid low.
That woman, the Great Mother imaging,
Cut out his heart.

The "sacrificial death" of the pierced boy at the hands of a "representative priestess" of the "Mother-Goddess," Vacher Burch told Yeats, "symbolized the death and resurrection of the Tree-spirit, or Apollo."[33] Yeats applies the myth to the death of Parnell, at whose funeral, Maud Gonne told him, "a star fell in broad daylight." Characteristically skeptical and open-minded, Yeats wondered if it "was a collective hallucination or an actual event." But he also knew that well over a hundred thousand people had attended that funeral, the largest in the history of a land not unfamiliar with burial rites, and he immediately recorded the famous description of Standish O'Grady: "I state a fact—it was witnessed by thousands. While his followers were committing Charles Parnell's remains to the earth, the sky was bright with strange lights and flames" (VP 834).

In the poem, amid the brightness remaining in a tempestuous and cloudy sky, "a brighter star shoots down; / What shudders run through all that animal blood? / What is this sacrifice?" The lines are allusive: once more Thomas Nashe's "brightness falls from the air," and Yeats has telescoped the questions from the first and fourth stanzas of the "Ode on a Grecian Urn" ("What men or gods are these? . . . Who are these coming to the sacrifice?"). He had asked in his note to the poem "If the fall of a star may not, upon occasion, symbolize an accepted sacrifice?" (VP 834). The sacrifice was, of course, Parnell himself, that noble quarry dragged down by "popular rage," the "*Hysterica passio*" of Catholics outraged by disclosure of the love affair with a married woman. Katherine O'Shea as Eve as Devorgilla (see U 29): Ireland, it seemed, had once again been betrayed by a woman. But it was Ireland herself who destroyed this male sinner, a Parnell fallen from grace and soon to die, exhausted and heartbroken. In the poem, Yeats refers to Irish heroes of the past, victims of the British. "Strangers murdered Emmet, Fitzgerald, Tone"; but in the case of Parnell, the Irish had destroyed their own deliverer:

None shared our guilt; nor did we play a part
Upon a painted stage when we devoured his heart.

This guilt is clearly collective, one shared by Irish men and women; at the same time, these heart-devourers are mythologically associated with the priestess of the Mother-Goddess whose barb pierces and lays low the star-hero and who is described in the preceding stanza as having "Cut out his heart." Vacher Burch notwithstanding, Yeats was thinking of Blake's "The Mental Traveller," the gnomic poem that underlies much of Yeats's *A Vision* and, in its grim deterministic cyclicism, threatened the later poet's imaginative freedom. A "Boy"—Blake's Orc as Christ, Dionysus, Loki, and Prometheus—is given to a "Woman Old," the Triple Goddess as Crone, who "nails him down upon a rock

/ Catches his shrieks in cups of gold," and, like the rejuvenated Old Woman of *Cathleen ni Houlihan,* "grows young" as she drinks:

She binds iron thorns around his head
She pierces both his hands and feet
She cuts his heart out at his side. . . .
To make it feel both cold & heat

Her fingers number every Nerve
Just as a miser counts his gold
She lives upon his shrieks & cries
And she grows young as he grows old.

"Parnell's Funeral" ends with an embittered litany suggestive of both primitive rituals in which a dead chief's heart is eaten by his potential successors and of the dismembering and devouring of the primal father by his sons, the myth at the root of all subsequent mythology and culture according to Freud's *Totem and Taboo* (1912). "Had de Valéra eaten Parnell's heart . . . Had Cosgrave eaten Parnell's heart. . . Had even O'Duffy . . . ." But he will "name no more" of these politicians: their school is "a crowd," while Parnell's master was "solitude." The poem, an uneven one, ends greatly: "Through Jonathan Swift's dark grove he passed, and there / Plucked bitter wisdom that enriched his blood" (VP 543). Parnell's rite of passage is in part replicated by the Irish people. Yeats ends his note to the poem: "We had passed through an initiation like that of the Tibetan ascetic, who staggers half dead from a trance, where he has seen himself eaten alive and has not yet learned that the eater was himself" (VP 835).

In the penultimate sentence of his note to "Parnell's Funeral," Yeats referred to "James Joyce" and "that dinner table scene" in *A Portrait of the Artist as a Young Man,* "when after a violent quarrel about Parnell and the priests, the host sobs, his head upon the table; 'My dead King.' " The bowed sobber is not the host, Mr. Dedalus (whose eyes are also filled with tears), but the Fenian Mr. Casey. Yeats was right, however, to associate his own myth of Parnell devoured with the Christmas dinner scene in *Portrait,* which also features unlikely but still recognizable priestesses of the Mother-Goddess in her negative aspect. In this, the most unforgettable of literary evocations of Parnell, the role of destructive female, the harridan-embodiment of the devourers of Parnell's heart, is played, at the dinner table, by Mrs. Riordan and, in the anecdote of a Parnell meeting, by the old woman shrieking denunciations of the Chief in Mr. Casey's face.

Dante Riordan is the right choice to play the role of Terrible Mother devouring the male hero. The novel's first instance of the cruel female, she is allied with predatory, castrating forces from the outset. She sadistically threatens Stephen as a child, borrowing her "eagles" who "will come and pull out his eyes" from Isaac Watts's hymn ("The ravens shall pick out his eyes / And eagles eat the same") and from the first of Joyce's "epiphanies."[34] She thus introduces themes to be developed in *Ulysses*: Ireland as the carrion-crow croaking for vengeance, and related forces—usually connected with Stephen's mother and with that "crazy queen," the Catholic Church—conspiring to induce devouring guilt in Stephen ("agenbite of inwit") and to threaten his vision. In Watts's hymn, though it is Protestant rather than Catholic, the eyes to be picked by ravens and devoured by eagles are those of him who "breaks his father's law / *Or mocks his mother's word*," which should remind us that, while Stephen's mother is "nice" in this opening episode of *Portrait,* and the authority figures seem to be the father and Dante, Mrs. Dedalus does insist, "Stephen will apologize" (P 8). Stephen, as Chester Anderson notes of this scene, "is threatened with 'castration' in the most classic way: by having his eyes pulled out, as Oedipus himself pulled out his with Jocasta's brooch." He is right to identify Dante with the castrating "terrible mother," but his distinction—"it is important that the threat comes from Dante, the 'bad' mother split from the 'nice'6"—is only partially accurate since, as Suzette Henke has remarked, it "obscures the revelation of Mary Dedalus as a female authority figure." Still, as Henke also observes, it is the "rabid" Dante Riordan, supporting "ecclesiastical authority in the name of moral righteousness," who, "like the 'sow that eats her farrow,' . . . is willing to sacrifice Parnell as a political scapegoat."[35]

The "negative" character of the Mother-Goddess is well represented by Dante, the 'bad' mother split from the 'nice' "—is only partially accurate since, as Suzette Henke has remarked, it "obscures the revelation of Mary walk in the fresh air, a "good breath of ozone." Mr. Dedalus turns to Dante and asks:

—You didn't stir out at all, Mrs Riordan?
Dante frowned and said shortly:
—No. (P 28)

The circumscribed, narrow world of this "spoiled nun" (35) is indeed airless; and she sustains her negativity. Offered sauce for her turkey, Dante "covered her plate with her hands and said:—No thanks" (30). Dante had been from the first a catastrophic mother, a moral guardian threatening Stephen's most vulnerable organ, his eyes. Here she is the representative of the forces that brought down vulnerable Parnell, a spokeswoman for "religion" and "public morality" who will *not* let up:

Nice language for any catholic to use! . . . And am I to sit here and listen to the pastors of my church being flouted? . . . The bishops and priests of Ireland have spoken, . . . and they must be obeyed. . . . He was no longer worthy to lead, said Dante. He was a public sinner. (31–32)

The ghost of the Chief had haunted Joyce's "Ivy Day in the Committee Room." Again Parnell is an absent but formidable presence—at this table as he was in turn-of-the-century Irish politics. When Mr. Dedalus and Mr. Casey criticize two Irish archbishops, Dante cries "hotly" that young Stephen will "remember all this when he grows up . . . the language he heard against God and religion and priests in his own house." Ironically, she is right. But Mr. Casey, who refuses to reject "the man that was born to lead" Ireland out of colonial bondage (38), is the more accurate prophet, for it is his position and that of Mr. Dedalus that Joyce (in Herbert Howarth's phrase) "burned into the world's memory."

—Let him remember too, cried Mr Casey to her from across the table, the language with which the priests and the priests' pawns broke Parnell's heart and hounded him into his grave. Let him remember that too when he grows up.
—Sons of bitches! cried Mr Dedalus. When he was down they turned on him to betray him and rend him like rats in a sewer. Lowlived dogs! And they look it! By Christ, they look it!
—They behaved rightly, cried Dante. **They** obeyed their bishops and their priests. Honour to them! (33–34)

A would-be peacemaker, Mrs. Dedalus tries again to calm the situation, but Mrs. Riordan, in a nice double negative, "will not say nothing. I will defend my church and my religion when it is insulted and spit on by renegade catholics" (34). Mr. Casey seizes on the words "renegade" and "spit." Flushed, but speaking with "quiet indignation," he refutes the implication that he is a renegade Catholic, while "spit" triggers the hilarious anecdote he tells about a political meeting in Arklow "not long before the chief died." "Before he was killed, you mean," Mr. Dedalus interjects. The story centers on a truly Terrible Woman, one of the crowd "booing and baaing" Parnell as he and his entourage made their way to the train station after the meeting.

"There was one old lady," says Mr. Casey, "and a drunken old harridan she was surely, that paid all her attention to me. She kept dancing along beside me in the mud bawling and screaming into my face: *Priesthunter! The Paris Funds! Mr Fox! Kitty O'Shea!"* He endures her charges, including Parnell's alleged misappropriation of funds and the scandalmongering reference to the alias he used in his liaisons with his inamorata; but when the old hag called "that lady" a name he will not repeat at table, Mr. Casey spat into that symbolically crucial organ, her eye.

> —I had my mouth full of tobacco juice. I bent down to her and *Phth*! says I to her like that . . . right into her eye. . . .
> —*O Jesus, Mary and Joseph!* says she. *I'm blinded! I'm blinded and drowned!*
> He stopped in a fit of coughing and laughing, repeating
> —*I'm blinded entirely.* (36–37)

Though she is not amused by Casey's "braggadocio" in recounting his "tale of heroism" and "masculine prowess," Suzette Henke has it right; Casey here "conquers the malevolent crone—the folkloric witch [or] hag. . . . Spitting into her eye, he symbolically achieves a talismanic victory through sexual violation of the phallic mother."[36]

The spit will be returned, or "almost," by Mrs. Riordan, one harridan, in effect, championing another. When her defense of the Catholic clergy, "the apple of God's eye," reaches its crescendo ("traitor, an adulterer! The priests were right to abandon him. The priests were always the true friends of Ireland. . . . God and religion before everything! Dante cried. God and religion before the world!"), Mr. Casey raises his clenched fist and brings it down on the table with a crash.

> —Very well, then, he shouted hoarsely, if it comes to that, no God for Ireland!
> —John! John! cried Mr Dedalus, seizing his guest by the coatsleeve.
> Dante stared across the table, her cheeks shaking. Mr Casey struggled up from his chair and bent across the table towards her, scraping the air from before his eyes with one hand as though he were tearing aside a cobweb.
> —No God for Ireland! he cried. We have had too much God in Ireland. Away with God!
> —Blasphemer! Devil! screamed Dante, starting to her feet and almost spitting in his face.
> Uncle Charles and Mr Dedalus pulled Mr Casey back into his chair again, talking to him from both sides reasonably. He stared before him out of his dark flaming eyes, repeating:
> —Away with God, I say!

Priestesses of the Great Mother

Dante shoved her chair violently aside and left the table, upsetting her napkinring which rolled slowly along the carpet and came to rest against the foot of an easychair. Mrs Dedalus rose quickly and followed her towards the door. At the door Dante turned round violently and shouted down the room, her cheeks flushed and quivering with rage:
—Devil out of hell! We won! We crushed him to death! Fiend!
The door slammed behind her.
Mr Casey, freeing his arms from his holders, suddenly bowed his head on his hands with a sob of pain.
—Poor Parnell! he cried loudly. My dead king!
He sobbed loudly and bitterly.
Stephen, raising his terrorstricken face, saw that his father's eyes were full of tears. (39)

The setting—Christmas dinner—is religiously and mythologically appropriate. "Parnell is dead," wrote Hélène Cixous, "but it is Christmas and the Christ Child is about to be born." Joyce's theme, however, is not birth but death:

> The King of the Jews and the uncrowned King of Ireland are to be slain after a meal at which they are dismembered . . . . The adults' conversation involves the dishes of a ritual meal that seems related to the cannibalism of hatred rather than to that of the eucharist. It is a special dinner, but there are ghostly guests present too. . . . The menu is only apparently innocent, and the communion made here is perfidious and treacherous.[37]

The Christmas dinner scene does more than connect the Christ *Child* with Parnell, the "man . . . *born* to be" Ireland's savior and messiah. Beyond that, the "cannibalism of hatred," that parody of the eucharist that nevertheless reveals the primordial origins of the symbolism, allies Christ and Parnell as archetypal hero-victims betrayed by their own: scapegoat saviors rejected and dismembered by their own treacherous and perfidious people. And Joyce goes out of his way, as he will in the parody-execution of the young rebel in "Cyclops," to connect the theme of perfidious Erin with the myth of the Devouring Female.

Dinner is, as Simon Dedalus complains, "spoiled." (When, notes Yeats, "Church and State" are "the mob that howls at the door, / Wine shall run thick to the end, / Bread taste sour.") Most of the turkey goes uneaten, and the pudding will never be served. But in this Last Supper become a repetition-with-a-difference of that totemic meal Freud thought the primal myth, the dead Parnell's heart, a heart broken by the priests and the priests' pawns before he was hounded into the grave, is once again devoured by a vindictive female.[38]

Destructive from the outset, Dante represents, like the "old lady" of Mr. Casey's more-than-amusing anecdote, Ireland at her worst. "Devil out of hell!" she cries in triumph over the corpse of Parnell, "We won! We crushed him to death!" The villains are the priests and the male God they allegedly serve in what Mr. Dedalus calls this "priestridden Godforsaken" land (P 37). But Joyce, for reasons mythic and perhaps misogynistic, has chosen to put the position of the priests and their pawns into the mouths of two harridans who seem appropriate hag-priestesses of the Terrible Mother. In a rending reenactment of the myth, the male hero has once again been crushed to death, dismembered, and consumed by Mother Ireland—this time, in the form of *two* Devouring Females.

Devouring Ireland

Nightmare leaves fatigue:
    We envy men of action
Who sleep and wake, murder and intrigue
    Without being doubtful, without being haunted.
And I envy the intransigence of my own
    Countrymen who shoot to kill and never
See the victim's face become their own
    Or find his motive sabotage their motives.
So reading the memoirs of Maud Gonne,
    Daughter of an English mother and a soldier father,
I note how a single purpose can be founded on
    A jumble of opposites:
Dublin Castle, the vice-regal ball,
    The embassies of Europe,
Hatred scribbled on a wall,
    Gaols and revolvers.
. . . .
Kathleen ni Houlihan! Why
    Must a country, like a ship or a car, be always female,
Mother or sweetheart? A woman passing by,
    We did but see her passing.
Passing like a patch of sun on the rainy hill
    And yet we love her for ever and hate our neighbour
And each one in his will
    Binds his heirs to continuance of hatred.
. . . .
Odi atque amo:
    Shall we cut this name on trees with a rusty dagger?
Her mountains are still blue, her rivers flow
    Bubbling over the boulders.
She is both a bore and a bitch;
    Better close the horizon,
Send her no more fantasy, no more longings which

Are under a fatal tariff.
For common sense is the vogue
   And she gives her children neither sense nor money
Who slouch around the world with a gesture and a brogue
   And a faggot of useless memories.
   —Louis MacNeice[1]

Aha! I know you, grammer! Hamlet, revenge! The old sow that eats her farrow!
   —James Joyce[2]

Dante and the harassing harridan from Arklow are folkloric hags, Irish women as devourers. Later in *Portrait*, in the fifth and final chapter, Ireland is specifically referred to as a Devouring Female, "the old sow that eats her farrow."[3] The occasion is perhaps the pivotal moment for any understanding of Joyce's own relation to Mother Ireland, Mother tongue, Mother Church. Stephen Dedalus is talking with an ardent young Nationalist for whom he feels considerable personal affection; revealingly, Davin alone is permitted to call him by his "Christian name," a rather touching "Stevie."[4] But Stephen is not to be seduced, religiously or politically. As the conversation develops, Davin, a chaste young man, admits to having had his Catholic sensibilities disturbed by Stephen's sexual revelations.

   A tide began to surge beneath the calm surface of Stephen's friendliness.
   —This race and this country and this life produced me, he said. I shall express myself as I am.
   —Try to be one of us, repeated Davin. In your heart you are an Irishman but your pride is too powerful.
   —My ancestors threw off their language and took another, Stephen said. They allowed a handful of foreigners to subject them. Do you fancy I am going to pay in my own life and person debts they made? What for?
   —For our freedom, said Davin.
   —No honourable and sincere man, said Stephen, has given up to you his life and his youth and his affections from the days of Tone to those of Parnell but you sold him to the enemy or failed him in need or reviled him and left him for another. And you invite me to be one of you. I'd see you damned first.
   —They died for their ideals, Stevie, said Davin. Our day will come yet, believe me.
   Stephen, following his own thought, was silent for an instant.
   —The soul is born, he said vaguely, first in those moments I told you of. It has a slow and dark birth, more mysterious than the birth of the body. When the soul of a man is born in this country there are nets flung at it to hold it back from flight. You talk to me of nationality, language, religion. I shall try to fly by those nets.
   Davin knocked the ashes from his pipe.

—Too deep for me, Stevie, he said. But a man's country comes first. Ireland first, Stevie. You can be a poet or mystic after.
—Do you know what Ireland is? asked Stephen with cold violence. Ireland is the old sow that eats her farrow.[5]

The litter devoured by Ireland consists of the patriot-martyrs who have died for her. Designated an "old sow," however, she has a history. Beo and other litter-devouring Celtic sow-goddesses represent the insatiable female as threatening and desirable, an obvious projection of male fantasies. Her classical lineage goes back to Egyptian and other Mediterranean Goddesses of Earth and Sky. The earth is the Goddess's womb, and into "this womb-pit" according to Herodotus, "offerings were thrown, namely . . . live pigs, these being the offspring of the gravid Earth Mother, the sow." This emblem of the Great Mother is also a cosmic projection. An early Egyptian text, according to Herman Kees, depicts "the sky woman as a sow, . . . the star-children going into her mouth in the manner of a sow eating her young." The Egyptian Sky-Goddess Nut, her body marked with stars, is "the sow, who devours her own children, sun, moon, and stars in the west." She appears on some steles as "a white sow"; the same is true of Great Mother Isis. Troy's excavator, Heinrich Schleimann, "found the figure of a pig dotted with stars, evidently representing the sky-woman as a sow." Not only has "the cult of the sow," as Neumann says, "left numerous traces"; the "swine-figure of the Great Mother" can cross sexual lines and yet remain recognizably the Great Mother:

the open womb is the devouring symbol of the uroboric mother, especially when connected with phallic symbols. The gnashing mouth of the Medusa with its boar's tusks betrays these features most plainly. . . . Just as beard and phallus are parts of her androgynous nature, so she is the sow that farrows and the boar that kills.[6]

Fusing the Great Mother's creative and destructive aspects, Joyce makes her the old sow that *eats* her farrow.

That image of Ireland as farrow-eating sow returns in *Ulysses*, a "jocoserious" (U 553) novel in which the Devouring Female appropriately assumes comic, tragicomic, and tragic forms: from the passionate "Sheila, my own" of "Cyclops" to the phantasmagoric "Bella/Bello" and the terrifying "corpse-chewer"-of-a-mother Stephen confronts both in "Telemachus" and, climactically, in "Circe," all culminating in the appearance of Ireland as "Old Gummy Granny."

* * *

Ireland as Devouring Woman appears in her least phantasmagoric yet most comic role in "Cyclops," the chapter in *Ulysses* whose "art" is specifically designated in Joyce's schema as "politics." There, in the funniest and most sustained of the narrative-interrupting parodies, an Irish rebel is about to go under the headsman's ax: more severed heads on the painted stage of politics-as-drama, this time in the form of gallows humor.

The execution-of-the-rebel parody is triggered by the Citizen's rant, "in the best Fenian style" (LJ 1:126), as synopsized by the barfly-narrator of the "Cyclops" episode. The "men of sixty seven and who fears to speak of ninety eight" allude to the abortive Fenian Rising of 1867 and to the failed United Irishman rebellion of 1798, the latter the historical setting of *Cathleen ni Houlihan*. Predictably, Joyce has Yeats's play on the mind and lips of the bellicose Citizen. At one point he declares, echoing Yeats's old Woman, "we want no more strangers in our house" (U 265), and he refers to the overseas Irish in America (who in "the land of the free remember the house of bondage") as saviors who will "come again and with a vengeance, no cravens, the sons of Grunuaile, the champions of Kathleen ni Houlihan" (270).

Bloom, the prudent member and man of commensense reason, is of course making no headway with the Citizen, glorifying the dead in his own "glory hole," Barney Kiernan's pub:

And the citizen and Bloom having an argument about the point, the brothers Sheares and Wolfe Tone beyond on Arbour Hill and Robert Emmet and die for your country, the Tommy Moore touch about Sara Curran and she's far from the land.

The execution scene is in large part a parody of Emmet's execution; it also plays on the connection with Sarah Curran. Emmet, the United Irishman who led the furtive 1803 rebellion and march on Dublin Castle, having been captured, escaped—only to be recaptured when he delayed his flight from the country to sentimentally and stupidly pay a celebrated "last farewell" to his fiancée. A perfect transition to the execution parody it would seem; but Joyce suspends it for a moment to allow the narrator to recall a "queer story" about Bloom and "three women" who "near roast[ed] him" for a scheme that backfired. Of the three, two are named (one is Molly, the other a Mrs. O'Dowd); the third, referred to three times as the "old one," is none other than Mrs. Riordan, the Dante of the Christmas dinner scene in *Portrait*, still "thumping her craw" with ostentatious piety. The story is no less amusing but rather less "queer" once we see it as yet another variation on the Triple

Devouring Ireland 53

Goddess, with Dante as the Crone. (Bloom's real "roasting" at the hands of vindictive women will come, of course, in the "Circe" chapter.)

Immediately following this inserted anecdote we have the resumption of the cliché-ridden, one-eyed politics of the Nationalist Citizen:

> —The memory of the dead, says the citizen taking up his pintglass and glaring at Bloom.
> —Ay, ay, says Joe.
> —You don't grasp my point, says Bloom. What I mean is. . . .
> —*Sinn Fein*! says the citizen. *Sinn fein amhain*! The friends we love are by our side and the foes we hate before us. (251)

Joyce had spared us the "Tommy Moore touch" about Sarah Curran, sentimentalized in the maudlin "She Is Far from the Land," but he puts in the Citizen's mouth another and more rousing poem ("Where Is the Slave?") from Moore's *Irish Melodies* (melodies Joyce knew by heart, as *Finnegans Wake* demonstrates). Though that poem too involves leaving Ireland ("Farewell, Erin"), the Citizen naturally prefers the lines immediately preceding:

> We tread the land that bore us,
> Her green flag glitters o'er us,
> The friends we've tried
> Are by our side,
> And the foe we hate before us.

The Citizen's allusion, with "love" substituted for "tried," leads directly to the execution scene parody, beginning, "The last farewell was affecting in the extreme." In addition to the Robert Emmet–Sarah Curran takeoff (partly indebted to Washington Irving's story "The Broken Heart"), Joyce's theatrical tableau also parodies the Calvary-like phenomena that had attended Parnell's interment in Glasnevin, Standish O'Grady's account of which I have already quoted from Yeats. Here is Joyce in his best pseudo-Miltonic journalese:

> The deafening claps of thunder and the dazzling flashes of lightning which lit up the ghastly scene testified that the artillery of heaven had lent its supernatural pomp to the already gruesome spectacle. (252)

The high point of the "spectacle" comes with the arrival of the hero's betrothed:

The *nec* and *non plus ultra* of emotion were reached when the blushing bride elect burst her way through the serried ranks of the bystanders and flung herself upon the muscular bosom of him who was about to be launched into eternity for her sake. The hero folded her willowy form in a loving embrace murmuring fondly *Sheila, my own*. Encouraged by this use of her christian name she kissed passionately all the various suitable areas of his person which the decencies of prison garb permitted her ardour to reach. She swore to him as they mingled the salt streams of their tears that she would ever cherish his memory, that she would never forget her hero boy who went to his death with a song on his lips as if he were but going to a hurling match in Clonturk park. She brought back to his recollection the happy days of blissful childhood together on the banks of Anna Liffey when they had indulged in the innocent pastimes of the young and, oblivious of the dreadful present, they both laughed heartily, all the spectators, including the venerable pastor, joining in the general merriment. That monster audience simply rocked with delight. But anon they were overcome with grief and clasped their hands for the last time. A fresh torrent of tears burst from their lachrymal ducts and the vast concourse of people, touched to the inmost core, broke into heartrending sobs, not the least affected being the aged prebendary himself. Big strong men, officers of the peace and genial giants of the royal Irish constabulary, were making frank use of their handkerchiefs and it is safe to say that there was not a dry eye in that record assemblage. A most romantic incident occurred when a handsome young Oxford graduate, noted for his chivalry towards the fair sex, stepped forward and, presenting his visiting card, bankbook and genealogical tree, solicited the hand of the hapless young lady, requesting her to name the day, and was accepted on the spot. Every lady in the audience was presented with a tasteful souvenir of the occasion in the shape of a skull and crossbones brooch, a timely and generous act which evoked a fresh outburst of emotion: and when the gallant young Oxonian (the bearer, by the way, of one of the most timehonoured names in Albion's history) placed on the finger of his blushing *fiancée* an expensive engagement ring with emeralds set in the form of a fourleaved shamrock the excitement knew no bounds. Nay, even the stern provostmarshal, lieutenantcolonel Tomkin- Maxwell ffrenchmullan Tomlinson, who presided on the sad occasion, he who had blown a considerable number of sepoys from the cannonmouth without flinching, could not now restrain his natural emotion. With his mailed gauntlet he brushed away a furtive tear and was overheard, by those privileged burghers who happened to be in his immediate *entourage*, to murmur to himself in a faltering undertone:— God blimey if she aint a clinker, that there bleeding tart. Blimey it makes me kind of bleeding cry, straight, it does, when I sees her cause I thinks of my old mashtub what's waiting for me down Limehouse way. (254-55)

Beneath the hilarity loom less-than-amusing, even somber motifs. "Sheila, my own" combines Sarah Curran, love of whom was the immediate cause of Robert Emmet's recapture and execution, with Sheila-ni-Gara, another of the many female names for Ireland, the beloved for whose "sake" Emmet and so many other rebel heroes were "launched into eternity." And Sheila is hardly the victim's "own." All those who, in Davin's words, had "died for their ideals," were, from Stephen's perspective, betrayed by the very Nationalists who identified themselves with Ireland's cause: "No honourable and sincere man . . . has given up to you his life and his youth and his affections from the days of Tone to those of Parnell but you sold him to the enemy or failed him in need or reviled him and left him for another." The gallant and wealthy Oxonian who proposes to Sheila is "accepted on the spot" by a woman who, protesting too much, has just sworn that she "would ever cherish" the "memory" of her "hero boy who went to his death with a song on his lips." We know what *sort* of song. The Fenian poets were forever singing of "thy hapless fate, dear Ireland," to quote a line reviled by Yeats for its conventional sentimentality (Au 151). But, like the historical Sarah Curran, Joyce's "hapless young lady," her hand solicited by the bearer of "one of the most timehonoured names in Albion's history," posts with dexterity not just to "another" but to the enemy.[7] And this theme of perfidious Erin—ever ready to compromise herself by coming to a collaborative arrangement with perfidious Albion—is interwoven both with the story of Parnell, whose party and countrymen succumbed to English pressure and betrayed their leader, and with a central theme of *Ulysses* itself, since Sheila-Ireland here resembles Molly Bloom, unfaithful Penelope to Bloom's victimized, cuckolded Ulysses, adulterate Queen Gertrude to his proletarian King Hamlet.

Sheila also presents a comic variant on *our* central theme of the Devouring Female. As her name suggests, she is a form of Sheela-na-gig, a devouring woman who hangs on the doomed man as if appetite had grown by what it fed on. As a clinging vine whose comic lust is insatiate and voracious—"she kissed passionately all the various suitable areas of his person which the decencies of prison garb permitted her ardour to reach"—she is allied with Yeats's tragic version of the femme fatale and Consuming Woman, the queen who presses her lips to man's severed head. The force of the underlying mythic archetype may explain why it is that Joyce chose to parody the execution of Robert Emmet in particular; for Emmet, in a memorable scene of rare brutality, was hanged *and beheaded*, "the beheading done with a common knife, and apparently while Emmet's heart was still beating."[8] To be sure, our hero's head is still attached, though Sheila seems less interested in his lips than in kissing other "areas," particularly those the "decencies" of prison garb do *not* permit "her ardour to reach." But severing, in any case, is imminent. We should not forget the blood-soaked circumstances in which Sheila's ardor is aroused; nor, funny as the description is, should we forget how profoundly James Joyce was repelled by bloodshed:

by the block stood the grim figure of the executioner, his visage being concealed in a tengallon pot with two circular perforated apertures through which his eyes glowered furiously. As he awaited the fatal signal he tested the edge of his horrible weapon by honing it upon his brawny forearm or decapitated in rapid succession a flock of sheep which had been provided by the admirers of his fell but necessary office. On a handsome mahogany table near him were neatly arranged the quartering knife, the various finely tempered disembowelling appliances (specially supplied by the world-famous firm of cutlers, Messrs John Round and Sons, Sheffield), a terra cotta saucepan for the reception of the duodenum, colon, blind intestine and appendix etc when successfully extracted and two commodious milkjugs destined to receive the most precious blood of the most precious victim. (253-54)

The allusion to the shedding of Christ's blood, precious because redemptive, is combined with a parodic reversal of woman's nurturing breasts. The "commodious milkjugs" destined to receive the blood of the victim prepare us for the arrival, at the zenith of the sacrifice, of Sheila, "that there bleeding tart" who in fact sheds no blood, redeems nothing, and is not nurturing but devouring, flinging herself upon *his* "muscular bosom." The "milkjugs" also look before and after: back to the opening chapter's old milkwoman, the shrunken-papped crone who gives milk that is "not hers," and ahead, not to Molly, whose ample breasts Bloom "wanted to milk . . . into the tea" (621), but to the novel's most horrific image of the Great Mother as Devourer. I refer to the ghostly manifestation of Stephen's own mother, who "suckled me with a bitter milk" (322): a "ghoul" and "corpsechewer" first encountered in the opening chapter but fully confronted, and repudiated, in the hallucinatory "Circe" episode.

*   *   *

In this opening chapter, "Telemachus," the Goddess appears—in a parody of her triple nature as beloved, nurturer, and crone—as an old woman who delivers the morning milk to the tower occupied by Stephen Dedalus, Buck Mulligan, and the Englishman Haines, an Oxford dilettante equally intrigued by the Irish "folk" and by Stephen's "sayings." Steeped in the very mythology and folklore he repudiates, Stephen sees in the old woman Ireland herself—an impoverished, ignorant, sterile, and utterly subject form of the Old Woman of Yeats's *Cathleen ni Houlihan*.

He watched her pour into the measure and thence into the jug rich white milk, not hers. Old shrunken paps. She poured again a measureful and a tilly. Old and secret she had entered from a morning world, maybe a messenger. She praised the goodness of the milk, pouring it out. Crouching by a patient cow at daybreak in the lush field, a witch on her toadstool, her wrinkled fingers quick at the squirting dugs. They lowed about her whom they knew, dewsilky cattle. Silk of the kine and poor old woman, names given her in old times. A wandering crone, lowly form of an immortal serving her conqueror and her gay betrayer, their common cuckquean, a messenger from the secret morning. To serve or to upbraid, whether he could not tell: but scorned to beg her favour. (12)

"Silk of the kine" and "poor old woman" (the Shan Van Vocht) are, of course, names given Ireland "in old times." Like "Sheila, my own," and the seduced servant girl of "Two Gallants," but *un*like Yeats's Cathleen ni Houlihan, this old woman literally "serves" her British conqueror. Whether she is to "serve" or "upbraid" *him* Stephen cannot tell. But, though an Irishman, as Davin had said in *Portrait*, his "pride is too powerful" to permit him to serve *her* in the way demanded by Nationalists; so, though he alone "recognizes" her, he "scorned to beg her favour." Nor can Joyce's personified Ireland expect much from the likes of Mulligan, for whom, revealingly, she has more respect than she has for Stephen ("her medicineman: me she slights"). Again unlike Yeats's Old Woman ("It's not silver I want"), she wants and needs money. Mulligan pays two shillings, reducing their debt for milk to twopence. When she leaves, Mulligan's silver in her hand and curtsying to her Judas, that "gay betrayer" tenderly chants, "Heart of my heart, were it more, / More would be laid at your feet" (13).

Mulligan's aubade is borrowed. It is Swinburne's "The Oblation," from *Songs before Sunrise*, which he had also quoted when he passed the coin along the table to the old woman: "Ask nothing more of me, sweet. / All I can give you I give." There is a doubled Yeatsian allusion here. First, Joyce has Mulligan quote the very poem Yeats seems to have been echoing when he informed Maud Gonne that, "being poor," he had only his dreams (rather than the heaven's embroidered cloths) to spread "under your feet"; Swinburne's penultimate line is, "Mine is the heart at your feet." Second, and more important, remembering the total sacrifice demanded by the Old Woman played by Maud Gonne in *Cathleen ni Houlihan* ("if anyone would give me help he must give me himself, he must *give me all*"), Joyce is commenting both on the gay betrayal of Irishmen like Mulligan and on his own unwillingness to make that total sacrifice in the form demanded. In another *non serviam*, Stephen scorns to beg the favor of this betrayed and self-betraying "cuckquean," a far cry from the "queen" the Old Woman is transformed into in the resonant final word of Yeats's play.

Stephen's Ireland is almost as sterile as the waste land Bloom imagines *his* Motherland to be—"A barren land. . . . It lay there now. Now it could bear no more. Dead: an old woman's: the grey shrunken cunt of the world" (U 50). The Old Woman who is Ireland has "old shrunken paps" and the dugs squeezed by her "wrinkled fingers" yield "rich white milk, not hers"—a painful parody of the archetype of the nurturant Great Mother and of an Ireland incapable of being rejuvenated. Yeats's "woman from beyond the world" became a young girl with the walk of a queen, a part "magnificently" played by Maud Gonne, whose great height, said Yeats, "made Cathleen seem a divine being fallen into our mortal infirmity." Joyce's personified Ireland, "a wandering crone, lowly form of an immortal," walks the earth as a divine being permanently fallen into our mortal infirmity, beyond hope of redemption. True, she had "entered from a morning world, a messenger perhaps"—in Joyce's Homeric parallel, an Athena (disguised as Mentor) come to Telemachus-Stephen. But whether she has come "to serve or to upbraid," both of which Athena did in advising Telemachus to assert himself in his mother's house, Stephen will neither serve nor upbraid *her.*

Besides, there is a more formidable "messenger" come from the other world to upbraid Stephen, one whose "wasted body" makes her both more heartbreaking and more terrifying than this old witch with shrunken paps and wrinkled fingers. The same mixture of sympathy, fear, and awe—and the same *non serviam*—marks Stephen's response to the most terrifying form of the Great Mother in this opening chapter. Though, alluding to Cranley's remarks in *Portrait*, Stephen will speculate in "Proteus" that maternal love "may be . . . the only true thing in life" (P 241-42; U 23), he has come to feel the terrible weight, the devouring force, of *amor matris.*

Reliving the nightmare that has come to him repeatedly since his mother's illness and eventual death of cancer (the crisis that compelled him to return to Ireland and to the center of the paralysis from which he had fled), Stephen is consumed by guilt and remorse, by "agenbite of inwit" (U 14). Yet he struggles fiercely to retain his independence—from her, and from the Holy Mother Church she is identified with in Stephen's mind, both of whom he turned from by refusing to make his Easter duty and, finally, by refusing to pray at her bedside, singing instead the beautiful poem of Yeats ("Who Goes with Fergus?") that haunts him throughout the day:

And no more turn aside and brood.

Folded away in the memory of nature with her toys.
Memories beset his brooding brain. Her glass of water from the kitchen tap when

she had approached the sacrament.... Her shapely fingernails reddened by the blood of squashed lice from the children's shirts.

In a dream, silently, she had come to him, her wasted body within its loose graveclothes giving off an odour of wax and rosewood, her breath, bent over him with mute secret words, a faint odour of wetted ashes.

Her glazing eyes, staring out of death, to shake and bend my soul. On me alone. The ghostcandle to light her agony. Ghostly light on the tortured face. Her hoarse loud breath rattling in horror, while all prayed on their knees. Her eyes on me to strike me down. *Liliata rutilantium te confessorum turma circumdet: iubilantium te virginum chorus excipiat.*

Ghoul! Chewer of corpses!
No, mother! Let me be and let me live.[9]

But she will not let Stephen be. The sea described by Mulligan (echoing Swinburne) as "our great sweet mother" is also the "scrotumtightening sea," suggesting a castration anxiety associated not with Dublin Bay but with "our mighty mother" in general and May Dedalus in particular (U 4, 5). "Beastly dead," as Mulligan has called her (7), she returns in the bestial episode of *Ulysses*. Her manifestation in "Circe" is also mythologically appropriate. For "the Great Mother is . . . the sorceress who transforms men into animals—Circe, mistress of wild beasts, who sacrifices the male and rends him."[10] I will return in a moment to the attempt to fling nets to hold back Stephen's soul from flight, to rend him—as Parnell had been "rent" by "low-lived dogs" and "hounded into his grave"—even from *beyond* the grave. First, though, a few words about the rending of Leopold Bloom, his humiliation and enslavement at the hands, and under the hoofs and heels, of Joyce's primary Circe, Bella Cohen.

*   *   *

Bella is the "massive whoremistress" (429) who runs the brothel into which Bloom has come in his protective, or unconsciously homosexual, pursuit of the drunken Stephen. In her, Bloom, himself sexually ambivalent, will encounter the Terrible Mother in all her phallic hideousness, though he will, of course, take perverse pleasure in his emasculation. Joyce's immediate sources were Krafft-Ebing's *Psychopathia Sexualis* and *its* principal source, Sacher-Masoch's *Venus in Furs*.[11] But when—to borrow the names of Sacher-Masoch's characters—Joyce has Bloom play a subservient and adoring Severin to Bella/Bello's dominant Wanda, he is also drawing, beyond Homer's transforming Circe, on aspects of the primordial Mother, particularly on her phallic aspects and on her androgynous role as both boar and sow.

Bella enters this "higgledypiggledy" chapter (410) "all in a mucksweat." "Fullnosed," she has "a sprouting moustache" not far removed from the "boar's tusks" of the phallic Great Mother, the Medusa (in fact, earlier in "Circe," Stephen had been propositioned by an "elderly bawd" whose "famished snaggletusks" protruded from a doorway.)[12] The emasculation begins at once. The young queen in Yeats's "The Cap and Bells" took up "her fan from the table" and "waved . . . off on the air" the heart of the jester; Bella's castrating "fan," "half opening, then closing," ridicules cuckolded and uxorious Bloom: "And the missus is master. Petticoat government." To which Bloom, subject to Molly as phallic Earth Mother, can only reply, "with a sheepish grin," "That is so" (430). A onetime shoefitter, he is soon kneeling before her, gently lacing up her "hoof and a full pastern, silksocked." "Bello," though suddenly masculine, remains female, addressed by an "infatuated" Bloom as "Empress!" (432).

Bloom's own "nose" has already "thicken[ed]" (432); now, himself fully transformed to a sow, "on all fours, grunting, snuffling," rooting for "truffles" at his Empress's feet, Bloom is mounted and ridden by Bello, "his" heel grinding cruelly into "her" neck: "Feel my entire weight. Bow, bondslave, before the throne of your despot's glorious heels, so glistening in their proud erectness" (433). Not only is the transformation into phallic Goddess complete; thanks to Bloom's foot fetish we can register the "entire weight" of what had been so delicately implicit in Yeats's obeisant submission before and beneath the "feet" of *his* Goddess. Of course, Bloom, who has just promised "never to disobey," would never petition *his* glorious-heeled despot of an Empress to "tread softly."

At this point Bloom resembles those theriomorphic consorts of the Goddess who, like the Greeks turned to swine by Circe, take the form of beasts, "those pigs of men," in Molly's phrase (638). One last change, also traditional, is required. Having just described himself as "Not man," but "Woman," Bloom is unmanned fully:

BELLO
(*Stands up*.) No more blow hot and cold. What you longed for has come to pass. Henceforth you are unmanned and mine in earnest, a thing under the yoke. Now for your punishment frock. You will shed your male garments . . . and don the shot silk luxuriously rustling over head and shoulders. And quickly too! (436)

Amid the transvestite fantasy and some genuine Joycean feminism ("You will be laced with cruel force into viselike corsets, . . . restrained in nettight frocks"), Bloom is here enlisted among the male consorts of the Mother Goddess, her priests and victims, who "prostituted themselves in her name and wore women's clothing."[13] The clothing was appropriate because these sacerdotal victims were eunuchs, men who had castrated themselves at the command of the Goddess. Yeats, describing "he that Attis' image hangs between / That staring fury and the blind lush leaf" ("Vacillation," II), was alluding to the high priest of the principal Great Mother, Cybele, who induces Attis to castrate himself to prevent his marriage to another; he metamorphoses after death into a pine tree. In the passage Yeats is echoing, Frazer describes the Attis-ritual, in which "the effigy of a young man was attached to the middle [of a ceremonial pine tree as] a representation of his coming to life again in tree form,"[14] material not irrelevant to the ritual enacted in "The Cap and Bells," in which stars "grew" out of the air following the symbolic castration and death of the young queen's devotee.

Bloom himself comes to "life again" in "Circe." Having emerged from the crucible of his masochistic ordeal and regaining his manhood as a consequence, he is, like those turned into beasts by Homer's Circe, reborn a better man, one capable of acting decisively and helping Stephen in the final action of "Circe." And Stephen *needs* help—both in Bella's and on the street. Having fled the whorehouse in terror, he is quickly entangled in a fight with two British soldiers. He ran from the brothel after being assaulted by the Great Mother in a form far more horrifying even than the bestial Bella, a "shaven mouth" and "suckeress" (436) who pales into insignificance beside this blood-sucking "ghoul." Bloom was born again; Stephen, born once, wants to be reborn but not re*borne* by a dead mother who threatens to crush and rend him as Parnell had been posthumously "crushed to death" and again devoured in the rending reenactment at the Christmas dinner Mrs. Dedalus prepared years before.

*   *   *

There is only one genuine hallucination in "Circe," genuine in the sense that others respond to what is happening in the mind of either Bloom or Stephen. "Look!," cries one of the whores, pointing to Stephen (474). "He's white." And with good reason. For Stephen is, as Hugh Kenner says, "haunted by a dead woman who is his Cathleen ni Houlihan and demands not less than all."[15] The ghost of Stephen's mother, related to but far more terrifying than the lady of the Trieste sketchbook, has risen from the floor of the brothel in which a drunken Stephen, whirling giddily in a "Dance of death," himself "stops dead."

STEPHEN
Ho!
(*Stephen's mother, emaciated, rises stark through the floor, in leper grey with a wreath of faded orangeblossoms and a torn bridal veil, her face worn and noseless, green with gravemould. Her hair is scant and lank. She fixes her bluecircled hollow eyesockets on Stephen and opens her toothless mouth uttering a silent word. A choir of virgins and confessors sing voicelessly.*)

THE CHOIR
Liliata rutilantium te confessorum . . .
Iubilantium te virginum . . .

(*From the top of a tower Buck Mulligan, in particoloured jester's dress of puce and yellow and clown's cap with curling bell, stands gaping at her, a smoking buttered split scone in his hand.*)

BUCK MULLIGAN
She's beastly dead. The pity of it! Mulligan meets the afflicted mother. (*he upturns his eyes*) Mercurial Malachi!

THE MOTHER
(*with the subtle smile of death's madness*) I was once the beautiful May Goulding. I am dead.

STEPHEN
(*horrorstruck*) Lemur, who are you? No. What bogeyman's trick is this?

BUCK MULLIGAN
(*shakes his curling capbell*) The mockery of it! Kinch dogsbody killed her bitchbody. She kicked the bucket. (*tears of molten butter fall from his eyes on to the scone*) Our great sweet mother! *Epi oinopa ponton.*

THE MOTHER
(*comes nearer, breathing upon him softly her breath of wetted ashes*) All must go through it, Stephen. More women than men in the world. You too. Time will come.

STEPHEN
(*choking with fright, remorse and horror*) They say I killed you, mother. He offended your memory. Cancer did it, not I. Destiny.

THE MOTHER
(*a green rill of bile trickling from a side of her mouth*) You sang that song to me. *Love's bitter mystery.*

STEPHEN
(*eagerly*) Tell me the word, mother, if you know now. The word known to all men.

THE MOTHER
Who saved you the night you jumped into the train at Dalkey with Paddy Lee? Who had pity for you when you were sad among the strangers? Prayer is allpowerful. Prayer for the suffering souls in the Ursuline manual and forty days' indulgence. Repent, Stephen.

STEPHEN
The ghoul! Hyena!

THE MOTHER
I pray for you in my other world. Get Dilly to make you that boiled rice every night after your brainwork. Years and years I loved you, O, my son, my firstborn, when you lay in my womb.

ZOE
(*fanning herself with the gratefan*) I'm melting!

FLORRY
(*points to Stephen*) Look! He's white.

BLOOM
(*goes to the window to open it more*) Giddy.

THE MOTHER
(*with smouldering eyes*) Repent! O, the fire of hell!

STEPHEN
(*panting*) His noncorrosive sublimate! The corpsechewer! Raw head and bloody bones.

THE MOTHER
(*her face drawing near and nearer, sending out an ashen breath*) Beware! (*she raises her blackened withered right arm slowly towards Stephen's breast with outstretched finger*) Beware God's hand!

(*A green crab with malignant red eyes sticks deep its grinning claws in Stephen's heart.*)

STEPHEN
(*strangled with rage, his features drawn grey and old*) Shite!

BLOOM
(*at the window*) What?

STEPHEN
Ah non, par exemple! The intellectual imagination! With me all or not at all. *Non serviam!*

FLORRY
Give him some cold water. Wait. (*she rushes out*)

THE MOTHER
(*wrings her hands slowly, moaning desperately*) O Sacred Heart of Jesus, have mercy on him! Save him from hell, O Divine Sacred Heart!

                    STEPHEN
No! No! No! Break my spirit, all of you, if you can! I'll bring you all to heel!

                    THE MOTHER
(*in the agony of her deathrattle*) Have mercy on Stephen, Lord, for my sake! Inexpressible was my anguish when expiring with love, grief and agony on Mount Calvary.

                    STEPHEN
Nothung!

(*He lifts his ashplant high with both hands and smashes the chandelier. Time's livid final flame leaps and, in the following darkness, ruin of all space, shattered glass and toppling masonry.*) (473-75)

Powerful as it is on its own, the episode requires some commentary, especially if we are to perceive the connection between the ghost of Stephen's mother, that Devourer with "toothless mouth," and "Old Gummy Granny," the pantomime-form in which that farrow-eating sow, old Ireland, appears to Stephen when he escapes into the street—and into a fight with two drunken British soldiers—in his headlong flight from his mother's ghoulish specter.

The ghost's "bluecircled hollow eyesockets," the graveyard version of "her eyes on me to strike me down" at the deathbed, are more terrifyingly lethal than the "two circular perforated apertures through which [the headsman's] eyes glowered furiously" in the executioner scene in "Cyclops." And rightly so, since it is a matter here of more than physical life and death, a matter of Stephen's "head" as the seat of that "reason" with which he will resist both inducements to "repent" and incitements to "remove" Ireland's enemies. Now truly "beastly dead," Stephen's mother would "save" him by suffocating him or by devouring the hero's heart: "A green crab with malignant red eyes sticks deep its grinning claws in Stephen's heart." That crab stands not only for cancer; the great-clawed "crab woman" is also a type of the devouring Goddess.[16] Buck Mulligan is present in Stephen's hallucination because it was he who had described Stephen's mother as "beastly dead" back in "Telemachus"; here he materializes to repeat the phrase, along with his charge that Stephen, by refusing to pray for his mother at her deathbed, had killed her: "Kinch dogsbody killed her bitchbody." Weeping the butter he had lavishly applied to his scones while the old milkwoman was trying to get paid, he repeats his allusions earlier in that chapter to Swinburne and Homer on the sea: "Our great sweet mother! *Epi oinopa ponton.*" But the Great Mother of the "Circe" chapter, more terrifying and far more hideous than in her initial ghostly appearance in "Telemachus," is May Dedalus.

Devouring Ireland

The Goddess, as we know, from Neolithic times on takes three forms. She might be "the beautiful nubile Virgin or the tender nurturing Mother; on the other hand she was a hideous ghoul, herself corpse-like and a devourer of corpses."[17] Like the lady of *Giacomo Joyce*, Stephen's mother assumes, in this chapter of Circean metamorphoses, all three forms of the Triple Goddess. "I was once the beautiful May Goulding. I am dead." But she still retains the aspect of the nurturing Mother, praying for Stephen in her "other world" and reminding him of the "pity" she had for him "when you were sad among the strangers" and of the "Years and years I loved you, O my son, my firstborn, when you lay in my womb." Both reminders of times "when" are deeply moving. Joyce is in fact putting in the toothless mouth of Stephen's dead mother words he had himself put in the mouth of the living mother who came to him in an actual dream when he was twenty and alone and hungry in Paris, a dream he recounted to his brother and memorialized among his early "epiphanies":

> She comes at night when the city is still; invisible, inaudible, all unsummoned. She comes from her ancient seat to visit the least of her children, mother most venerable, as though he had never been alien to her. She knows the inmost heart; therefore she is gentle, nothing exacting; saying, I am susceptible of change, an imaginative influence in the hearts of my children. Who has pity for you when you are sad among the strangers? Years and years I loved you when you lay in my womb.[18]

This mother most venerable, come unsummoned from her ancient seat, is not only Mary Murray Joyce but also the nurturing Great Mother who—"gentle, nothing exacting"—is the precise opposite of the blood-exacting Devourer. But while it may well be that mother love is the only true thing in life, *amor matris* ("subjective and objective genitive") is ambiguous in ways more than linguistic (U 23). The same nurturing Mother *becomes* the Devourer, the uroboros with her own tail in her mouth, fulfilling the bitter lamentation in which Stephen, fusing biblical rhetoric with the mythology of the Dark and Terrible Mother, cried out in the agony of a child left alone in the dark:

> But thou hast suckled me with a bitter milk: my moon and my sun thou hast quenched for ever. And thou hast left me alone for ever in the dark ways of my bitterness: and with a kiss of ashes hast thou kissed my mouth. (322)

(The specific reference here is to "Erin," who fornicates with "a stranger" while making Stephen "the slave of servants"; but the bitter spike "in his bosom" [323] combined with this "kiss of ashes" confirms the coalescence of Motherland and mother.)[19]

In his hallucination, Stephen shrinks from the "ashen breath" of a ghost who has modulated into the quintessentially Irish form of the Terrible Mother, the posthumous incarnation of that "crazy queen, old and jealous," the holy Roman catholic and apostolic church. James Joyce's devoutly Catholic mother and the child who is now truly "alien to her" are alike at least in that neither is any longer "susceptible to change"; consequently, her "imaginative influence" in the heart of her fictional firstborn can only be negative. The mother who had been gentle, "nothing exacting," the light in her eyes benignant, is now malign, demanding repentance.[20] At first, Stephen shifts blame to Mulligan. "Choking with fright, remorse and horror," he denies the charge of matricide: "They say I killed you, mother. He offended your memory. Cancer did it, not I. Destiny." But that is no more persuasive than Haines's earlier shuffling off of responsibility for England's treatment of Ireland ("It seems history is to blame"). Stephen continues to be eaten by remorse—in his own devouring archaism, "agenbite of inwit." If there is salvation for him it is also in a "word." When the ghost repeats the phrase "Love's bitter mystery" from the Yeats poem Stephen sang to her in place of the deathbed prayer, he turns to her eagerly: "Tell me the word, mother, if you know now. The word known to all men." As Yeats's phrase suggests, and as the new edition of *Ulysses* confirms, the word is "Love,"[21] yet the word actually spoken by his mother's ghost is "Repent!" Reminders of his sojourn in her womb and her threats of hellfire alike, however, draw the same response. Beyond the Buck's "beastly dead" (for there are more things in heaven and earth than are dreamt of in Mulligan's philosophy), she is "lemur," "ghoul! Hyena! . . . corpsechewer! Raw head and bloody bones."

To fully grasp this brutal rejection, horrified and horrifying, we must understand exactly what is being rejected. Stephen goes far beyond Joyce's Homeric analogue (Odysseus's initial harshness when he encounters the ghost of his mother)[22] because, herself devoured by the "green crab" of cancer, *this* Anticlea has become the Terrible Mother herself, a fusion of everything—mother-love and love of mother, family duty, Catholicism and Ireland—that would devour *him*. Old Gummy Granny will rise up in a moment as the grotesque caricature of Cathleen ni Houlihan; the church is the particular province of Stephen's mother, allied with her phantom to the point of identification. Raising her "blackened withered right arm slowly towards Stephen's breast with outstretched finger," she cries out, "Beware God's hand!" And the "anguish when expiring with love, grief and agony on Mount Calvary" was "*my* anguish." The crucifixion of Christ, associated in *Portrait* with the death and dismembering of Parnell, is here associated with the final agony and death of the mother Stephen is accused of killing. No wonder his remorse and terror are transformed to needful defiance, for this is the ultimate, and most formidable, attempt to break his spirit.

"Strangled with rage, his features drawn grey and old" (recalling the ghost, described as "emaciated, . . . in leper grey"), Stephen cries out, "Shite!" With him it is "all or not at all"; choosing the "not at all" rather than the "all" demanded by this mother as it was by his church and by the Old Woman of Yeats's play, he repeats from *Portrait* his Luciferian "*Non serviam*!" When his mother's ghost calls on the "Sacred Heart of Jesus" to "save him from hell," Stephen makes his great refusal and affirmation: "No! No! No! Break my spirit all of you if you can! I'll bring you all to heel!" Though it refuses the thrice-repeated prayer to the Sacred Heart and echoes Peter's denial of Christ, Stephen's triple denial is aimed less at Christ and the Father-Son-Spirit of the Blessed Trinity than at this Terrible Mother of a Triple Goddess, a carrion-eating ghoul and corpsechewer still praying for her son in the now posthumous "agony of her deathrattle."

* * *

The "Not at all," "*Non serviam*," and thrice-repeated "No!" are capped by Stephen's final exclamation, "*Nothung!*" Knowing Joyce's penchant for puns trivial and quadrivial, we cannot rule out *Nothung* as "not hung," castration at the hands of the Terrible Mother. But Stephen, still "able [Abel] to raise a cain [cane]" (FW 47), has *not* been "unmanned" in the encounter with the ghost, and his assertion of his manhood is surely not less, or less needful, than Bloom's reassertion after his far more humiliating encounter with his own fantasies projected onto Bella/Bello as phallic Terrible Mother. Stephen has, to be sure, engaged in as profound and climactic a conflict with the elements in his own nature as Bloom has—in Stephen's case, those elements "formed in loving submission to mother, family, Church and country."[23] He has almost buckled under the combined onslaught of fear, grief, remorse, and—most potent threat of all—his not-quite-extinguished belief that repentance is still possible if only he will submit to, and accept the merciful intervention of, that Jesus whose Sacred Heart is invoked by his ghostly mother as her final temptation.[24] It is all these that Stephen attempts to deny and extinguish in a single word and act.

The destructive act, smashing the gaslight, is, like his refusal to pray for his dying mother, an outward, conscious gesture of denial. The final act of resistance—against the violence urged on him by Ireland as Old Gummy Granny—is still to come; and that is an inward battle in which the ashplant-weapon must itself be denied. For the moment, however, Stephen utters the triumphant cry of both Siegmund and Siegfried in Wagner's *The Ring of the Nibelung.* "Nothung," German for "Needful," is the name of the magic sword Wotan had originally planted in the heart of Yggdrasil, the world ash tree (Stephen's stick is an "ashplant"), from which, in *The Valkyrie*, it was withdrawn, named, and victoriously held aloft in bright spring sunshine by Siegmund. This is the scene Joyce parodies when he has Stephen lift his ashplant "high with both hands," only to smash a brothel lamp. In a typically complex fusion, the ashplant-turned-sword also functions as the reforged *Nothung* used by Siegfried to slay the gold-guarding dragon Fafner in the third opera in the *Ring* cycle—here Stephen psychologically slays the bestial mother he has already been accused of killing—and as the *Nothung* Siegfried sees as the guardian of that unintentionally fatal blood oath in the *Dusk of the Gods,* whose music Stephen borrowed earlier in "Circe" to sing, his text edited from *The Valkyrie,* of *Hunger* (German for intense, unfulfilled desire) as that which destroys us all, "*Macht uns alle kaputt*" (U 457). He is responding to the question of one of the whores, Zoe, who had asked Bloom regarding Stephen, "Is he hungry?" Stephen, who has not eaten for forty-eight hours, is in fact destroyed with hunger; but his most profound unfulfilled longing, his true *Hunger,* is for a spiritual father and a nurturing woman. When Zoe asks if he is hungry, Stephen "extends his hand to her smiling" and, "to the air of the bloodoath in the *Dusk of the Gods*," addresses her, as Siegmund had addressed Sieglinde in act 1, scene 2 of *The Valkyrie,* as *Fragende Frau,* questioning wife.[25] A few moments later, he will murmur to her as she reads his palm, "Hold me. Caress." But Zoe is disturbed by what she reads in Stephen's palm: "You'll meet with a . . . (*She peers at his hands abruptly.*) I won't tell you what's not good for you. Or do you want to know?" (457–58)

What Stephen is to "meet with" is a double figure: the ghost of a mother who is not a nurturer but a devourer, and Bloom himself, a maternal father who will take Stephen home and share with him, in sacramental "jocoserious silence," one of Joyce's favorite beverages from the days when he was starving in Paris, "Epps massproduct, the creature cocoa" (553). Wagnerian redemption is the work of a woman, Brünnhilde, who restores the ring to the Rhine Maidens and so makes at least possible the birth of a new world out of the destruction of the old; but when, at the end of his "meeting" with his mother's ghost, Stephen cries out *"Nothung!,"* he sees woman only as the Terrible Mother, a Devourer feeding on *him*, in part because of his own remorse, his "agenbite of inwit."

Wagner's *Götterdämmerung,* his dusk or twilight of the gods, is accompanied by "Time's livid final flame," the going up in flames of Valhalla. There is redemption in the final music, but what we *see* is the return to primordial chaos, the blue-green of the inundating Rhine. Stephen's implicit redemption takes another form. What follows his comic-Wagnerian blow seems, in fact, less a *Götterdämmerung* than the *Götzen-dämmerung* ("Twilight of the Idols") of Wagner's earlier parodist, Nietzsche, who turned on the master when, with *Parsifal,* he allegedly "went Christian." Stephen's "Not at all," *"Non serviam,"* repeated "No!," and *"Nothung!"* are the very opposite of the Schopenhauerian pessimism that shaped Wagner's decision to end his *Ring* cycle with the renunciation of the world, an apocalyptic ruin from which new life may or may not arise. Stephen's No is in effect a Nietzschean Yes to life, an affirmation made jocoseriously explicit when he proclaims in the midst of the violent encounter with the British tommies, "Down with death. Long live life!" (482)

Asserting the crucial interaction in his own creative life, Yeats declared, "Nietzsche completes Blake and has the same roots" (LY 379). And it is Blake, the precursor he shares with Yeats, that Joyce summons up in the climactic phrase: "Time's livid final flame leaps and, in the following darkness, ruin of all space, shattered glass and toppling masonry." These stage directions, having turned a modest gaslamp into a grandiose "chandelier," now mythologize Stephen's blow into an apocalypse, the partially Blakean nature of which is made clear by this echo of Stephen's earlier allusions—in the classroom ("Nestor") and during his walk along Sandymount strand ("Proteus").

At the outset of "Nestor," questioning his students about the Battle of Tarentum before moving on to Milton's "Lycidas," Stephen—who is shortly to inform the headmaster that "history is a nightmare from which I am trying to awake"—thinks of the "corpsestrewn" battlefield in his "gorescarred book" as

> Fabled by the daughters of memory. And yet it was in some way if not as memory fabled it. A phrase, then, of impatience, thud of Blake's wings of excess. I hear the ruin of all space, shattered glass and toppling masonry, and time one livid final flame. What's left us then? (20)

The "phrase," that "phrase the world had remembered," is Phyrrus's famous "Another victory like that and we are done for." For Stephen as for

Joyce himself, every act of physical violence is either a defeat or a Phyrric victory. His image of "shattered glass and toppling masonry" is framed by "the ruin of all space" and "time one livid final flame," the Kantian forms in images of Blakean apocalypse. For what matters to Joyce and Blake, for all their differences, is genuine vision, which is not, in Blake's words, "Fable . . . Form'd by the daughters of Memory" but an inner truth perceived or created by the "Imagination . . . surrounded by the daughters of Inspiration." If we cleanse the doors of perception, "Eternity will appear," for "Error" is "Burnt up the Moment Men cease to behold it."[26] The temperament of Joyce, celebrator of the everyday, is obviously less apocalyptic than that of Blake, for whom "the outward Creation... is as the Dirt upon my feet, No part of Me," a vegetative world to be "consumed in fire." Yet both are visionary artists "melting apparent surfaces away," as Blake says, "and displaying the infinite which was hid."[27] Revealing the eternal implicit in the mundane: What else were the Joycean epiphanies? What else is *Ulysses*?

Further, Joyce's word *ruin*, though applied to space, surely echoes Blake's celebrated axiom combining temporal consolation with imaginative compensation: "every Mortal loss is an Immortal Gain. The Ruins of Time builds Mansions in Eternity."[28] Aware that he was "building the great myth of everyday life" in *Ulysses*, Joyce told another novelist in 1937:

> I wrote the greater part of the book during the war. There was fighting on all fronts, empires fell, kings went into exile, the old order was collapsing with a crash; and I had, as I sat down to work, the conviction that in the midst of all these ruins I was building something for the most distant future.[29]

The horrors of World War I are reflected not only in Stephen's "corpsestrewn" battlefield and image of shattered glass and toppling masonry but also in his conjuring up of the "uproar of battles, the frozen deathspew of the slain, a shout of spear spikes baited with men's bloodied guts" (27). But the violent history that formed the nightmare he was trying to escape was also specifically Irish. When the "shattered glass and toppling masonry" next appear, in "Proteus," the context is Fenian: a portrait of the Fenian dynamitard Joseph Casey, whom Joyce met in Paris and immortalized as Kevin Egan. In the course of trying to enlist Stephen—"to yoke me as his yokefellow, our crimes our common cause"—Egan refers to "Maud Gonne, beautiful woman," here yoked with Lucien Millevoye, her French lover. Of this collocation ("Maud Gonne, beautiful woman, *la Patrie*, M. Millevoye," U 36), Malcolm Brown perceptively remarks: "Kevin Egan strains toward a fantasy female vampire." In his association of Maud Gonne, Yeats's Cathleen ni Houlihan, with an Irish version of Joan of Arc (her bedfellow Millevoye had urged Maud to seize her destiny "in the role of *la pucelle* of Ireland"), Egan's "patriotic and sexual fantasies interchange with each other as forms of death."[30] Joyce was being sarcastic when he referred, in a 1905 letter to Stanislaus, to Maud Gonne as "the Irish Joan of Arc" (LJ 2:85), but as the contemporaneous "A Mother" suggests, he was aware even then of the sinister power of nationalism as *la Patrie* incarnate in a woman. The "fantasy female vampire" Kevin Egan strains toward was precisely the figure rejected by James Joyce.

Even Egan's lighting of his "gunpowder" cigarette is a violence-charged act: "The blue fuse burns deadly between hands and burns clear. Loose tobacco shreds catch fire: a flame and acrid smoke light our corner" (U 36). Casey/Egan is another who has sacrificed all for love of Ireland. "Lover, for her love," he conspired in a plot to free Irish prisoners from Clerkenwell Prison in 1867, a plot involving a keg of gunpowder that exploded, killing a dozen innocent people and wounding over a hundred. Stephen imagines him as he, "crouching, saw a flame of vengeance hurl them upward in the fog. Shattered glass and toppling masonry" (36).

This excursus has seemed necessary both to fully elucidate this image cluster in its climactic repetition in "Circe" and to prepare for what is immediately to come: Stephen's demonstration that he, like Blake, prefers spiritual to corporeal warfare. When he smashes the chandelier, Mother-haunted Stephen is caught between the physical violence of shattered glass and toppling masonry, associated with the history-fabling daughters of memory, and the apocalyptic visionary imagination associated by Blake with fire and the daughters of inspiration. Yet that act of Siegfriedian violence initiates, and is the necessary prelude to, Stephen's response to the physical violence he encounters when he runs from the brothel—violence triggered by Private Carr's misunderstanding of Stephen's drunken greeting to the tommies: "you are my guests. The uninvited. . . . History to blame. Fabled by mothers of memory" (479). Stephen has, significantly, replaced Blake's "daughters" with "*mothers* of memory." Stephen's "mothers" are personal and Nationalist; above all, Ireland as Terrible Mother, raped by her uninvited guests, and then—in a fusion of justifiably bitter memory and imagination—fabling history into the lethal mythology of Romantic Ireland, a myth for whose sake so many have died. If Stephen has altered Blake, he also remains faithful. For while "mothers" is doubtless the word that initiates the confrontation ("was he insulting you?" Carr asks Cissy Caffrey, the Irish girl on his arm), the Wagnerian sword is dismissed in favor of the Blakean "Sword" of "Mental Fight."[31]

At the moment, though, his putting out of the light and plunging things into "darkness" is decidedly masculine, a kind of preemptive strike in which he usurps the mythological role of the Mother Goddess who traditionally devours time and light: her own star-children, along with the sun and moon. Of his own mother, Stephen had complained, "My moon and my sun thou hast quenched for ever" and "left me alone for ever in the dark" (U 322). In *The Wind Among the Reeds,* Yeats's boar without bristles comes from the west, roots "sun and moon and stars out of the sky," and lies in the "darkness, grunting," symbol, as we shall see in Chapter 4, of that "Armageddon that shall quench all things in the Ancestral Darkness again." But Yeats's boar, like his Black Pig whose valley was the prophesied site of the apocalyptic battle in which Ireland was to defeat at last her English enemy, is cognate with Joyce's farrow-eating sow, phallic aspects of the Great Mother who shall devour time and shall quench all things in darkness. Indeed, she *is* darkness. The gender is clear in the final line of "Darkness," that terrifying nightmare in which Byron, Stephen's youthful favorite, had "a dream, which was not all a dream"; sun, moon, and stars were "extinguished," tides, winds, and clouds had perished: "Darkness had no need / Of aid from them—*She* was the Universe." On one level, then, Stephen's mythological plunging of the universe into darkness is the appropriate blow—final and phallic—against the rejected mother. However, as he flees the brothel, Stephen, "his head and arms thrown back stark," is described as "abandoning his ashplant" (476). That is significant. For the next threat to be resisted is the violence urged on him by the Terrible Mother as Ireland herself, a scene in which ashplant gestures can have no place.

*   *   *

In rejecting his mother, Stephen is rejecting two other Crones as well, two "queens" first encountered in "Telemachus." Not only that "crazy queen, old and jealous," the "holy Roman catholic and apostolic church," but Ireland herself, the old shrunken-papped witch on her toadstool who, at the climax of Yeats's play, has the "walk of a queen." It is, as they say, no accident that toward the climax of the "Circe" episode, during Stephen's altercation with the drunken British soldiers, Ireland should suddenly appear before him, seated like the "witch" of "Telemachus" on a toadstool, the "deathflower" of the potato famine on her breast. Now she is "Old Gummy Granny," recalling the "toothless mouth" of Stephen's ghostly mother and "Gap-toothed Kathleen, her four beautiful green fields, the stranger in her house" (U 152). That is Stephen's earlier allusion, in "Scylla and Charybdis," to Yeats's *Cathleen ni Houlihan*, to which, of course, he was also alluding in his depiction of the opening chapter's old milkwoman, of which Old Gummy Granny is the ultimate caricature.

The presentation of Old Gummy Granny may be pantomime, but Joyce was never more serious. The network of allusions, even more labyrinthine than usual, reveals Ireland as a Devourer on several levels:

(The women's heads coalesce. Old Gummy Granny in sugarloaf hat appears seated on a toadstool, the deathflower of the potato blight on her breast.)

STEPHEN
Aha! I know you, g[r]ammer! Hamlet, revenge! The old sow that eats her farrow!

OLD GUMMY GRANNY
(rocking to and fro) Ireland's sweetheart, the king of Spain's daughter, alanna. Strangers in my house, bad manners to them! *(she keens with banshee woe)* Ochone! Ochone! Silk of the kine! *(she wails)* You met with poor old Ireland and how does she stand?

STEPHEN
How do I stand you? The hat trick! Where's the third person of the Blessed Trinity? Soggarth Aroon? The reverend Carrion Crow. (485–86)

The "women" whose "heads coalesce" are the three whores (484) who are looking on at the confrontation between Stephen and Private Carr: Biddy the Clap, who is more interested in Stephen's eloquence than his nationality; The Virago, who is pro-Irish ("Green above the red . . . Wolfe Tone"); and The Bawd ("The red's as good as the green, and better. Up the soldiers! Up King Edward!"). Out of the coalescence of this trinitarian unity-within-diversity emerges the form of Old Gummy Granny. The death-flower of the Great Hunger upon her, she is herself hungry for revenge. In another coalescence, the cry of the ghost in *Hamlet* (1.5.23–25) merges with that of Hamlet himself: "Come, the croaking raven doth bellow for revenge!" (3.2.244–45). And to Hamlet's carrion-eater, Stephen adds his old image of Ireland as farrow-eating sow.

If Stephen is bored (485) by the British soldier threatening him ("O, this is too monotonous! Nothing. . . . some brutish empire of his"), he has, as usual, no illusions about the nature of those who have been brutalized by that empire. Irish chauvinism, buttressed by a formidable memory of English oppression, was epitomized in "Cyclops" by the Citizen, who had appropriately appeared a moment earlier, with "a huge emerald muffler and shillelagh," to pray for the descent of a bird traditionally associated with peace:

May the God above
Send down a dove
With teeth as sharp as razors
To slit the throats
Of the English dogs
That hanged our Irish leaders. (484)

Ireland's hanged patriots had instantly materialized in the form of "The Croppy Boy," hero of one of the ballads of the 1798 uprising. With the "rope noose round his neck" and gripping "his issuing bowels with both hands," he manages to quote two lines from his own ballad ("I bear no hate to a living thing, / But love my country beyond the king") before being dispatched by the headsman/hangman brought in from the executioner scene in "Cyclops." The last line he gets out, his tongue protruding violently just before he "gives up the ghost," is *Horhot ho hray ho rhother's hest*, a strangled version, in the agony of *his* deathrattle, of his confession in the ballad that, before he went off to fight, he had "forgot to pray for my mother's rest." (Stephen, of course, had not forgotten to pray for *his* mother; he had refused.) These caricatures and jocoserious allusions to the violence and futility of physical-force movements in Irish Nationalism reveal not only Stephen's reasons for refusing to fight with the British soldiers but also his awareness that Ireland as Old Gummy Granny is, as she will shortly prove yet again, little better than the strangers she would drive from her house through violence.

If Stephen's mother is beastly dead, Old Gummy Granny is beastly alive, at once Hamlet's croaking raven, a carrion crow, a teethed dove, and Stephen's old sow that eats her farrow. She also of course allies herself with Yeats's Cathleen ni Houlihan (keening with banshee woe of "Strangers in my house") and with "poor old Ireland" from "The Wearin' of the Green": "You met with poor old Ireland and how does she stand?" Standing on its patriotic head Napper Tandy's question about how Ireland stands, Stephen asks rhetorically, "How do *I* stand *you*?" His next reference, to "the hat trick," alluded to earlier in "Circe," has been explained as "a dirty Irish trick: an Irishman covers a turd on a curb with his hat. Telling a policeman it is a bird, the Irishman goes off for help, asking the policeman to stand guard."[32] The hallucinatory appearance of Old Gummy Granny is also, like that of the ghost of Stephen's mother, a "bogeyman's trick," but the implication of the specifically Irish trick is that this manifestation of Ireland is also a case (made explicit in *Finnegans Wake*, where "Kate Strong" wheels a "dungcart") of a worthless turd masquerading as a bird. If so, this "hat trick" debases not only the "dove" sent down from above and Ireland as a young girl with the walk of a queen but even, perhaps, the central icon of *Portrait*: the "dove"-plumaged bird-girl whose thighs are wound in "emerald" seaweed (P 171).

Yet, on a still deeper level, Old Gummy Granny *is* a bird, a carrion crow. When Stephen asks, "Where's the third person of the Blessed Trinity?," he alludes to the Holy Ghost, the Paraclete as dove, that "bird" from Mulligan's "Ballad of Joking Jesus": "I'm the queerest young fellow that ever you heard. / My mother's a jew, my father's a bird" (U 16). But the religious reference is multiple since, as Stephen had bitterly informed Haines while they were listening to Mulligan's blasphemous ballad, he has a trinity of masters: English, Italian, and "a third," Ireland, who "wants me for odd jobs." Ireland is present here, in the person of Old Gummy Granny, and so is the first master, "the imperial British state," in the form of Private Carr. The missing third is therefore "the holy Roman catholic and apostolic church," which explains Stephen's allusion—"*Soggarth Aroon*"—to the "priest, Dear" of John Banim's nineteenth-century poem. I quote the first, second, and final stanzas:

Am I the slave they say,
    Soggarth aroon?
Since you did show the way,
    Soggarth aroon!
Their slave no more to be,
While they would work with me
Old Ireland's slavery,
    Soggarth aroon!

Why not her poorest man,
    Soggarth aroon!
Try and do all he can,
    Soggarth aroon!
Her commands to fulfil
Of his own heart and will,
Side by side with you still,
    Soggarth aroon?
   . . . .

Och! you, and only you,
    Soggarth aroon!
And for this I was true to you,
    Soggarth aroon!
In love they'll never shake,
When for ould Ireland's sake
We a true part did take,
    Soggarth aroon!

But the patriot-priest so beloved by Banim's peasant, the priest through whom enslaved Old Ireland conveys "Her commands," is for Stephen a death figure, "the reverend Carrion Crow." It has been plausibly suggested that Joyce may be recalling a character in Flaubert's *Madame Bovary* who, as Emma is dying, compares "all priests to carrion-crows attracted by the smell of death."[33] There is more than a suggestion of the theme—brilliantly condensed in the "blind mouths!" of Milton's "Lycidas," the poem Stephen taught earlier in the day—of pastors, who ought to feed their flock, as devourers. In Stephen's telescoped allusions, the nineteenth-century patriot-priest becomes a raven of war—feeding, by implication, on the carrion left when the peasant to whom he has shown the militant "way" to political freedom has, instead, died in the attempt to play a "true part" and break "Old Ireland's slavery." Though death is the ultimate escape from servitude, it was presumably not the priest's intention that his parishioner rather than the English enemy should die.

In his preaching of violent rebellion, the Fenian priest become Carrion Crow has missed his mark—as had the tailor in the nursery rhyme about the crow. From the outset of this exchange with Old Gummy Granny, Stephen had identified her as "the old sow that eats her farrow"; he seems also to have floating in his echo chamber of a mind the *Mother Goose* rhyme "Heigh-ho, the Carrion Crow," in which a tailor, aiming an arrow at a crow in an oak tree, "missed his mark" and "shot his own sow quite through the heart." But just as Stephen's mother returns as ghost, so his "old sow," Romantic Ireland, keeps rising from the grave. Indeed, as Old Gummy Granny, she survives, as the Carrion Crow survived, to feed upon the dead as she had upon the living. Drunk as he is, Stephen has no trouble perceiving what Yeats had adumbrated in *Cathleen ni Houlihan*: that beneath the manifestations of Ireland as a poor old woman or even as the young girl with the walk of a queen there prevails the "third person" in the Celtic Trinity of the Triple Goddess: The Celtic goddess of war and destruction, that "woman who is headed like a crow." As Devouring Female, Ireland is at once the old sow that eats her farrow and the Morrigu, the female version of "reverend Carrion Crow."

*   *   *

Preparing the way for the climactic appearance of Old Gummy Granny are several Irish women who either side with the British (repeating the disloyalty of "Sheila, my own") or prove inadequate, or debased, embodiments of the nurturant aspects of the Great Mother. Private Carr's companion, Cissy Caffrey, is at first excited by the prospect, and imagined motive, of the incipient violence: "They're going to fight. For me" (487). When the whore Cunty Kate, "blushing deeply," pronounces for the tommies in the chivalry-mocking medieval lingo given her ("The gules doublet and merry St. George for me"), Stephen—still, as Davin said, "an Irishman"—varies Blake's "Auguries of Innocence": "The harlot's cry from street to street / Shall weave old *Ireland's* winding sheet." While Private Carr prepares for unknightly battle (loosening his belt, he shouts, "I'll wring the neck of any fucking bastard says a word against my bleeding fucking king"), Bloom appeals to Cissy Caffrey as potential peacemaker and still recognizable incarnation of the Mother Goddess: "Speak, you. Are you struck dumb? You are the link between nations and generations. Speak, woman, sacred lifegiver" (488). Alarmed, the girl seizes Private Carr's sleeve and, though she hardly links nations, does try to avert violence by reassuring the soldier: "Amn't I with you? Amn't I your girl? Cissy's your girl." But Stephen, "ecstatically" reciting his favorite canting song, is less interested in her words than in the "red" mouth they proceed from;[34] and woman as "sacred lifegiver" is about to be profaned. With violence imminent, Stephen's chandelier-smashing is reenacted: Dublin's "on fire," the "midnight sun is darkened," and it "rains dragon's teeth. Armed heroes spring up from furrows." Apocalypse is attended by a Black Mass centering on the mother-to-be from the preceding episode, "The Oxen of the Sun": "On the altarstone Mrs Mina Purefoy, goddess of unreason." On her naked "swollen belly" rests a chalice from which the celebrant, a version of blasphemous Mulligan, removes and elevates a "blooddripping host" (488–89). The stage is set for the appearance of Ireland herself as a goddess of unreason demanding blood.

Old Gummy Granny may be all gums, but she is sharp-teethed just the same. Her equivalent of the ghost's arm and finger stretched "towards" Stephen is even more immediately lethal. With Private Carr on the verge of throwing a punch, Old Gummy Granny reappears. "She thrusts a dagger towards Stephen's hand," a kind of decrepit Lady Macbeth materializing along with the dagger she had planted in the mind of her susceptible husband, "its handle towards [his] hand." Her accompanying command—vengeful, wheedling, pious, promising; above all, lethal, especially to those who *do* her bidding—is a parody, at once funny and embittered, of the tradition of physical force in Irish political history and, in particular, of the violence demanded, and the immortality promised, by the bloodthirsty Old Woman in Yeats's *Cathleen ni Houlihan*: "Remove him, Acushla. At 8:35 a.m. you will be in heaven and Ireland will be free. (*she prays*.) O good God, take him!" (490).

Old Gummy Granny, in effect, answers the question she had herself raised, as the Shan Van Vocht, in that song of '98: "Oh! the French are on the sea, / Says the Shan Van Vocht, / And *will Ireland then be free*?" She also answers two prayers: that of Stephen's mother that he be saved "from hell" ("at 8:35 a.m. you will be in heaven") and the more immediate prayer of the Citizen, that Stephen be sent from heaven a "dove / With teeth as sharp as razors / To slit the throats of the English dogs." Ireland, dove as avenging raven and carrion crow, is indeed a Paraclete armed, her dagger out-thrust. In the apocalyptic prelude to her appearance, it had rained "dragon's teeth" and "armed heroes" had sprung up from furrows—a Greek myth with specifically Irish resonance since Joyce's allusion is less to Cadmus than to the celebrated peroration of a 1779 speech in the Irish Parliament by Walter Hussey de Burgh, an orator unequaled, according to Lord Plunket, "in power of stirring the passions." "Talk not to me of peace," Burgh had declaimed in a characteristic fusion of the Bible and mythology. "Ireland is not at peace. It is smothered war. England has sown her law as dragon's teeth and they have sprung up armed men."[35]

Even in his drunkenness, however, Stephen makes his decision, another affirmative "no," about being one of those "armed men." Trying to extricate Stephen, Bloom hands him his ashplant: "Come along with me now before worse happens. Here's your stick." Mistakenly thinking he is being given it as a shillelagh, Stephen—reflecting Joyce's own deep-seated aversion to brute force and his anti-Fenian preference for nonviolent resistance over what he sarcastically described as "the persuasive faculty of the knife or the bomb"[36]—makes his Blakean declaration: "Stick, no. Reason. This feast of pure reason" (490).

The quadrivial allusion fuses Blake's "mental fight," his preference of

Devouring Ireland

"spiritual" to "corporeal warfare," with Pope's Horatian retreat from the world's "din" into a "grotto" featuring the "Feast of Reason"—indeed (with a glance at Kant's first *Critique*) of *"pure* reason," philosophy untainted by "practical reason" in either its noumenal or its commonsense forms. The result is a "feast" that—if not quite Pope's "friendly Bowl, / The Feast of Reason and the Flow of Soul"—is, like Pope's feast, served to men "out of War," and thus the very opposite of the meal planned by that Carrion Crow, Old Gummy Granny as the Morrigu.[37] Repudiating both his Siegfried-sword and the dagger thrust toward him by Old Gummy Granny, Stephen grips instead Pope's rapier ("Satire's my weapon") and Blake's unsleeping "sword" of "mental fight." As he had said a few moments earlier, tapping his "brow"—and tapping in the process another cluster of Blakean allusions—"in here it is I must kill the priest and the king."[38]

Though in the very next moment Stephen will be punched flat by Private Carr, he is neither coward nor defeatist. Blake himself, in the episode Joyce is recalling, pushed the British soldier out of his garden,[39] and Stephen does not walk away: "I don't avoid it. He provokes my intelligence" (484). Again alluding to Blake, Joyce once wrote Ibsen to tell him how much he had been inspired by the dramatist's mental fight, "not the obvious material battles but those that were fought and won behind your forehead" (LJ 1:52). The most celebrated weapons of Joyce and of Stephen Dedalus—the "only arms I allow myself to use," as Stephen says—were those nonviolent three: "silence, exile, and cunning" (P 247). But the principal weapon is love—unfortunately, as the situation in Northern Ireland demonstrates daily, *not* the word known to all men. As Yeats wrote during the Irish Civil War, in the year *Ulysses* was published and *Finnegans Wake* begun:

We had fed the heart on fantasies,
The heart's grown brutal from the fare;
More substance in our enmities
Than in our love. . . . (VP 425)

When Stephen turns from force and hatred, and affirms "life," he replicates Bloom's triumphant moment, standing up—nonviolently—to the one-eyed Fenian Citizen in his cave: that grotto of unreason, Kiernan's pub. Discussing persecution, Bloom turns from the English oppression of the Irish (and Ireland is his nation too; "I was born here") to the mistreatment of his own race.

—Are you talking about the new Jerusalem? says the citizen.

—I'm talking about injustice, says Bloom.
—Right, says John Wyse. Stand up to it then with force like men.

But Bloom, whom the barfly narrator imagines more comfortable with a "sweepingbrush" than with "the business end of a gun," wants no part of the physical-force movement either as Irishman or as Jew:

—But it's no use, says he. Force, hatred, history, all that. That's not life for men and women, insult and hatred. And everybody knows that it's the very opposite of that that is really life.
—What? says Alf.
—Love, says Bloom. I mean the opposite of hatred.[40]

Bloom understands the Fenian position; can even acknowledge (in "Eumaeus") "a certain kind of admiration for a man who had actually brandished a knife, cold steel, with the courage of his political convictions." But "personally, he would never be a party to any such thing" (524). Nor would Stephen. In refusing Bloom's misinterpreted offer of his stick and the phantasmagoric dagger thrust toward him by Old Gummy Granny, Stephen again rejects the Terrible Mother, Ireland herself as the Morrigu. As in the exchange with Davin in *Portrait*, Stephen proves less susceptible to the siren call to arms of the Old Woman who "wants me for odd jobs" than had Michael Gillane in Yeats's play, or all those others in Irish history who chose physical force rather than mental fight, most of them offering themselves up only to be sold, failed, reviled, abandoned. The only thing certain is that they will all "be launched into eternity" for the sake of a victimized but bloodthirsty Shan Van Vocht who seems to crave martyrs as much as she does freedom.

The Ireland-as-Devourer theme must have been painfully evident to Joyce in the autumn of 1922 when, with *Ulysses* published, he began thinking about what would become *Finnegans Wake*. Ireland's "eatupus complex" (FW 128) seems in fact to have provided the genesis of his "work in progress," which Joyce "first began to imagine in Nice in late October and early November 1922, when the Irish Revolution began to devour its own children."[41] Among them was Rory O'Connor, executed by the Free State government in early December on the reluctant but unyielding order of Justice Minister Kevin O'Higgins, at whose wedding O'Connor had been best man, and who was himself (to Yeats's grief) shortly to be assassinated. The first sketch of the *Wake*, written in March 1923, centers on Ireland's last high king, Roderick (Ruidri or Rori) O'Conor, and, as both Hugh Kenner and Edmund

Epstein have pointed out, the coincidence of the names reveals the genesis of Joyce's final work in his response to contemporary Irish history: the death of O'Connor at the hands of his former brothers-in-arms, a Shem-Shaun rivalry at its most murderous. Yet it was all part of a national awakening from the eight hundred years of oppression that had begun when "Roderick O'Conor, the paramount chief polemarch and last preelectric king of Ireland" (FW 380), had been reduced to a shadow monarch by the invading Normans under Strongbow.

Eventually, the Roderick O'Conor fragment, having indirectly generated the new book's opening paragraph,[42] became part of the "tavern" chapter (part 2, chap. 3), the longest and most dramatic section of *Finnegans Wake*, as "Circe," also set at midnight, had been of *Ulysses*. As drunk as Stephen in "Circe," Earwicker-O'Conor, dismembered and devoured by his tavern customers (FW 378), also passes out. But he will awaken. After he is knocked down by Private Carr at the end of "Circe," Stephen too assumes the fetal position, waiting to be reborn. In the case of Ireland as well, it is possible that out of death and dismemberment will come resurrection to new life. "Let my country die for me," Stephen had announced in a drunken exchange with Carr. But, really, he doesn't want *that* either: "I don't want it to die. Damn death. Long live life!"[43] But to Ireland, as to his own mother, he cries out, "No, mother! Let me be and let me live." The trinitarian Terrible Mother—as maternal ghost, as Holy Mother Church, and as Old Gummy Granny, Ireland herself—will have to find other corpses to chew. No more than James Joyce will Stephen Dedalus number himself among the heroic and betrayed—or the fantasy-fed and brutalized—litter to be eaten by that old sow, "another lineage" to "feed the crow."

4

The Cries of the Perishing

How with this rage shall beauty hold a plea,
Whose action is no stronger than a flower?
    —Shakespeare, Sonnet 65

But is there any comfort to be found?
Man is in love and loves what vanishes,
What more is there to say?
    —Yeats, "Nineteen Hundred and Nineteen"

But hush, for I have lost the theme,
Its joy or night seem but a dream;
Up there some hawk or owl has struck,
Dropping out of sky or rock,
A stricken rabbit is crying out,
And its cry distracts my thought.
    —Yeats, "The Man and the Echo"

The end of art is peace.
    —Coventry Patmore[1]

    The preceding section ended with two Yeatsian allusions, both to *Tower* poems of the twenties. The last is to Yeats's sardonic variation on Virgil's "Messianic" Eclogue in the first of "Two Songs from a Play": "Another Troy must rise and set, / Another lineage feed the crow." The other is to the sixth and most poignant section of his sequence *Meditations in Time of Civil War,* in which the lineage that feeds Carrion Crow is specified as the self-consuming Irish:

A barricade of stone or of wood;
Some fourteen days of civil war;
Last night they trundled down the road
That dead young soldier in his blood.

The Cries of the Perishing

Writing during the Irish Civil War, in the same year in which *Ulysses* was published, Yeats meditated on the Nationalist fantasies Romantic Ireland had devoured, "fare" that had brutalized hearts with one sacrificial purpose alone:

We had fed the heart on fantasies,
The heart's grown brutal from the fare;
More substance in our enmities
Than in our love; O, honey-bees,
Come build in the empty house of the stare.

Yeats's hope here, as he said in a note to his Nobel Prize acceptance speech, was that out of the bitterness and desolation of civil war there might yet come that constructive sweetness and light he associated with the bees who had built a comb in the crevice next to his bedroom window in the tower, a crevice abandoned by a starling.[2] The invocation to the honeybees is particularly moving in the case of a poet capable of glorifying violence, one whose Old Woman, metamorphosed into a young girl with the walk of a queen, had certainly thrilled, and brutalized, the national heart. (Indeed, she walked again in Stockholm, where the play was put on as part of the Nobel festivities.) But Yeats was capable of even more profound metamorphoses. His Cuchulain ends, for all his violence, by submitting himself to the mystical community of serene obedience, obeying the "ancient rule" of the Shrouds in the underworld of "Cuchulain Comforted" and awaiting his metamorphosis from warrior to sweet singing-bird.

A similarly quiescent note was struck forty years earlier in a poem associating Ireland with a destructive pig—not, in this case, the old sow that eats her own farrow, but the Black Pig whose valley was to be the site of an apocalyptic battle between Ireland and her English enemies. In this chapter, I will briefly examine "The Valley of the Black Pig," intrinsically and in a variety of contexts: in the context of the volume in which it appears, in the context of the elaborate notes Yeats appended to it over the years, and, finally, in the context of the responses of Yeats and Joyce to Cathleen ni Houlihan's summons to battle. We began Chapter 2 with "The Cap and Bells"; we end with "The Valley of the Black Pig." They seem worlds apart, and they are. But Yeats placed them back-to-back in *The Wind Among the Reeds*: poems of submission with quite different implications.

*   *   *

When "The Valley of the Black Pig" first appeared, in *The Savoy* for April 1896, it was accompanied by a two-sentence note. The operative statement gives us the potentially violent political myth:

> The Irish peasantry have for generations comforted themselves, in their misfortunes, with visions of a great battle, to be fought in a mysterious valley called, "The Valley of the Black Pig," and to break at last the power of their enemies.

This sentence was expanded to a thousand-word essay when the poem was reprinted three years later in *The Wind Among the Reeds*. There Yeats speaks of "prophecies," repeated "all over Ireland," of "the coming rout" of her enemies, prophecies that, as in "the Fenian days," are a "political force." He tells of one man who would not contribute to Michael Davitt's Land League (1879–1881) "because the Battle could not be until the close of the century"—an instance either of myth superseding practical politics or of cunning parsimony.

Yeats was of course aware that, "as a rule, periods of trouble bring prophecies of [the Battle's] near coming" (a phrase recalling the local clairvoyant's prophecies of the Old Woman in *Cathleen ni Houlihan*); that, as so often in the history of the biblical West, apocalyptic prophecies are allied with local dreams of political revolution. But the battle is not merely political. Yeats repeats the anecdotes first trotted out in the *Savoy* note:

> [one Sligo man] used to fall down in a fit and rave out descriptions of the Battle, [another told the poet that] it will be so great a battle that the horses shall go up to their fetlocks in blood, and that their girths, when it is over, will rot from their bellies for lack of a hand to unbuckle them. (VP 161)

Then he goes on to describe it as "a mythological battle." A long, clotted exposition follows, a discussion brilliantly distilled in yet another note, added in 1908 and polished in 1922. I quote the latter:

> If one reads Rhys' *Celtic Heathendom* by the light of Frazer's *Golden Bough*, and puts together what one finds there about the boar that killed Diarmuid, and other old Celtic boars and sows, one sees that the battle is mythological, and that the Pig it is named from must be a type of cold and winter doing battle with the summer, or of death battling with life. (VP 811)

In short, the apocalyptic black pig, a "bad sign" in Irish folklore, can be either Celtic boar or sow. Yeats seems to be aware that the androgynous Great Mother is both the "sow that farrows and the boar that kills."[3] Indeed, its role as winter battling summer, death battling life, allies the Black Pig specifically with the Terrible Mother who destroys the solar hero, "the mother goddess and the slain god" enacting "the old ritual of the year" (VP 840). Thus Yeats's Adonis poem, "Her Vision in the Wood," in which we hear of "the beast that gave the fatal wound," is the monologue of a blood-bedabbled old crone once tortured by a hero who is nevertheless "my heart's victim."

That the Black Pig is akin to Stephen Dedalus's farrow-eating old sow, to the mother who has "quenched for ever . . . my sun and moon," and to the star- and time-devouring Goddess herself is suggested by a point omitted in this the note's final form, but salient in both its 1899 and 1908 versions. Echoing Wordsworth on his "use" of Platonism in the Immortality ode, Yeats notes that, making the best use he could of this material "for the purposes of poetry," he took the battle as "a symbol of the darkness that will destroy the world"—what he had referred to, after quoting the first four lines of "The Valley of the Black Pig" in 1902, as the "Armageddon which shall quench all things in the Ancestral Darkness again" (Myth 110–11).

In *The Wind Among the Reeds,* Yeats both longs for that darkness and resists it; for the "purposes of poetry" served by these "old Celtic boars and sows" is precisely that: plural. This characteristically Yeatsian dialectic is embodied in "The Valley of the Black Pig" and in the poem in the volume with which it is most obviously connected, and from which it is most subtly detached.

I would that the Boar without bristles had come from the West
And had rooted the sun and moon and stars out of the sky
And lay in the darkness, grunting, and turning to his rest.

The poem's long title—"He Mourns for the Change that has come upon Him and his Beloved, and longs for the End of the World"—provides the autobiographical key to *The Wind Among the Reeds* as a whole: the sexual torment underlying the elaborate poetic, mythological, occult, and religious trappings of the Yeatsian apocalypse. In addition, it explains why the poet longs to turn to his own "rest," to return to that Ancestral Darkness in which all things, including the frustration of unrequited sexual desire, are quenched. It is a consummation devoutly to be wished, whatever the violence of the Armageddon that must precede the return of that primordial darkness. Here Yeats is at the opposite pole from Joyce, though both depend on the same archetypal material. Yeats's darkness is symbolized by the boar's devouring of sun and moon and stars, a variant on the "star-children going into [the Great Mother's] mouth in the manner of a sow eating her young," the same archetype played on in Stephen's repeated image of Ireland as the old sow that eats her farrow and in his reference to his own mother and Motherland: "my moon and my sun thou hast quenched for ever."

The same complex of emotions underlies the power of the greatest single passage in *The Wind Among the Reeds*. The six-line climax of "The Secret Rose" lifts into greatness a poem matted with allusions to the Irish mythological heroes (Cuchulain among them) enfolded in the "great leaves" of a Rose emblematic of the terrible beauty shared by spiritual revelation, Ireland, and Maud Gonne, the latter a Rose in whose leaves Yeats also longs to be "enfolded":

> I, too, await
> The hour of thy great wind of love and hate.
> When shall the stars be blown about the sky,
> Like the sparks blown out of a smithy, and die?
> Surely thine hour has come, thy great wind blows,
> Far-off, most secret, and inviolate Rose?

This celestial imagery is also employed in the final lines of "The Valley of the Black Pig," but there we encounter something very different from this apocalypse quarried from Yeats's occult and Blakean sources. Indeed, following this top-heavy mythological preamble, the poem itself will seem considerably less than the promised end:

> The dews drop slowly and dreams gather: unknown spears
> Suddenly hurtle before my dream-awakened eyes,
> And then the clash of fallen horsemen and the cries
> Of unknown perishing armies beat about my ears.
> We who still labour by the cromlech on the shore,
> The grey cairn on the hill, when day sinks drowned in dew,
> Being weary of the world's empires, bow down to you,
> Master of the still stars and of the flaming door.

Was it for this that all that mythological ink was shed? The mountain of comparative mythology and Celtic folklore would seem to have labored only to bring forth a mouse rather than the formidable Black Pig. But then that is precisely what happens in the poem as well: the dreamt-of great battle simply fails to materialize. Whatever the "political force" Yeats said attended the apocalyptic prophecies, the peasants and poets who labor by Celtic cromlech and cairn end in a Celtic twilight; "day sinks drowned in dew," and "we,"

> Being weary of the world's empires, bow down to you,
> Master of the still stars and of the flaming door.

This occult description of God momentarily recharges the poem with light—the "still stars" are *not* devoured by the Boar/Sow—and apocalyptic excitement. But the fact is that "we" end in crepuscular exhaustion and submission. A divine Master may be preferable to English masters, the traditional "enemies of Ireland," but the quietism with which the poem ends seems less mystical than, simply, apolitical.[4] Yeats's Armageddon comes to nothing; the mythological battle of summer and winter, light and darkness, sunrise and sunset—the whole solar drama identified by Max Müller, the great Vedic scholar and chief nineteenth-century champion of solar mythology, as "the principal subject of early mythology"—collapses into a dusk that is hardly that Wagnerian "dusk of the nations" Yeats had envisaged the previous year (and which, rather preposterously, he thought might be initiated by the 1895 border dispute between the United States and Venezuela [LY 259–60]). As Yeats tells us, oppressed people dream apocalyptic dreams of deliverance, of what Rufus Jones has memorably called "the fierce comfort of a relief expedition from the skies."[5] In this poem, the relief expedition is evoked only to be recalled by a poet perhaps weary of what Nietzsche called "the ephemeral babble of politics," a poet certainly, for the moment, less concerned with terrestrial than with celestial "empires," the occult mysteries of that "flaming door" Yeats hoped would swing open for him in the nineties.

Shortly before Yeats wrote the poem, MacGregor Mathers, the chief figure in Yeats's occult society, the Order of the Golden Dawn, "began to foresee changes in the world, announcing in 1893 or 1894 the imminence of immense wars. . . . It may have been some talk of his," Yeats adds, "that made me write the poem that begins . . . ." And he quotes, significantly, only the first four lines of "The Valley of the Black Pig," the lines depicting a visionary glimpse of the great battle in which Ireland was to overthrow her enemies (Au 336). Interestingly enough, however, the submissiveness of the second half of the poem is anticipated even in these opening lines, with their emphasis not on the victors but on the defeated: the clash of "*fallen* horsemen" and "the cries / Of unknown *perishing* armies."

Those armies may have been "unknown" to the visionary poet; they were known precisely by Cathleen ni Houlihan and her surrogates. In the section of *The Celtic Twilight* entitled "War," Yeats tells of a poor Sligo widow who—obsessed by a fusion of biblical prophecy and traditions of the "great rebellion" of 1798, the rebellion ostensibly glorified in Yeats's play—interpreted the battle of the Black Pig as "a battle between Ireland and England." Though he recorded her conversation in 1902, the same year he wrote *Cathleen ni Houlihan,* Yeats felt compelled to amend her interpretation; it seems "to me," he added in his own fusion of biblical prophecy with comparative mythology and the occult, "an Armageddon which shall quench all things in the Ancestral Darkness again" (Myth 110–11).

Yeats's "Armageddon" is related to that "magical Armageddon" prophesied by Mathers—with a crucial difference. Yeats here avoids that specifying of "definite . . . nations and individuals" indulged in during the mid-nineties by Mathers and, occasionally, by Yeats himself—and, in 1902, by that old Sligo widow. To be sure, Yeats shared something of that old woman's and of Mathers's "imagination brooding upon war" (Au 336); but whatever the misplaced concreteness of *their* visions or pre-visions, the spears and armies that "Suddenly hurtle before my dream-awakened eyes" in the opening lines of "The Valley of the Black Pig" are, in Yeats's repeated adjective, "unknown."

The "unknown" is, precisely, the occult. In part, and this is paradoxical, Yeats was saved from his own apocalyptic recklessness by his occult obsessions, obsessions that were also a considerable factor in distancing him from the Irish political crisis. For one thing, as Allen Grossman notes in his study of *The Wind Among the Reeds*, the Golden Dawn symbolism itself provided Yeats "with a stable hierarchy by which he was protected from the violence of his desire to overthrow all order."[6] For another, that symbolism, secret and elitist, excluded the many, including political literalists of the imagination. As a contemporary reviewer of *The Wind Among the Reeds*, William Sharp, observed in referring to the final line of "The Valley of the Black Pig," "only the few may apprehend 'the flaming door.' "[7]

Not that Yeats was merely wrapping himself in mantic robes. Clairvoyance is always mysterious ("*somewhere* in sands of the desert"); the sign of the Sublime, as Longinus notes, is always the mark of interrogation. What Whitehead was later to call the Fallacy of Misplaced Concreteness is a fallacy worth evading since the cost, in the case of a poet, is the diminished evocativeness and resonance that attends the overspecifying of symbols. As a man who was simultaneously a poet, an occultist, and a comparative mythologist, Yeats was unwilling to delimit the vision of an apocalyptic battle—even one he admits he appropriated from Irish "peasants and visionaries"—to a struggle between Ireland and England in which the Irish "will break at last the power of their enemies." Thus, in his various notes and comments on "The Valley of the Black Pig," he universalizes the specifically Irish battle and beast by allying them with similar beasts and battles in world mythology, while, in the poem itself, he aligns specifically Irish peasants and poets, laboring by

Celtic "cromlech" and "cairn," with those who bow down, not to any local or even temporal masters, but to the spiritual "Master" of all.[8]

Characteristically, Yeats has things both ways, at once including and excluding his Irish audience. The "Master of the still stars and of the flaming door," though God of all, is known by such an appellation only to the privileged "few." In a specifically Irish context, it seems as alien a depiction of God as (at the opposite pole of the inside joke) that of Buck Mulligan in his response to the opening words of the Old Woman representing Cathleen ni Houlihan in the first chapter of *Ulysses*:

—That's a lovely morning, sir, she said. Glory be to God.
—To whom? Mulligan said, glancing at her. Ah, to be sure.
Stephen reached back and took the milkjug from the locker.
—The islanders, Mulligan said to Haines casually, speak frequently of the collector of prepuces. (U 12)

Like most of her fellow "islanders," the Old Woman would be no more familiar with Jehovah's commandment regarding circumcision (Genesis 17:10–14) than she is with the Irish language itself ("I'm told it's a grand language by them that knows"). Similarly, "only the few," as Yeats's fellow occultist William Sharp pointed out, would be capable of apprehending what Yeats meant by that Master of the "flaming door." The Covering Cherub with his fiery sword excludes us from the Eden we have been ejected from by guarding that "flaming door." Yeats is similarly exclusive. Though drawing on peasant visions of a battle popularly associated with the victory of Ireland over England, he hieratically distances himself from those peasants and retreats from that battle, in both its political and even its mythological versions. In doing so, he distances himself far from the madding crowd, those "islanders" who, six years later, would thunderously applaud his *Cathleen ni Houlihan*, clapping proleptically bloody hands, blissfully unaware that Yeats's crone-turned-queen was still a death-hag eventually capable of exacting their own blood.

*   *   *

The Easter Rising and the martyrdom of its sixteen leaders might not quite amount to the long-prophesied Battle of the Black Pig, "so great a battle that the horses shall go up to their fetlocks in blood," but it *was* a "terrible beauty" that was born, one requiring their "own red blood," even if "excess of love / Bewildered them till they died." Yeats is recalling, in this contemporary bewilderment, Emmet, Fitzgerald, Tone, and "all that delirium of the brave" in "September 1913," his premature burial of "Romantic Ireland." It turned out to be an Ireland very much alive, for even if its heart was "enchanted to a stone," it had been "fed . . . on fantasies," those very fantasies he had stimulated and exploited years before in *Cathleen ni Houlihan*. The "love" motivating those fantasies is made clear in the final stanza of "September 1913." Could we call back Ireland's dead and exiled heroes, "as they were / In all their loneliness and pain,"

You'd cry, 'Some woman's yellow hair
Has maddened every mother's son':
They weighed so lightly what they gave.

That "woman" is Ireland as Triple Goddess, not only beloved and mother, but she who, demanding "all," lures her sons and lovers to their death. Of course, the exalted madness, the erotic frenzy, of the dead heroes who lightly gave all is to be preferred to "you," the Catholic middle-class Paudeens who, in "September 1913," "fumble in a greasy till / And add the halfpence to the pence / And prayer to shivering prayer"—rather as Michael Gillane's parents do in *Cathleen ni Houlihan*. And yet, as usual, there are Yeatsian reservations. Like Michael Gillane, who suddenly "has the look of a man that has got the touch," the heroes of "September 1913" and "Easter 1916" are delirious, bewildered, maddened—and dead: all of them launched into eternity by the "excess of love" they bear Cathleen ni Houlihan, that "terrible beauty" and Great Mother of every Irish hero, of "every mother's son" who is also "a servant of the queen."

There were alternative, rational forms of Irish patriotism. The chief of staff of the Irish Volunteers, the scholar Eoin MacNeill, sensing that his director of organization, Padraic Pearse, was planning an insurrection based on the mythology of Cathleen ni Houlihan and the cult of blood sacrifice, wrote an eloquent memorandum in February 1916 opposing a romantic and fatalistic plunge into military action. The memorandum, read in his absence and quickly forgotten, concluded:

We have to remember that what we call our country is not a poetical abstraction, as some of us, perhaps all of us, in the exercise of our highly developed capacity for figurative thought, are sometimes apt to imagine—with the help of our patriotic literature. There is no such person as Caitln N Uallachan or Roisn Dubh or the Seanbhean-Bhoct, who is calling us to serve her. What we call our country is the Irish nation, which is a concrete and visible reality.⁹

But realism is of no avail against the allure of the terrible beauty of Cathleen and Dark Rosaleen. After the Rising that MacNeill was unable to prevent, and as the Troubles ground on, that terrible beauty began, in Sean O'Casey's phrase, "to lose her good looks." He himself saw her at her ugliest during the Abbey uproar over *The Plough and the Stars* in 1926. He re-creates for us in his *Autobiographies* the whole chaotic scene: "Yeats . . . shouting out his scorn, his contempt," an "aged Cuchullain in his hero-rage" conjuring up a vision of O'Casey's "triumphant apotheosis" while men tried to tear down the front curtain and uproot theater seats and the "high, hysterical distorted voices of women kept squealing that Irish girls were noted over the world for their modesty, and that Ireland's name was holy." For "the first time in his life," O'Casey continues, he

felt a surge of hatred for Cathleen ni Houlihan sweeping over him. He saw now that the one who had the walk of a queen could be a bitch at times. She galled the hearts of her children who dared to be above the ordinary, and she often slew her best ones. She had hounded Parnell to death; she had yelled and torn at Yeats, at Synge, and now she was doing the same to him. What an old snarly gob she could be at times; an ignorant one too.¹⁰

Cathleen was a "terrible beauty" who had indeed lost much of her "good looks." Yet she never completely lost her allure for Yeats. He is, I suspect, the "solitary man" who "turned his stately head" (away from or toward?) the siren who beckons in "I am of Ireland." He knows, as she does, that "time runs on" and also that "the night grows rough," that "the fiddlers are all thumbs," that the trumpets and trombones have "burst." He may cock "a malicious eye"; yet her haunting song, combining invitation and command, like time itself, runs on, runs on:

'I am of Ireland,
And the Holy Land of Ireland,
And time runs on,' cried she.
'Come out of charity,
Come dance with me in Ireland.'

Yeats was ambivalent in his response to the invitation to that dance, a dance of life and death not unrelated to the dance "arranged" by the Morrigu in *The Death of Cuchulain,* or to the ritual of the Yeatsian queens who, resembling Kali and Salome, dance before and kiss severed heads. But the "call of country" remained seductive. Whatever his scholarly distancing in his early handling of the Black Pig material, for example, he never completely forgot that battle as symbol of a specifically Irish apocalypse. The drafts of his very last poem, written on his deathbed, reveal that the defiant Irish heroes gathered in the Black Tower for the last battle wait, as Yeats had waited forty years earlier in *The Wind Among the Reeds,* for the apocalyptic "wind" to blow, a wind specified in "The Black Tower" manuscripts as coming "from the black pig's dike."[11]

But that allusion was eventually deleted; in any case, this poem, for all its eerie power, lacks the authentic greatness of Yeats's true deathbed poems, "Cuchulain Comforted" and "The Man and the Echo."

In the first, the hawk-god and warrior Cuchulain—"son of that clean hawk out of the air" (VPl 485)—is transformed in the underworld. At first a man "violent and famous," he "strode among the dead," frightening the linen-carrying Shrouds who timidly peer out of the branches at him; "the rattle of those arms makes us afraid." But he is soon sewing his own shroud in this community of his opposites, "convicted cowards all." Yeats's own arms-rattling ends here—the Yeatsian equivalent of Stephen's rejection of violence and of the ashplant as weapon. In this most mysteriously beautiful of Yeats's poems, the final metamorphosis—"They had changed their throats and had the throats of birds"—is not only an appropriate transformation of Cuchulain, from hawk-god to sweet singing-bird, but also an evocation of Yeats's own avian image of himself as one who "ruffled in a manly pose / For all his timid heart" (VP 489). Opposites meet: Yeats, dropping the mask of violent Cuchulain, becomes one with Stephen Dedalus and James Joyce, opponents of violence.

For one can oppose to violence—specifically, to the blood-cult of the Devouring Female as Cathleen ni Houlihan—values that are also "female." Of Joyce two contemporary feminist critics have declared: "His values are not only humanistic but traditionally female in their disdain for war, violence, and aggression."[12] We cannot quite say this of Yeats, part of whose divided sensibility was attuned to, and attracted by, violence and the predatory birds of war. But in his most profound moments, as in "Cuchulain Comforted" and in the second of the death poems referred to, "The Man and the Echo," Yeats too adopts "humanistic [and] traditionally female" values.

In "The Man and the Echo," Yeats's thought is interrupted and his timid heart goes out, not as it had so often in the past to the heroic bird of prey, but to its helpless victim:

Up there some hawk or owl has struck,
Dropping out of sky or rock,
A stricken rabbit is crying out
And its cry distracts my thought.

It is appropriate that this deeply moving expression of empathy and uncertainty (that repeated Keatsian "or"[13] is one of Yeats's subtlest triumphs) should come at the end of a self-questioning poem that consists of an old man's final anguished uncertainties, the most memorable of which have to do with "that play" of his that sent out men the English shot.

Yeats's sense of responsibility regarding those incited to violence by his *Cathleen ni Houlihan,* his sympathy for her (and his) victims, is poignant enough. Even more poignant is that empathy with the stricken rabbit in the final lines of "The Man and the Echo." The image recalls Yeats's "The Death of the Hare," poem IV of *A Man Young and Old,* which Yeats himself, in a rare explication, interpreted as expressing a lover's "sympathy with his beloved's dread of captivity" (LY 840–41), a remarkable shift of perspective in which the conventional male "victim" of the first three poems in the *Man* sequence suddenly recognizes female victimage in the cruelty of the love hunt.

In "Cuchulain Comforted," the hero who was himself the victim of the Morrigu lays down his arms; in "The Man and the Echo," Yeats empathizes with the victim of the hunt, its "cry" resembling the "cries / Of unknown perishing armies" in "The Valley of the Black Pig." In the context of our theme, these poems seem rejections of those goddesses of the hunt and of war that have always been the universal images of the "Dark and Terrible Mother," described by Neumann as she who, having generated "all living things on earth," devours them and "takes them back into herself." According to Neumann's synopsis, she

pursues her victims and captures them with snare and net. . . . Among all peoples the goddesses of war and the hunt express man's experience of life as a female exacting blood. This Terrible Mother is the hungry earth, which devours its own children and fattens on their corpses.[14]

In the greatest of his death poems, Yeats, like Stephen Dedalus, flies by those snares and "nets" flung at the soul to hold it back. The Terrible Mother yields to a kindlier goddess, the goddess of that nurturing "Love" which is "the word known to all men" but which remains unspoken by that ghostly and ghastly corpsechewer-of-a-mother Stephen Dedalus confronts in "Circe," the familial equivalent of his Motherland, Cathleen ni Houlihan, the old sow that eats her farrow.

We do not have to go to Yeats's deathbed to find resistance to devouring violence. In the three early works in which he most directly invokes Irish political mythology (the poem from "Kathleen-ny-Houlihan," "The Valley of the Black Pig," and *Cathleen ni Houlihan* itself), Yeatsian reservations are—overtly or covertly—present. "Angers" may have "set our hearts abeat" in the first; "But we have all bent low and low and kissed the quiet feet / Of Cathleen, the daughter of Houlihan," a personified Ireland that here resembles the fatally adored "young queen" of "The Cap and Bells," with "the quiet of love in her feet." In the poem immediately following in *The Wind Among the Reeds*, the vision of Ireland's great battle ends in a similarly quiet submission, as "we," being "weary of the world's empires, bow down to you, / Master of the still stars and of the flaming door." We may be perplexed or even discomfited by this submission, not to Cathleen, the daughter of Houlihan, but to a spiritual "Master," as well as by the quiescent turning away from the final battle between Ireland and her enemies, a battle "The Valley of the Black Pig" evokes only to evade. We will appreciate the poem more if we see it as the rejection of those "Celtic boars and sows" who devour not only time but also their own "star-children," the warriors fed into their voracious maws. Like Joyce, who also submits himself to a more-than-mortal Master in the final words of *Portrait* ("Old father, old artificer, stand me now and ever in good stead"), Yeats prefers spiritual to corporeal war, the "mental fight" of their common "Master." Rejecting Blake's "Orc"—the fiery boy of violent revolution and, incidentally, Irish for "pig"—and siding with "Los," Blake's blacksmith god and figure of capable imagination, Yeats chooses, in the words of Stephen Dedalus, "to forge in the smithy of my soul the uncreated conscience of my race" (P 253).

Both writers, in short, choose to "serve," not Church or State, but their Art, though an art itself in service to the uncreated soul of Ireland.[15] Under the influence of Maud Gonne, Yeats, in *Cathleen ni Houlihan*, may have compromised his own soul by forging it in a more public and popular, certainly a more potentially violent, smithy. He did not, however, sell his soul. For beneath the appeal to romantic Nationalism, surviving even the electrifying climax in which the Old Woman seems changed, changed utterly, the primordial form of the Terrible Mother and Devouring Female persists. The Old Woman may have become, in the theater and especially in Maud Gonne's celebrated performance, a young girl with the walk of a queen, a far cry from the old sow that eats her farrow. But, as Yeats asked, referring to Maud Gonne herself, "who can tell / Which of her forms has shown her substance right?" Yeats ends that poem by imagining Maud Gonne "supernatural; / As though a sterner eye looked through her eye." With that "mysterious eye" British journalists thought "contained the shadow of battles yet to come," Maud Gonne, like the personified Ireland she portrayed, becomes at times indistinguishable from that one-eyed tomb haunter, the Morrigu.

When, acting out the inevitable, he cast Maud Gonne as Cathleen ni Houlihan, Yeats was anticipating those poems of his "where an always personal emotion was woven into a general pattern of myth and symbol" (Au 151). When he made his Cathleen a sympathetic old woman who is nevertheless a devourer akin to Sheela-na-gig or to Joyce's farrow-eating old sow, he went well beyond the merely conventional line of "the Fenian poet" he quoted immediately following the "myth and symbol" sentence, a rhythmically inert line ("For thy hapless fate, dear Ireland, and sorrows of my own") that "but follows tradition," says Yeats, "and does not move us deeply." Though Yeats's heart also aches for Ireland's hapless fate and sorrows of his own, he, unlike the Fenian poet, gives us an Ireland ultimately less hapless than terrifying, a drinker of man's blood.

And not only *man's* blood. For the final irony is that Cathleen ni Houlihan demanded "all" of certain *women* too—most notably, Constance Markiewicz and Maud Gonne. If Maud, who "took / All, till my youth was gone," devoured Yeats, she in turn—enslaved by an Anglophobic "fanaticism and hate" Yeats thought soul-destroying—was devoured by the all-consuming crone she portrayed in *Cathleen ni Houlihan* and to whom she submitted herself as servant of the queen. Yeats's play, personifying an Ireland embodied by Maud Gonne, may be the ultimate example of the literary work as self-consuming artifact. However one evaluates the life and lifelong political commitment of this remarkable woman, she was one who "had fed the heart on fantasies," fantasies of a "cause" that might be noble or something other than human life. Whether or not she had traded life's rich horn of plenty for an old bellows full of angry wind, Maud Gonne was a woman who became "pale-cheeked," as Cathleen ni Houlihan promised, in the service of her queen. Yeats described her in old age not only as a "dark tomb-haunter" but also as a hollow-cheeked eater of air, a skeleton-gaunt "image of such politics" as those she shared with Con. In what is perhaps his greatest single poem, Yeats presents her as a still voracious Devourer feeding on insubstantial fare:

Her present image floats into the mind . . .
Hollow of cheek as though it drank the wind
And took a mess of shadows for its meat.[16]

Yet, in the imagination of romantic Nationalists, an imagination fired by what Yeats and Maud Gonne put on the stage in 1902, Maud Gonne's Cathleen walks still with "the walk of a queen." That image, like the image of devoured Parnell in the work of Yeats and Joyce, can still stir us. And that is the problem—one Yeats and Joyce exacerbated even as they tried to resolve it through spiritual rather than corporeal warfare. Moved by what were more than "mere images," they too ran the risk of being consumed by all-devouring Ireland. As Yeats put it in acknowledging the intensity of hatred in a small country,

Out of Ireland have we come,
Great hatred, little room,
Maimed us at the start.
I carry from my mother's womb
A fanatic heart. (VP 506)

The Mother is Ireland, her devouring womb the earth hungering for her own fanatic- or stone-hearted children, those who die for love of her. In an 1881 play about Robert Emmet, the cult of the dead, the mystique of blood sacrifice as the necessary nourisher, achieved a kind of vulgar perfection: "The shamrock grows better when there's dead men at the roots."[17] While Yeats was decidedly not one for shamrocks, he resurrected Padraic Pearse after the execution of the leaders of the 1916 Rising to repeat the familiar fertilizing recipe for a less plebeian Celtic plant. "Our Rose Tree" needs only to be watered, James Connolly and Pearse agree, "To make the green come out again."

'But where can we draw water,'
Said Pearse to Connolly,
'When all the wells are parched away?
O plain as plain can be
There's nothing but our own red blood
Can make a right Rose Tree.'

That, like the logic-repudiating eloquence of "MacDonagh's bony thumb" in the immediately preceding poem, seems consistent with the blood sacrifice ostensibly glorified in *Cathleen ni Houlihan*, the play that helped speed Pearse, Connolly, MacDonagh, and the rest of the "Sixteen Dead Men" to their graves fourteen years later. "Such a sacrifice," wrote one student of the play's "ideological factors," was "not merely worthy of admiration, but actually advocated as the bounden duty of each Irish generation."[18]

So it would seem. But I have argued that Yeats's own misgivings, later explicit, were implicit even in 1902. Of course, those spellbound by the performance of Maud Gonne as Ireland herself, and other audiences whose infatuation with their own mythology of romantic Nationalism was fed by Yeats, were not likely to detect the "negative aspect" I have stressed. As Conor Cruise O'Brien remarks in a footnote toward the end of *States of Ireland*: "It doesn't seem to have occurred to earlier audiences of Yeats's *Cathleen ni Houlihan* that there might be something unhealthy about a mother who shuffles around promising her sons that 'they shall be remembered for ever,' providing they get themselves killed for mother's sake." It *had* occurred to Yeats, whose infatuation with his own mythmaking was both tempered and short-lived. "Yeats himself," as O'Brien had noted earlier, "almost immediately recoiled from *Cathleen ni Houlihan*. The being he had created continued to beckon others, but left her creator cold."[19]

She continues to beckon others, as O'Brien—hounded by the IRA—has more reason than most to know. He originally ended *States of Ireland* on a note of transcendent hope, a longing for the evaporation of the simplifying myths accepted and exploited, whether by Orangemen or the IRA:

Men and women who have quarrelled can learn through suffering how to live together and apart. . . . People can wake up in the morning and find an imprisoning myth no longer imprisoning but just plain silly. Cathleen ní Houlihan and King Billy are not necessarily immortal.

No, not necessarily. But, in an epilogue, meditating on a 1972 pronouncement by Cardinal Conway, the Primate of All Ireland ("Irish society, both Catholic and Protestant, is not a secular society; it is a deeply religious one"), O'Brien himself was compelled to return to those two symbols, or pantomime figures, employing—as appropriate to the "callous brutality" of which both "deeply religious" sides have proved themselves capable—a devouring image:

The two varieties of intolerance, different as they are in tone and presentation, in fact feed on one another and feed their cruel children, ultra-nationalism and sectarianism, Cathleen and King Billy.[20]

The same mythological pairing occurs in a 1974 lecture in which Seamus Heaney connects Cathleen ni Houlihan with the Mother Goddess of *The Bog People*, in which P. V. Glob had argued that the naked bodies preserved under the Jutland peat were those of ritual victims sacrificed to the goddess. The book was published in 1969, the year the killing began again in Northern Ireland. Archaeology, mythology, and contemporary politics naturally coalesced in the mind of a poet from Northern Ireland struggling "to encompass the perspectives of a humane reason and at the same time to grant the religious intensity of the violence its deplorable authenticity and complexity." To some extent, Heaney told his audience at the Royal Society of Literature,

the enmity can be viewed as a struggle between the cults and devotees of a god and goddess. There is an indigenous territorial numen, a tutelar of the whole island, call her Mother Ireland, Kathleen Ni Houlihan, the poor old woman, whatever; and her sovereignty has been temporarily usurped or infringed by a new male cult whose founding fathers were Cromwell, William of Orange and Edward Carson. . . . This idiom is remote from the agnostic world of economic interest . . . and remote from the political manoeuvres of power-sharing; but it is not remote from the bankrupt psychology and mythologies implicit in the terms Irish Catholic and Ulster Protestant.

Heaney's question is Shakespeare's: "How with this rage shall beauty hold a plea?" His answer is to offer what Yeats called, in *Meditations in Time of Civil War*, "befitting emblems of adversity." He found such emblems in Glob's book, especially in the Tollund Man, described in Heaney's poem of that title as "Bridegroom to the goddess," his severed head preserved in a museum. He was among the

ritual sacrifices to the Mother Goddess, the goddess of the ground who needed new bridegrooms each winter to bed with her in her sacred place, in the bog, to ensure the renewal and fertility of the territory in the spring. Taken in relation to the tradition of Irish political martyrdom for that cause whose icon is Kathleen Ni Houlihan, this is more than an archaic barbarous rite: it is an archetypal pattern.[21]

It is a pattern that has persisted. The insatiability of Ireland as Terrible Mother was powerfully conveyed in Heaney's 1974 poem "Kinship." "Our mother ground / is sour with the blood / of her faithful," who "lie gargling / in her sacred heart." Those who come to Ireland to "report us fairly" must tell "how we slaughter / for the common good, . . . / how the goddess swallows / our love and terror."[22]

The Cries of the Perishing

The faithful are still being swallowed, in even greater numbers. A decade and a half later, the gun and bomb continue—like the bony thumb and the icons of Cathleen and King Billy—to outweigh logic. The troubled ghettos of the North have become a permanent war zone, and the economy of the Republic, promising when O'Brien and Heaney wrote in the early seventies, is now afflicted by high unemployment and a massive foreign debt. But King Billy and Cathleen ni Houlihan are alive and well. Indeed, with more than twenty-six hundred men, women, and children dead since 1969 and another twenty-five thousand maimed and injured, with another lineage "to feed the crow," Cathleen ni Houlihan and her counterpart seem to be not only well, but well-fed. Ireland continues, like the Dark and Terrible Mother of mythology, to devour her own children and fatten on their corpses.

What links of responsibility, if any, were forged in the workshop of the author of *Cathleen ni Houlihan*? The political situation in the North—religious hatred and a Partition that the 1985 Anglo-Irish Agreement has certified in practice if not in principle—is hardly to be laid at Yeats's doorstep. But the stereotypes inherited by the Protestant and Catholic communities—self-images that, "subconsciously, they live and die to resemble"—are in turn based on "a presumed spirit or essence which is to be identified with the very soul of Ireland." While Denis Donoghue (whose *We Irish* I am quoting) agrees with his fellow Catholic Northerner Seamus Deane that Yeats "did much to present the question of Irishness as a moral criterion," he knows that the Yeatsian description of the destiny of Irishness "would not be invoked by either of the communities in conflict in the North today."[23]

Nevertheless, as Yeats himself acknowledged, "We had fed the heart on fantasies, / The heart's grown brutal from the fare." Though, as Donoghue remarks, nobody is "obliged to coincide with a stereotype," the fantasies and stereotypes, political and lethal, persist. Indeed, hearts in the North have, if anything, grown even more brutal than they were when Yeats wrote these lines sixty-five years ago, meditating in time of Civil War and longing for the honeybees to come build in the empty house of the stare. "The one enlivening truth that starts out of it all," Yeats wrote H. J. C. Grierson at the time, "is that we may learn charity after mutual contempt" (LY 691). Refusing to plunge into "this whirlpool of hate" for which "both sides are responsible"[24] and hoping to "learn charity," Yeats sounds rather like Leopold Bloom, championing Love in Kiernan's pub. Tragically, in Northern Ireland the lesson about mutual charity, let alone love, is still to learn.

Epilogue

Conor Cruise O'Brien wrote the final chapter and the epilogue to *States of Ireland* in the immediate aftermath of "Bloody Sunday," that day in late January 1972 when British paratroops fired into an "anti-internment" rally in Derry killing thirteen men, all Catholics. Not long after that day, and the resumption of direct rule of the North from Westminster, Seamus Heaney, becoming an "inner émigré,"[1] moved his wife and children from Belfast to County Wicklow in the Republic. In August of the following year, he gave a lecture at the Yeats International Summer School in Sligo. His talk, the highlight of the conference for me, focused on the compassionate humanity—not the most familiar gesture of the cold-eyed Yeats—of the final movement of "The Man and the Echo." In Yeats's concern not with the violent hawk but with the stricken rabbit, Heaney found a point at which "Christ and Caesar are hand in glove" in Yeats's work.

Though altered in meaning, the phrase was borrowed from Joyce;[2] significantly, it was with the hand-in-hand blessing of Joyce that Heaney himself later implied that he had, perhaps, broken free from the poetic burden of the violence in the North. In the final poem of his Dantesque sequence "Station Island" (1985), the poet finds, gripping his, a "helping hand . . . fish-cold and bony, but whether to guide / or to be guided I could not be certain." The echo of Stephen Dedalus's response to Cathleen ni Houlihan's arrival in the form of an old milkwoman ("To serve or to upbraid, whether he could not tell") is appropriate since the helping hand is that of the ghost of James Joyce, a tall man who "seemed blind, though he walked straight as a rush / upon his ash plant" and who, striking "a litter basket / with his stick," tells Heaney,

> "your obligation
> is not discharged by any common rite.
> What you must do must be done on your own
> so get back in harness."

Epilogue

The poet should "write / for the joy of it" and not be "so earnest, / let others wear the sackcloth and ashes"; and stop "raking at dead fires, / a waste of time for somebody your age." That "subject people stuff is a cod's game" in which "you lose more of yourself than you redeem." He is therefore to

> "Keep at a tangent.
> When they make the circle wide, it's time to swim
>
> out on your own and fill the element
> with signatures on your own frequency,
> echo soundings, searches, probes, allurements,
>
> elver-gleams in the dark of the whole sea."[3]

It is moving and beautiful, but the reader is tempted to say, with T. S. Eliot, "That was a way of putting it—not very satisfactory." Seamus Heaney would probably agree; he is, after all, not a detached, ghostly James Joyce. Nor, despite his formidable powers, is he Dante, the Yeats of the Dantesque "Cuchulain Comforted," or the Eliot who encounters the ghost of Yeats in the Dantesque section of "Little Gidding." The real problem, however, is not aesthetic but political and human: no matter how "silly" or "bankrupt" the myth may be, it remains to some degree "imprisoning," and we are left wondering if even those Irish writers who try to keep at a tangent and swim out on their own can ever truly escape. Resisted by Yeats and Joyce, by O'Brien and Heaney, even, in their own ways, by Donoghue and Deane, the mythology survives, still threatening to devour men, women, and children in Ireland. As long as she remains a victim herself, Cathleen will go on claiming victims of her own.

We began, in the Dedication, by citing Yeats's prose version of reciprocal political dismemberment; we end with poetic images of that dismemberment. The greatest of Yeats's political poems, "Nineteen Hundred and Nineteen," fuses his reaction to the Black and Tan atrocities of that year with a vision of decapitating Salome and her sisters. This cyclical "dance of the daughters of Herodias, . . . Herodias doubtless taking the place of some old goddess" (VP 800), is a whirl of eternally recurrent eroticized violence that modulates into a climactic evocation of the fourteenth-century Kilkenny witch and murderess, Dame Alice Kyteler, and the demonic incubus to whom she and her coven offered dismembered animals in ritual sacrifices:

> Herodias' daughters have returned again,
> A sudden blast of dusty wind and after
> Thunder of feet, tumult of images,
> Their purpose in the labyrinth of the wind;
> And should some crazy hand dare touch a daughter
> All turn with amorous cries, or angry cries,
> According to the wind, for all are blind.
> But now wind drops, dust settles; thereupon
> There lurches past, his great eyes without thought
> Under the shadow of stupid straw-pale locks,
> That insolent fiend Robert Artisson
> To whom the love-lorn Lady Kyteler brought
> Bronze peacock feathers, red combs of her cocks.

In this barbarous dance of mutilated mutilators, blind daughters of the Terrible Mother and a destructive female herself become an amorous victim, we have, unfortunately, a befitting emblem not only of 1919's whirlpool of hatred but also of the rapidly accelerating vortex of violence in the North seventy years later—a widening gyre in which the Devouring Female herself is consumed in a tumult of blood-dimmed images. As the violence continues, a frenzy in which even the burials of the dead have become ceremonies stained with fresh blood, the conflict of Cathleen and King Billy threatens to become a maelstrom from which fewer and fewer may be able to keep at a tangent and swim out on their own.

Appendix: *Cathleen ni Houlihan*

Persons in the Play

Peter Gillane
Bridget Gillane, *Peter's wife*
Michael Gillane, *his son, going to be married*
Delia Cahel, *engaged to Michael*
Patrick Gillane, *a lad of twelve, Michael's brother*
The Poor Old Woman
Neighbours

> *Interior of a cottage close to Killala, in 1798. Bridget is standing at a table undoing a parcel. Peter is sitting at one side of the fire, Patrick at the other.*

Peter. What is that sound I hear?
Patrick. I don't hear anything. [*He listens.*] I hear it now. It's like cheering. [*He goes to the window and looks out.*] I wonder what they are cheering about. I don't see anybody.
Peter. It might be a hurling.
Patrick. There's no hurling to-day. It must be down in the town the cheering is.
Bridget. I suppose the boys must be having some sport of their own. Come over here, Peter, and look at Michael's wedding clothes.
Peter [*shifts his chair to table*]. Those are grand clothes, indeed.
Bridget. You hadn't clothes like that when you married me, and no coat to put on of a Sunday more than any other day.
Peter. That is true, indeed. We never thought a son of our own would be wearing a suit of that sort for his wedding, or have so good a place to bring a wife to.
Patrick [*who is still at the window*]. There's an old woman coming down the road. I don't know is it here she is coming.

Bridget. It will be a neighbour coming to hear about Michael's wedding. Can you see who it is?

Patrick. It think it is a stranger, but she's not coming to the house. She's turned into the gap that goes down where Maurteen and his sons are shearing sheep. [*He turns towards Bridget.*] Do you remember what Winny of the Cross-Roads was saying the other night about the strange woman that goes through the country whatever time there's war or trouble coming?

Bridget. Don't be bothering us about Winny's talk, but go and open the door for your brother. I hear him coming up the path.

Peter. I hope he has brought Delia's fortune with him safe, for fear the people might go back on the bargain and I after making it. Trouble enough I had making it.

> *Patrick opens the door and Michael comes in.*

Bridget. What kept you, Michael? We were looking out for you this long time.

Michael. I went round by the priest's house to bid him be ready to marry us tomorrow.

Bridget. Did he say anything?

Michael. He said it was a very nice match, and that he was never better pleased to marry any two in his parish than myself and Delia Cahel.

Peter. Have you got the fortune, Michael?

Michael. Here it is.

> *Michael puts bag on table and goes over and leans against chimney-jamb. Bridget, who has been all this time examining the clothes, pulling the seams and trying the lining of the pockets, etc., puts the clothes on the dresser.*

Peter [*getting up and taking the bag in his hand and turning out the money*]. Yes, I made the bargain well for you, Michael. Old John Cahel would sooner have kept a share of this a while longer. 'Let me keep the half of it until the first boy is born,' says he. 'You will not,' says I. 'Whether there is or is not a boy, the whole hundred pounds must be in Michael's hands before he brings your daughter to the house.' The wife spoke to him then, and he gave in at the end.

Bridget. You seem well pleased to be handling the money, Peter.

Peter. Indeed, I wish I had had the luck to get a hundred pounds, or twenty pounds itself, with the wife I married.

Bridget. Well, if I didn't bring much I didn't get much. What had you the day I married you but a flock of hens and you feeding them, and a few lambs

Appendix 105

and you driving them to the market at Ballina? [*She is vexed and bangs a jug on the dresser.*] If I brought no fortune I worked it out in my bones, laying down the baby, Michael that is standing there now, on a stook of straw, while I dug the potatoes, and never asking big dresses or anything but to be working.

Peter. That is true, indeed. [*He pats her arm.*]

Bridget. Leave me alone now till I ready the house for the woman that is to come into it.

Peter. You are the best woman in Ireland, but money is good, too. [*He begins handling the money again and sits down.*] I never thought to see so much money within my four walls. We can do great things now we have it. We can take the ten acres of land we have the chance of since Jamsie Dempsey died, and stock it. We will go to the fair at Ballina to buy the stock. Did Delia ask any of the money for her own use, Michael?

Michael. She did not, indeed. She did not seem to take much notice of it, or to look at it at all.

Bridget. That's no wonder. Why would she look at it when she had yourself to look at, a fine, strong young man? It is proud she must be to get you; a good steady boy that will make use of the money, and not be running through it or spending it on drink like another.

Peter. It's likely Michael himself was not thinking much of the fortune either, but of what sort the girl was to look at.

Michael [*coming over towards the table*]. Well, you would like a nice comely girl to be beside you, and to go walking with you. The fortune only lasts for a while, but the woman will be there always.

Patrick [*turning round from the window*]. They are cheering again down in the town. Maybe they are landing horses from Enniscrone. They do be cheering when the horses take the water well.

Michael. There are no horses in it. Where would they be going and no fair at hand? Go down to the town, Patrick, and see what is going on.

Patrick [*opens the door to go out, but stops for a moment on the threshold*]. Will Delia remember, do you think, to bring the greyhound pup she promised me when she would be coming to the house?

Michael. She will surely.

    Patrick goes out, leaving the door open.

Peter. It will be Patrick's turn next to be looking for a fortune, but he won't find it so easy to get it and he with no place of his own.

Bridget. I do be thinking sometimes, now things are going so well with us, and the Cahels such a good back to us in the district, and Delia's own uncle a priest, we might be put in the way of making Patrick a priest some day, and he so good at his books.

Peter. Time enough, time enough. You have always your head full of plans, Bridget.

Bridget. We will be well able to give him learning, and not to send him tramping the country like a poor scholar that lives on charity.

Michael. They're not done cheering yet.

> *He goes over to the door and stands there for a moment, putting up his hand to shade his eyes.*

Bridget. Do you see anything?

Michael. I see an old woman coming up the path.

Bridget. Who is it, I wonder? It must be the strange woman Patrick saw a while ago.

Michael. I don't think it's one of the neighbours anyway, but she has her cloak over her face.

Bridget. It might be some poor woman heard we were making ready for the wedding and came to look for her share.

Peter. I may as well put the money out of sight. There is no use leaving it out for every stranger to look at.

> *He goes over to a large box in the corner, opens it and puts the bag in and fumbles at the lock.*

Michael. There she is, father! [*An Old Woman passes the window slowly. She looks at Michael as she passes.*] I'd sooner a stranger not to come to the house the night before my wedding.

Bridget. Open the door, Michael; don't keep the poor woman waiting.

> *The Old Woman comes in. Michael stands aside to make way for her.*

Old Woman. God save all here!

Peter. God save you kindly!

Old Woman. You have good shelter here.

Peter. You are welcome to whatever shelter we have.

Bridget. Sit down there by the fire and welcome.

Old Woman [*warming her hands*]. There is a hard wind outside.

Appendix

> *Michael watches her curiously from the door. Peter comes over to the table.*

Peter. Have you travelled far to-day?

Old Woman. I have travelled far, very far; there are few have travelled so far as myself, and there's many a one that doesn't make me welcome. There was one that had strong sons I thought were friends of mine, but they were shearing their sheep, and they wouldn't listen to me.

Peter. It's a pity indeed for any person to have no place of their own.

Old Woman. That's true for you indeed, and it's long I'm on the roads since I first went wandering.

Bridget. It is a wonder you are not worn out with so much wandering.

Old Woman. Sometimes my feet are tired and my hands are quiet, but there is no quiet in my heart. When the people see me quiet, they think old age has come on me and that all the stir has gone out of me. But when the trouble is on me I must be talking to my friends.

Bridget. What was it put you wandering?

Old Woman. Too many strangers in the house.

Bridget. Indeed you look as if you'd had your share of trouble.

Old Woman. I have had trouble indeed.

Bridget. What was it put the trouble on you?

Old Woman. My land that was taken from me.

Peter. Was it much land they took from you?

Old Woman. My four beautiful green fields.

Peter [*aside to Bridget*]. Do you think could she be the widow Casey that was put out of her holding at Kilglass a while ago?

Bridget. She is not. I saw the widow Casey one time at the market in Ballina, a stout fresh woman.

Peter [*to Old Woman*]. Did you hear a noise of cheering, and you coming up the hill?

Old Woman. I thought I heard the noise I used to hear when my friends came to visit me.

> *She begins singing half to herself.*

I will go cry with the woman,
For yellow-haired Donough is dead,
With a hempen rope for a neckcloth,
And a white cloth on his head,—

Michael [*coming from the door*]. What is it that you are singing, ma'am?

Old Woman. Singing I am about a man I knew one time, yellow-haired Donough that was hanged in Galway.

She goes on singing, much louder.

> I am come to cry with you, woman,
> My hair is unwound and unbound;
> I remember him ploughing his field,
> Turning up the red side of the ground,
> And building his barn on the hill
> With the good mortared stone;
> O! we'd have pulled down the gallows
> Had it happened in Enniscrone!

Michael. What was it brought him to his death?

Old Woman. He died for love of me: many a man has died for love of me.

Peter [*aside to Bridget*]. Her trouble has put her wits astray.

Michael. Is it long since that song was made? Is it long since he got his death?

Old Woman. Not long, not long. But there were others that died for love of me a long time ago.

Michael. Were they neighbours of your own, ma'am?

Old Woman. Come here beside me and I'll tell you about them. [*Michael sits down beside her on the hearth.*] There was a red man of the O'Donnells from the north, and a man of the O'Sullivans from the south, and there was one Brian that lost his life at Clontarf by the sea, and there were a great many in the west, some that died hundreds of years ago, and there are some that will die to-morrow.

Michael. Is it in the west that men will die to-morrow?

Old Woman. Come nearer, nearer to me.

Bridget. Is she right, do you think? Or is she a woman from beyond the world?

Peter. She doesn't know well what she's talking about, with the want and the trouble she has gone through.

Bridget. The poor thing, we should treat her well.

Peter. Give her a drink of milk and a bit of the oaten cake.

Bridget. Maybe we should give her something along with that, to bring her on her way. A few pence or a shilling itself, and we with so much money in the house.

Peter. Indeed I'd not begrudge it to her if we had it to spare, but if we go running through what we have, we'll soon have to break the hundred pounds, and that would be a pity.

Bridget. Shame on you, Peter. Give her the shilling and your blessing with it, or our own luck will go from us.

> *Peter goes to the box and takes out a shilling.*

Bridget [*to the Old Woman*]. Will you have a drink of milk, ma'am?
Old Woman. It is not food or drink that I want.
Peter [*offering the shilling*]. Here is something for you.
Old Woman. This is not what I want. It is not silver I want.
Peter. What is it you would be asking for?
Old Woman. If any one would give me help he must give me himself, he must give me all.

> *Peter goes over to the table staring at the shilling in his hand in a bewildered way, and stands whispering to Bridget.*

Michael. Have you no one to care for you in your age, ma'am?
Old Woman. I have not. With all the lovers that brought me their love I never set out the bed for any.
Michael. Are you lonely going the roads, ma'am?
Old Woman. I have my thoughts and I have my hopes.
Michael. What hopes have you to hold to?
Old Woman. The hope of getting my beautiful fields back again; the hope of putting the strangers out of my house.
Michael. What way will you do that, ma'am?
Old Woman. I have good friends that will help me. They are gathering to help me now. I am not afraid. If they are put down to-day they will get the upper hand to-morrow. [*She gets up.*] I must be going to meet my friends. They are coming to help me and I must be there to welcome them. I must call the neighbours together to welcome them.
Michael. I will go with you.
Bridget. It is not her friends you have to go and welcome, Michael; it is the girl coming into the house you have to welcome. You have plenty to do; it is food and drink you have to bring to the house. The woman that is coming home is not coming with empty hands; you would not have an empty house before her. [*To the Old Woman.*] Maybe you don't know, ma'am, that my son is going to be married to-morrow.
Old Woman. It is not a man going to his marriage that I look to for help.
Peter [*to Bridget*]. Who is she, do you think, at all?

Bridget. You did not tell us your name yet, ma'am.

Old Woman. Some call me the Poor Old Woman, and there are some that call me Cathleen, the daughter of Houlihan.

Peter. I think I knew some one of that name, once. Who was it, I wonder? It must have been some one I knew when I was a boy. No, no; I remember, I heard it in a song.

Old Woman [*who is standing in the doorway*]. They are wondering that there were songs made for me; there have been many songs made for me. I heard one on the wind this morning.

    [*Sings*]

Do not make a great keening
When the graves have been dug to-morrow.
Do not call the white-scarfed riders
To the burying that shall be to-morrow.

Do not spread food to call strangers
To the wakes that shall be to-morrow;
Do not give money for prayers
For the dead that shall die tomorrow . . . .

They will have no need of prayers, they will have no need of prayers.

Michael. I do not know what that song means, but tell me something I can do for you.

Peter. Come over to me, Michael.

Michael. Hush, father, listen to her.

Old Woman. It is a hard service they take that help me. Many that are red-cheeked now will be pale-cheeked; many that have been free to walk the hills and the bogs and the rushes will be sent to walk hard streets in far countries; many a good plan will be broken; many that have gathered money will not stay to spend it; many a child will be born and there will be no father at its christening to give it a name. They that have red cheeks will have pale cheeks for my sake, and for all that, they will think they are well paid.

    She goes out; her voice is heard outside singing.

They shall be remembered for ever,
They shall be alive for ever,
They shall be speaking for ever,
The people shall hear them for ever.

Bridget [*to Peter*]. Look at him, Peter; he has the look of a man that has got the touch. [*Raising her voice.*] Look here, Michael, at the wedding clothes. Such grand clothes as these are! You have a right to fit them on now; it would be a pity to-morrow if they did not fit. The boys would be laughing at you. Take them, Michael, and go into the room and fit them on. [*She puts them on his arm.*]

Michael. What wedding are you talking of? What clothes will I be wearing to-morrow?

Bridget. These are the clothes you are going to wear when you marry Delia Cahel to-morrow.

Michael. I had forgotten that.

> *He looks at the clothes and turns towards the inner room, but stops at the sound of cheering outside.*

Peter. There is the shouting come to our own door. What is it has happened?

> *Neighbours come crowding in, Patrick and Delia with them.*

Patrick. There are ships in the Bay; the French are landing at Killala!

> *Peter takes his pipe from his mouth and his hat off, and stands up. The clothes slip from Michael's arm.*

Delia. Michael! [*He takes no notice.*] Michael! [*He turns towards her.*] Why do you look at me like a stranger?

> *She drops his arm. Bridget goes over towards her.*

Patrick. The boys are all hurrying down the hillside to join the French.

Delia. Michael won't be going to join the French.

Bridget [*to Peter*]. Tell him not to go, Peter.

Peter. It's no use. He doesn't hear a word we're saying.

Bridget. Try and coax him over to the fire.

Delia. Michael, Michael! You won't leave me! You won't join the French, and we going to be married!

> *She puts her arms about him, he turns towards her as if about to yield.*
>
> *Old Woman's voice outside.*

They shall be speaking for ever,
The people shall hear them for ever.

Michael breaks away from Delia, stands for a second at the door, then rushes out, following the Old Woman's voice. Bridget takes Delia, who is crying silently, into her arms.

Peter [*to Patrick, laying a hand on his arm*]. Did you see an old woman going down the path?

Patrick. I did not, but I saw a young girl, and she had the walk of a queen.

THE END

Notes

Notes to Preface

1. Seamus Heaney, part 1 of "Sheelagh na Gig," in *Station Island,* 49. In *Celtic Mysteries: The Ancient Religion,* John Sharkey reproduces the "grotesque effigy" Heaney is describing, one of the strange stone carvings known collectively as "Sheela-na-gigs." The Sheela-na-gig, "a graphic representation of the Celtic goddess of creation and destruction," is a figure common in Irish castles and churches, though Sharkey and Heaney both choose the Romanesque effigy in the Church of St. Mary and St. David, Kilpeck, Herefordshire, England. A particularly well-preserved carving, this sheela has the most universal feature, the grotesquely exaggerated and prominently displayed genitalia. But she lacks the characteristic skeleton ribs and the often gaping mouth that make other examples—notably the celebrated and ferocious Cavan sheela now in the National Museum in Dublin—so immediately menacing. Her sexual display is, however, ugly—and widespread in both senses, since, as Sharkey remarks: "This repellent Kali-like aspect of the goddess recurs throughout Indo-European myth and ritual" (plate 6). It should be added that many of these carved "vulva-women," which appeared all over Irish churches and castles built before the sixteenth century and were largely in place during the nineteenth century, were defaced or removed in the Victorian period. According to G. R. Scott, some have been found buried near the churches they had previously adorned (*Phallic Worship,* 239–43). For more on the sheelas, including photographs and bibliographies, see Edith M. Guest's 1930s articles in the *Journal of the Royal Society of Antiquities of Ireland,* especially "Irish Sheela-na-gigs in 1935." Helen Hickey devotes a few pages to the sheelas (57–58, 70) in *Images of Stone: Figure Sculpture of the Lough Erne Basin,* and there is work in progress by Yvette Sencer.

An exhaustively documented catalog of the sheelas of the British Isles and France is available in Jørgen Andersen's valuable *The Witch on the Wall,* whose epigraph comes from Joyce's *Ulysses*: "without a stitch on her, exposing her person, open to all comers, fair field and no favor." While this certainly suggests the sheelas, with their exaggerated and elaborately exposed genitalia, Joyce never explicitly mentions Sheela-na-gig in his work. The same is true of Yeats, though his Crazy Jane (like Joyce's Molly Bloom) has been suggested, by Vivian Mercier, as analogous to the archetype (*The Irish Comic Tradition,* 72). See the same work (53–56) for a brief but illuminating discussion of the sheelas as exemplifying an amalgam of the "macabre and grotesque." As

Mercier also points out, while Yeats and Joyce may not mention Sheela-na-gig by name, other modern Irish writers do—for example, Austin Clarke, in his erotic novel of medieval Ireland, *The Bright Temptation*—and Mercier describes Moll in Samuel Beckett's *Malone Dies* as "the hag-like Sheela-na-gig in person" (76). Heaney's poem continues a tradition.

2. Erich Neumann, *The Great Mother: An Analysis of the Archetype*, trans. Ralph Mannheim, 2d ed., title of chapter 11.

3. John Sharkey, *Celtic Mysteries: The Ancient Religion*, pl. 6.

4. "Irish Fairies, Ghosts, Witches, etc.," rpt. in UP 1:130–37 (136).

5. VPl 1061. In the passages cited (*Great Mother*, 162, 164–65), Neumann quotes from Sir E. A. Wallis Budge's translation of *The Book of the Dead*, 2d ed. rev., chap. CLXIV, and Wolfgang Krause's *Die Kelten*, 22.

The gaunt, skeleton-ribbed torso of the typical Sheela-na-gig, along with the often ferociously gaping mouth, suggests a connection with the devouring war-goddess. Like the sheelas, the Celtic war-goddesses are also sexual hags. What Marie-Louise Sjoestedt calls "the link between the mother-goddesses and the goddesses of war" is the rite of childbirth, associated with Badb, along with the Morrigu, an aspect of the Celtic war-goddess (*Gods and Heroes of the Celts*, 35). Like Sjoestedt (35) and Vivian Mercier (*The Irish Comic Tradition*, 54–55), Anne Ross sees a connection between the grotesquely sexual war-hags in the early Irish tale *The Destruction of Da Derga's Hostel* and the Sheela-na-gig. Of the sheela figures, Anne Ross speculates: "I would like to suggest that, in their earliest iconographic form, they do in fact portray the territorial or war-goddess in her hag-like aspect" ("The Divine Hag of the Pagan Celts").

6. See *Great Mother*, 66, 177; and Jung, *Psychology and Alchemy* (1944); in *The Collected Works of Carl G. Jung*, trans. R. F. C. Hull 12:207 and fig. 108.

7. See Sydney Bolt, *A Preface to James Joyce*, 131.

8. Darcy O'Brien, in two places: *The Consciousness of James Joyce*, 211, 207, and "Some Determinants of Molly Bloom," in *Approaches to "Ulysses*," ed. Thomas F. Staley and Bernard Benstock, 148, 143, 140. His diatribe makes O'Brien the shrillest if not the first of the anti-Molly revisionists (the first was Hugh Kenner in *Dublin's Joyce*, 1955). O'Brien's denunciation has been described as "patriarchal" and "puritanical" by Bonnie Kime Scott, who offers, in *Joyce and Feminism*, a balanced treatment of Molly: though still a "male-projected entity," through "Joyce's female voice," she has reordered the "male-centered, rational world" of the novel, "changed literature and aroused criticism" (159, 183). For Suzette Henke, too, Molly "exists as a female projection of the male psyche," "her monologue limited to . . . libidinous preoccupations" (*Joyce's Moraculous Sindbook: A Study of* Ulysses, 234, 235).

9. William Safire, "On Language," *New York Times Magazine*, 3 May 1987.

10. Despite the characteristically vague reference ("somewhere") and his confusion of Salome with her mother, Yeats is probably right. The poem Yeats has in mind is Heine's "Atta Troll" (1841). Condemned to hell for her "bloody love" ("Would a woman want the head of / Any man she did not love?"), the specter of Herodias rides with the bleeding trophy in her hand. Yet with "woman's maniac frenzy,"

Sometimes, she, with childish laughter,
Whirls it in the air above her,

Then again will nimbly catch it,
Like a plaything as it falls.

   Wilde's debt to Heine is argued in a famous work published the year before Yeats wrote his note, Mario Praz's *The Romantic Agony*. The title of both the book and the particular chapter ("Byzantium") would have obvious appeal to Yeats, especially since Praz goes on immediately to discuss Mallarmé's *Hérodiade*, a work echoed in *A Full Moon in March*. *The Romantic Agony*, trans. Angus Davidson, 2d ed., 298–305.
   11. See Joseph Hone, *W. B. Yeats, 1865–1939*, 2d ed., 321. Hone notes that Yeats, choosing these two as representative of his "love poetry," declined to read anything more personal, though invariably asked to do so." On one occasion, "the usual request was made, and the usual refusal given. But the request was repeated so many times that at last he lost his temper and announced 'Under no circumstances will I read you a poem that may be taken as a personal utterance'" (321–22). The irony, of course, is that, however seemingly distanced, there could hardly *be* "anything more personal" than these two poems, especially (as we shall see) "The Cap and Bells."
   12. Armand Silvestre on Tony Noël's sculpture; cited in Bram Dijkstra, *Idols of Perversity: Fantasies of Feminine Evil in Fin de Siècle Culture*, 380; see also 396.
   13. The poem now appears, entitled "Red Hanrahan's Song about Ireland," in Yeats's 1904 collection, *In the Seven Woods*. Yeats's spelling in the *National Observer* version approximates that of Yeats's and Joyce's favorite nineteenth-century Irish poet, James Clarence Mangan. His "Kathaleen-ny-Houlahan" contains lines that, I suggest below, influenced the electrifying final lines of Yeats's play.
   Not so incidentally: to read Maud Gonne's tribute to "Willie" Yeats in *Scattering Branches: Tributes to W. B. Yeats*, ed. Stephen Gwynn, one would think that his major works were *Cathleen ni Houlihan* and "Red Hanrahan's Song about Ireland."
   14. Suzette Henke, at a July 1987 conference held at the University of Leeds, Yorkshire, as reported by Brenda Maddox, "Wakers of the World, Unite! You Have Nothing to Lose But Your Theory," *New York Times Book Review*, 20.
   15. Scott, *Joyce and Feminism*, 206.
   16. Annette Kolodny, "Some Notes on Defining a 'Feminist Literary Criticism,'" 90–91. See also Kolodny's later "Dancing through the Minefield: Some Observations on the Theory, Practice and Politics of Feminist Literary Criticism" and the responses of three feminists in *Feminist Studies* 8 (1982): 629–75. For a still more recent critique of Kolodny, see Toril Moi, *Sexual/Textual Politics*.
   17. Denis Donoghue, *We Irish: Essays on Irish Literature and Society*, 22, 153–55. See also Thomas Flanagan's review of *We Irish*, "The Quaking Bog," and my own review, "A Balanced Stance."
   18. The best brief response to the decisions to reinstate the soldier, Ian Thain, and not to prosecute the Royal Ulster Constabulary officers is that of the London *Times*: "simply wrong," it declared editorially. According to John Stalker, the Manchester constable who headed the R.U.C. inquiry for two years until his dismissal in 1986, the evidence indicated a "police inclination, if not policy, to shoot suspects dead without warning, rather than arrest them." For details, see his book, *The Stalker Affair: One Man's Battle with Power and Politics in Northern Ireland*, published in February 1988.

Notes to Chapter 1: Cathleen ni Houlihan

1. Journal, March 1909, in Mem 183–84.
2. Spoken by Larry Doyle in *John Bull's Other Island* (1904).
3. Maire Cruise O'Brien, "The Female Principle in Gaelic Poetry," in *Woman in Irish Legend, Life and Literature*, ed. S. F. Gallagher, 26–37 (36).
4. George Russell, "Some Characters of the Irish Literary Movement"; *Letters from AE*, ed. Alan Denson, 44. Both quoted by Richard Ellmann, *James Joyce*, New and Revised Edition, 100.
5. Quoted by Ellmann, *James Joyce*, 102.
6. Ben L. Collins, "Joyce's Use of Yeats and of Irish History: A Reading of 'A Mother,'" 54, 51. Though Collins's essay is rather too ingenious in its quest for parallels, it clearly establishes Joyce's parody of Yeats's play. Taking for granted the link between "A Mother," the Revival, and Yeats's play, Hugh Kenner observes, "Wracked between Kathleen Kearney and Mr. Holohan, . . . Kathleen ni Houlihan is divided indeed" ("The Look of a Queen," in *Woman in Irish Legend, Life and Letters*, 115–24 [120]). Originally a paper presented at the Fourteenth International Seminar of the Canadian Association for Irish Studies (21 March 1981), Kenner's essay has provoked a feminist response; see next note.
7. Kenner, "The Look of a Queen," 120. The first of the anti-Molly revisionists and a lifelong monitor of the threat presented by females in Joyce's work, Kenner goes on in this paper to suggest destructiveness even in Anna Livia Plurabelle. Resisting Kenner's depiction of Mrs. Kearney, Mrs. Dedalus, and others as "devourers who work to the detriment and division of their nation, their families, and even themselves," Bonnie Kime Scott argues that, despite his characteristically impressive gathering of evidence, Kenner's thesis "seems to be grounded on male-centered psychological theory, Freud's castrating mother." In keeping with one overall conclusion of her book ("I have seen less of the temptress and devourer in Joyce's depiction of female sexuality, and more of the female's sense of her magical power to arouse and revive the male"), she insists that Joyce, though "no great admirer of the literary revival," did not reject strong women and depicted nationalist women in ways "more varied than Kenner suggests" (*Joyce and Feminism*, 22, 203). I agree with her that, for example, Molly Ivors in "The Dead" has a "dignity and decency that are missed when she is summarized by Kenner as 'aggressively patriotic,'" but Kenner certainly seems to me right in emphasizing Joyce's sustained literary rejection of the lethal mythology incarnate in Yeats's Cathleen. She is not only "temptress and devourer" but, as a woman from beyond the world, is also in possession of "magical power to arouse and revive the male"—though the arousal paradoxically leads to death.
8. Kenner, "The Look of a Queen," 117–18.
9. Yeats's "The Circus Animals' Desertion," the familiar final stanza of which I quote here, was first published in January 1939; the contents of Kate Strong's cottage, like the contents of Yeats's foul rag-and-bone shop, probably echo the gutter sweepings and refuse of Swift's "Description of a City Shower."
10. Donoghue, *We Irish*, 32–33.
11. The precise degree of Lady Gregory's contribution is conjectural, but we do

have the testimony of the collaborators. In dedicating the play to her, Yeats notes that "*we* turned my dream" into drama, and Lady Gregory herself says (in *Our Irish Theatre*, 82), "we wrote together *Kathleen ni Houlihan*." According to her biographer, whenever Lady Gregory's family urged her to "stake her claim," she "always refused with a smile, saying that she could not take from him any part of what had proved, after all, his one real popular success" (Elizabeth Coxhead, *Lady Gregory: A Literary Portrait*, 2d ed., 65). One might be skeptical of Coxhead, who is unsympathetic to Yeats; but another Gregory scholar, Daniel Murphy, told me in 1975 that most of the dialogue was Lady Gregory's. What matters in the present context, however, are the initial "dream" and, above all, the symbolic speeches of Cathleen; and these, everyone agrees, were Yeats's alone.

12. Máire nic Shiublaigh, "First Annual Report of Inghinidhe na hEireann [Daughters of Erin]," 1–2. It should be added that Maud gradually moderated her political position. She resigned from the Irish Republican Brotherhood and began working with Arthur Griffith and (in 1905) Sinn Fein, a movement still ardently Nationalist but opposed to conspiracy and physical force—at least until taken over by the Republicans after 1916.

13. Máire nic Shiublaigh and Edward Kenny, *The Splendid Years*, 19.

14. Nancy Cardozo, *Lucky Eyes and a High Heart: The Life of Maud Gonne*, 216.

15. Leonard E. Nathan, *The Tragic Drama of William Butler Yeats: Figures in a Dance*, 88, 89. John Rees Moore, *Masks of Love and Death: Yeats as Dramatist*, 9.

16. Moore, *Masks of Love and Death*, 9.

17. Yeats associates the "call of the heart" with his play *The Land of Heart's Desire* (1894); says of *Cathleen ni Houlihan*, "this play is the call of country"; and concludes: "I have a plan of following it up with a little play about the call of religion, and printing the three plays together some day" (VPl 235). While Yeats attended to all three calls, that of the heart and its own desires was clearly the most persistent.

18. See *Collected Works of Padraic Pearse: Political Writings and Speeches*, 25, 38, 128.

19. Elizabeth Cullingford, *Yeats, Ireland and Fascism*, 52.

20. The poem quoted is "The Statues." But even Cuchulain underwent the baptism of the gutter. A month before he died, Yeats told William Rothenstein that the "romantic movement" had survived in Ireland: "Some of the best known of the young men who got themselves [killed] in 1916 had the Irish legendary hero Cuchullain so much in their minds that the government has celebrated the event with a bad statue" (Rothenstein, *Since Fifty: Men and Memories, 1922–1938*, 305).

21. Stephen Gwynn was a Protestant constitutional nationalist; for the whole of his memorable description of the play's impact, see *Irish Literature and Drama*, 158–60.

22. *The United Irishman* (12 April 1902): 4.

23. William Irwin Thompson, *The Imagination of an Insurrection: Dublin, Easter 1916*, 63.

24. "The People" (VP 353). It was in comparing himself with Maud that Yeats described himself as having a "more skeptical intelligence."

25. Griffith, "All Ireland," *The United Irishman* (17 October 1903): 1. A month later, to Yeats's distress, Maud Gonne resigned from the National Theatre Company in protest over the production of Synge's play. Her own idea of theater appropriate to Ireland

came the following year. *Dawn, A Play in One Act and Three Tableaux,* was Maud's propagandistic response to Synge, a short play modeled on *Cathleen ni Houlihan* and featuring a self-sacrificing mother who spurs the men in her family to rise up against the invading "Stranger" to the music of "bright swords . . . that clash the battle welcome" as the "red sun" of dawn rises on Ireland's freedom.

26. Hilary Berrow, "Eight Nights in the Abbey," in *J. M. Synge: Centenary Papers 1971,* ed. Maurice Harmon, 75–87. Parodying the same lines in "The Holy Office," Joyce declared, "I must not accounted be / One of that mumming company" (CW 149).

27. See Robert Brennan, *Allegiance,* 202–3.

28. Anne Ross, "The Divine Hag of the Pagan Celts," 146. James Clarence Mangan, "Kathaleen-ny-Houlahan (A Jacobite Relic from the Irish)," opening lines of the second stanza (John Cooke, ed., *The Dublin Book of Irish Verse, 1728–1909,* 137). The last line quoted and the line following appear, unattributed, as the epigraph to *Cathleen Ni Hoolihan* (London, 1902); see VPl 214. Rumors of Griffith's frustrated love fueled Sean O'Casey's account of a rivalry between Yeats and Griffith in *Drums Under the Window,* 117–19.

29. VPl 233, fusing Yeats's 1908 note to *The Unicorn from the Stars and Other Plays* with appendix II to *Cathleen ni Houlihan,* from vol. 4 of the 1908 *Collected Works.*

30. Gwynn, *Irish Literature and Drama,* 159.

31. See Maud's contribution to the memorial volume, *Scattering Branches,* ed. Gwynn, 29–30.

32. Moore, *Masks of Love and Death,* 12.

33. Yeats, *Plays and Controversies* (New York: Macmillan, 1924), 160–61; Hugh Kenner, *A Colder Eye: The Modern Irish Writers,* 59.

34. *Prison Letters of Countess Markiewicz,* 63–4, 155. If so, Yeats thought it was a gospel for the "blind" and "bitter." See "On a Political Prisoner" (VP 397).

35. Lady Gregory, *Seventy Years,* 444. She refers to her 1919 performances, occasioned by the unavailability of Máire nic Shiublaigh for the first three nights, in *Lady Gregory's Journals, 1916–1930,* ed. Lennox Robinson, 56–58. She reports that Yeats "came up to the gallery afterwards and said coldly it was 'very nice, but if I had rehearsed you it would have been much better' " (57). The comment from Shaw is telling, given the remark of Larry Doyle from *John Bull's Other Island* (see the epigraph to Chapter 1).

36. Andrew Parkin, *The Dramatic Imagination of W. B. Yeats,* 86.

37. *A Servant of the Queen,* 7, 350. Maud's autobiography was published in Dublin in 1938; a second volume was planned but was left incomplete at her death in April 1953.

38. He ends this unpublished passage from a draft of his *Autobiography* by observing that until some political project came into her head, "she was [circa 1890] the woman I had come to love." A page later he adds: "I came to hate her politics, my one visible rival" (Mem 60, 61, 63).

39. L. A. G. Strong, "William Butler Yeats," in *Scattering Branches,* ed. Gwynn, 222.

40. O'Casey, *Inishfallen, Fare thee Well,* 88.

41. Yeats's Cathleen—a loathly lady transformed into a young beauty with the walk of a queen; a supernatural being who yet needs to be rescued, rescue and reju-

venation alike requiring the blood-sacrifice of her deliverer—has the ambiguity of the fairy queens and mistresses of Celtic myth, familiar to every modern reader from Keats's "La Belle Dame sans Merci." La Belle Dame sans Merci derives her ambivalent nature from a Celtic tradition characterized, as Roger Sherman Loomis has noted, by the "gross inconsistency" between the legends in which she is portrayed. She can be either "the fairy mistress or the tender foster mother or the malevolent sorceress or the efficient leech or the great queen." As Barbara Fass adds in her study of the fairy mistress theme in French, English, and German Romanticism: "Much will be made of this ambiguity by romantic writers not certain whether their muse is a demon or an agent of divine inspiration." Normally, the determination as to whether the lady is benevolent or malevolent depends on context, "the particular tale in which she appears." In Yeats's play, either/or yields to both/and; my present emphasis is on her role as leech, living on the blood of her now pale-cheeked martyrs. See Loomis, *Arthurian Tradition and Chrétien de Troyes*, 53, 182; cited by Fass, *La Belle Dame sans Merci and the Aesthetics of Romanticism*, 20.

42. Curran is cited by Ian Fletcher in "Yeats and Lissadell," in *W. B. Yeats, 1865-1965: Centenary Essays on the Art of W. B. Yeats*, ed. D. E. S. Maxwell and S. B. Bushrui, 62.

43. D. W. P. Knight, cited by Barbara G. Walker, *The Woman's Encyclopedia of Myths and Secrets*, 932.

44. David R. Kinsley, "The Hindu Goddess," in *The Encyclopedia of Religion*, ed. Mircea Eliade, 6:52. See also his *The Sword and the Flute: Kāli and Krsna, Dark Visions of the Terrible and Sublime in Hindu Mythology*. Along with his own Cathleen, the Hag of Beare is, as Yeats said, "very famous," the best known of all the Irish hags. Her pagan power is withered by contact with the new religion, Christianity, in a celebrated lament "almost certainly put into her mouth by a votary of the goddess," the "primaeval mother goddess" of pre-Christian Ireland. Maire Cruise O'Brien, "The Female Principle in Gaelic Poetry," 26, 31.

45. In addition to *The Great Mother*, see also chap. 2 of Neumann's *The Origins and History of Consciousness*.

46. Neumann, *Great Mother*, 148-49.

47. Heinrich Zimmer, in *The Mystic Vision*, 74; quoted in Neumann, *Great Mother*, 152. Zimmer and Neumann note that there is also a nurturant side to Kali, who, as mother of us all, combines beneficent and terrible qualities—unlike the totally evil Rangda, a Hindu witch-goddess worshiped in Bali. In "Kali, the Mad Mother," C. Mackenzie Brown notes that Kali is too inclusive to be categorized as evil; despite her destructive blood-lust, she gives birth to us and dazzles us with her splendor before she devours us in the dance of life. In his essay on "The Hindu Goddess," David Kinsley remarks, "Although she has a dark, destructive, blood-thirsty side, this aspect of the Great Goddess is seen as a natural part of an overarching orderliness that affirms the positive and necessary interaction of life and death, creation and destruction, vigor and rest, in the nature of the cosmos."

48. Lorna Reynolds, "Women in Irish Legend, Life and Literature," and Maire Cruise O'Brien, "The Female Principle in Gaelic Poetry," both in *Woman in Irish Legend, Literature and Life*, 12, 26.

49. Susan Bordo, "Anorexia Nervosa: Psychopathology as the Crystallization of Culture," 91–93. Lasch quotations cited in Bordo are from *The Culture of Narcissism*, 346, 343; Gay quotations, from *The Bourgeois Experience*, 1:197–201, 207.

50. Allesandra Comini, "Posters from the War Against Women," review of *Idols of Perversity*, *New York Times Book Review* (1 February 1987): 13–14. Cf. Praz, *The Romantic Agony*, 206: "the function of the flame which attracts and burns is exercised, in the first half of the century, by the Fatal Man (the Byronic hero), in the second half by the Fatal Woman; the moth destined for sacrifice is in the first case the woman, in the second the man. It is not simply a case of convention and literary fashion: literature, even in its most artificial forms, reflects to some extent aspects of contemporary life. It is curious to follow the parabola of the sexes during the nineteenth century: the obsession for the androgyne type towards the end of the century is a clear indication of a turbid confusion of function and ideal. The male, who at first tends towards sadism, inclines, at the end of the century, towards masochism."

51. Zimmer, in Neumann, *Great Mother*, 152.

52. *Fairy and Folk Tales of the Irish Peasantry*, ed. and selected by W. B. Yeats, 81, 146.

53. Joyce's more domestic and cajolable Goddess, Molly Bloom, has similar affiliations. Standing with Stephen in the garden of the "Ithaca" episode, worshipful Bloom speculates about the "special affinities" that seem to him "to exist between the moon and woman"; as the "luminous sign" of his wife's lamp in the window indicates, the moon certainly has affinities with Molly, whose mother's first name was in fact Lunita, little moon. *Ulysses* is quoted throughout from the new (but *still* not definitive) edition, here pp. 576, 627. For the citations from Graves earlier in this paragraph, see the "Amended and Enlarged Edition" of *The White Goddess*, 489, 491.

Notes to Chapter 2: Priestesses of the Great Mother

1. *The Complete Poetical Works of Samuel Taylor Coleridge*, ed. E. H. Coleridge, 1:295–97.

2. In a letter of 6 July 1803 to his friend Thomas Butts, Blake claimed to be able to praise his poem *Milton* "since I dare not pretend to be any other than the Secretary; the Authors are in Eternity" (*The Letters of William Blake*, ed. Geoffrey Keynes, 69).

3. Richard Ellmann, *The Identity of Yeats*, 2d ed., 251.

4. In a more celebrated "love song," another doomed erotic quester, intoxicated by "perfume from a dress," inexorably advances from thoughts of women's "voices," then of their "eyes," finally imagining, in a gradual access of intimacy, "arms that are braceleted and white and bare / (But in the lamplight, downed with light brown hair!)." The speaker of "The Love Song of J. Alfred Prufrock," though frightened rather than frustrated, resembles the Yeatsian jester in two ways. He too is a type of "the Fool" (line 119), and though "no prophet"—no John the Baptist whose head Salome demanded of Herod as reward for her dance—he *has* (line 82) "seen my head (grown slightly bald) brought in upon a platter."

5. Brenda Webster, *Yeats: A Psychoanalytic Study*, 113. But note that a pentimento

results from the cancellation. Forgetting to get her back into her "chamber," Yeats in effect has the queen still outdoors, yet opening door and window.

6. Ibid., 17; Zimmer, in *The Mystic Vision*; see note 45 to Chapter 1.

7. See below, Chapter 3. In other *Wind Among the Reeds* poems, dealt with in my final chapter, the "stars" are repeatedly blown out or devoured. Yeats's sources are to be found in Blake, the occult, and in Celtic myths of the pig, interchangeably boar or sow, who roots "the sun and moon and stars out of the sky" (VP 153). Like Joyce's "old sow that eats her farrow," this is ultimately the Great Mother as the Egyptian Sky Woman, her "star-children going into her mouth in the manner of a sow eating her young."

8. *The Golden Bough* 1:297–99. See also M. Renee Salzman, "Magna Mater: Great Mother of the Roman Empire," in *The Book of the Goddess, Past and Present: An Introduction to Her Religion*, ed. Carl Olson, 49–67 (64–65).

9. Neumann, *Origins*, 88–89.

10. I concur with Harold Bloom: "useful criticism" of these plays "must begin with Helen Vendler's insight: they are plays that concern the relation of Poet to Muse, and more particularly of Yeats to his own muse, the Shelleyan epipsyche he had confronted, or convinced himself he had beheld, in Maud Gonne. . . . Yet these savage plays, though they return again to that love and that trouble, are fearfully far in spirit from the young man's descriptions of his beloved's beauty." Bloom, *Yeats*, 338–39; cf. Vendler, *Yeats's* Vision *and the Later Plays*, 145.

11. For more on these matters, see my study of Graves, *A Wild Civility: Interactions in the Poetry and Thought of Robert Graves*, 86–87. Graves discusses the singing heads of Orpheus and Bran in *The Greek Myths*, 1:113–14.

12. Anne Ross, *Pagan Celtic Britain: Studies in Iconography and Tradition*, 126.

13. Mallarmé, *Hérodiade*, translated by Yeats's friend Arthur Symons. For the influence of *Hérodiade* on these two plays, as well as on *The Shadowy Waters* and several Yeats lyrics, see Stella Revard, "Yeats, Mallarmé, and the Archetypal Feminine."

14. Zimmer, *The Mystic Vision*, 74; in Neumann, *Great Mother*, 152. See also Dijkstra, *Idols of Perversity*, 382, 388. Oddly, the only text by Yeats referred to by Dijkstra is "Leda and the Swan."

15. Moore, *Masks of Love and Death*, 328.

16. Neumann, *Great Mother*, 164. The Celtic war goddess is a shifting triadic figure, though the dominant—and sometimes subsuming—member of the trinity is the Morrigu.

17. "A Bronze Head" (1938) is to "Among School Children" (1926) what *Purgatory* (also 1938) is to "A Dialogue of Self and Soul" (1927). In both cases, the late works provide the dark otherside. *Purgatory*, for example, animates the terror implicit in Nietzschean Eternal Recurrence, the reenactment "again, and yet again," embraced with such vitalistic relish in "Dialogue." Indeed, the quoted phrase, from the poem, appears in the drafts of the play.

18. *Hamlet* 3.2.92–94, 244–45; 2.2.564–65.

19. Yeats seems to have been deeply impressed by the apocalyptic darkness at the end of *Lear*, "the history of a whole evil time" (E&I 215). In "Lapis Lazuli," that "dread" will be transfigured by Nietzschean "gaiety."

20. Again, politics and mythology converge with psychology. Scrutinizing the "bisexual" imagery of "A Bronze Head," F. A. C. Wilson remarks of the opening lines of the final stanza: "a stern male eye looks through her eye; and Yeats abdicates from the role of the gentle father and responds with fascination and dread" to Maud as "phallic woman." "Yeats's 'A Bronze Head': A Freudian Investigation," 11. Though he traces no allusions, Wilson does refer to the poem's "Shakespearean cadences" (11).

21. "A Mother" has been discussed earlier. In *Dubliners*, a book framed by sterile sisters ("The Sisters," "The Dead"), Eveline is as paralyzed as Ireland ("Eveline"). The seduced servant girl of "Two Gallants" emerges as a pathetic and betrayed counterpart of Ireland herself, symbolized by a harp here compared to a violated woman. In "The Dead," Gabriel is nonplussed by the Nationalist Molly Ivors and fails to refute her taunt that he is a "West Briton"; his Joycean response ("literature was above politics") remains unspoken.

22. On this figure, see Bonnie Kime Scott, "The Woman in the Black Straw Hat: A Transitional Priestess in *Stephen Hero*." Scott concludes that at this stage of his development, Stephen's needs are better satisfied by the woman in the black straw hat than by the other females encountered in *Stephen Hero*, all of whom—Emma, his mother, his sister, the Virgin Mary—are "identified with Catholicism" (413).

23. Richard Ellmann had quoted from the manuscript in *James Joyce* (1959), and it was he who edited it for the much-publicized Viking edition of 1968.

24. Vicki Mahaffey, "Giacomo Joyce," in *A Companion to Joyce Studies*, ed. Zack Bowen and James F. Carens, 387–420 (414, 404). She also describes this lady as "the subject of Joyce's first experiments with the protean inclusiveness of Bertha Rowan, Molly Bloom, and Anna Livia Plurabelle, figures who come to embody the variety of life itself" (412–13).

25. Katherine Tynan, *Twenty Five Years: Reminiscences*, 345.

26. Indeed, Parnell was always bigger than life. In fact, many persisted in believing that he had not died; that his coffin was loaded with stones; that, like all mythic heroes, he would return in a moment of crisis, the Deliverer still.

27. CW 242–45. The purported speaker is Joyce's Irish publisher, but the occasion of the poem, Joyce's protest against the publishers who were reneging on their commitment to bring out *Dubliners*, reveals once again the artist's identification with the betrayed Parnell.

28. In its American edition, Howarth's book is titled *The Irish Writers: Literature and Nationalism, 1880–1940*.

29. F. S. L. Lyons, "The Parnell Theme in Literature," in *Place, Personality and the Irish Writer*, ed. Andrew Carpenter, 69–95 (69). Seamus Deane has observed that Joyce took the "brute fact" of Parnell's downfall and death "from the world of history and reestablished it in the world of fiction by unfettering it from actual circumstances and making of it a maieutic image which helped him to understand what he already knew—that in Ireland possibility would always be humiliated into squalid fact" ("Joyce and Nationalism," in *James Joyce: New Perspectives*, ed. Colin MacCabe, 168–83 [169]).

30. Lyons, "The Parnell Theme in Literature," 69.

31. Ibid., 74.

32. Conor Cruise O'Brien, *States of Ireland*, 28-29.

33. Au 578. For details, see Au 371-75, 576-79. The scholar is identified as Burch in Richard Finneran's note to "Parnell's Funeral" in his *W. B. Yeats, The Poems: A New Edition*, 664.

34. Stanza 3 of Watts's hymn, itself based on Proverbs 30:17, ends with these ravens and eagles who wreak punishment on the guilty law-breakers and mockers of their mothers' word. The eagles who will come and pull out the child's eyes appear in the very first of Joyce's "epiphanies." The threat seems to have deep roots in Joyce's psyche. Revealingly, though, even as a child, Stephen turns Dante's threat into a rhymed chant, an aesthetic act akin to his creation of a "green wothe," a green rose (P 7).

35. Chester G. Anderson, "Baby Tuckoo: Joyce's 'Features of Infancy,'" in *Approaches to Joyce's "Portrait": Ten Essays*, ed. Thomas F. Staley and Bernard Benstock, 149; Suzette Henke, "Stephen Dedalus and Women: A Portrait of the Artist as a Young Misogynist," in *Women in Joyce*, ed. Suzette Henke and Elaine Unkeless, 83, 103 n3, 85.

The mother as authority figure is a sociocultural problem, stemming from the female domination typical of the early childhood "normal" to most of us, a point stressed in the study Henke refers us to: Dorothy Dinnerstein's *The Mermaid and the Minotaur*. Bonnie Kime Scott makes a distinction that should be kept in mind when we encounter the ghost of Stephen's mother in *Ulysses*. Mrs. Dedalus, she notes, is "Joyce's most fully developed, realistic portrayal of the womanly woman," the nourishing mother. "Her threatening aspect after her death results from Stephen's guilt over using her in life and from his unconscious projections. Like most mothers, she was a first authority figure, and may have therefore remained an unconscious threat. She cannot be established as a devouring mother from behavior she has displayed" (*Joyce and Feminism*, 51).

36. Whatever one may think of the descriptions of Molly Bloom as a "manly" or "phallic" woman, she seems to have a "phallic eye." In "Calypso," we find uxorious, "henpecked" Bloom "glancing askance at her mocking eye," and in "Circe," Bloom is "at [the] service" of a fantasized Molly who wears trousers, orders him to call her "Mrs Marion" as token of his cuckoldry, and has a "slow friendly mockery in her eyes." (U 52, 359). The one-eyed Morrigu and Maud Gonne, through whose eye a "sterner eye" looks down in "A Bronze Head," participate in this motif of the phallic eye. See above, note 20 to this chapter.

37. Hélène Cixous, *The Exile of James Joyce*, trans. Sally A. J. Purcell, 187-88. As is well known, Joyce was obsessed with the central "mystery of the Mass," which he paralleled to what he was "trying to do" in his work, to "give people," as he told his brother Stanislaus, "some kind of intellectual pleasure or spiritual enjoyment by converting the bread of everyday life into something that has a permanent artistic life of its own." This secularizing of transubstantiation is repeated by Stephen, who envisions himself in *Portrait* "a priest of eternal imagination, transmuting the daily *bread* of experience into the radiant body of everliving life" (p. 221). This naturalizing of the supernatural is a reverent sacrilege; the parody of the eucharistic meal in the Christmas dinner scene involves a recognition of it as a survival of rites of blood-sacrifice and even of cannibalism. The parody enacted in the Christmas dinner passage,

though it has its funny moments, is charged with the tragedy of Parnell's mythological status as a devoured god; in the "Lotus-Eaters" chapter of *Ulysses*, Bloom, ignorant of Catholic ritual and bluntly materialistic, performs in Joyce's manipulation a *comic* reduction of the mystery. He has ducked into All Saints Church in order to read his letter from his secret correspondent, Martha. Communion is in progress: "Shut your eyes and open your mouth. What? *Corpus*: body. Corpse . . . they don't seem to chew it; only swallow it down. Rum idea: eating bits of a corpse. Why the cannibals cotton to it" (U 66). See also Stanislaus Joyce, *My Brother's Keeper*, 121, and Cixous, *Exile of James Joyce*, 116–17, 711.

38. Since Mrs. Riordan suffers from "heartburn" and is associated with "maroon" (she has torn the green emblematic of Parnell from her set of brushes), we may wish to associate her, as at least one critic has, with Dante's Beatrice who, in the *Vita Nuova*, wears crimson and devours Dante's "burning heart." Robert J. Andreach, *Studies in Structure: The Stages of the Spiritual Life*, 49.

Notes to Chapter 3: Devouring Ireland

1. Louis MacNeice, from *Autumn Journal: A Poem*.
2. James Joyce, Stephen Dedalus to Cathleen ni Houlihan as "Old Gummy Granny" in the "Circe" episode of *Ulysses*.
3. Though, as Richard Ellmann notes, that image was implicit even in Joyce's early fiction: "*Dubliners* is written on the assumption that Ireland is an inadequate mother, 'an old sow who eats her farrow,' and Joyce associates himself with the masticated children" (*James Joyce*, 295).
4. Davin is based on Joyce's college friend George Clancy, who founded the University College Dublin branch of the Gaelic League. (The league's course in Irish, which Joyce attended for a time, was taught by Padraic Pearse.) In 1921, Clancy was shot dead by disguised Black and Tans.
5. P 203. Bonnie Kime Scott, always resistant to the image of the Devouring Female in Joyce, acknowledges that the characterization of Ireland as a farrow-eating sow is a "degrading image"; but she makes a subtle point: "even in context, this line can assume a comic, ironic function for the reader in evaluating Stephen. Through Stephen, Joyce may represent the threatened male that he once had been" (*Joyce and Feminism*, 22). Perhaps; but Ireland as Devourer seems to have threatened the mature Joyce as much as she did the youthful Stephen. Chester Anderson stresses Stephen's, and Joyce's, ambivalence: "The fear that Stephen expresses" in calling Ireland the sow that eats her farrow "conceals the wish that precedes it—a wish and fear that we all share and handle in our different ways" ("Baby Tuckoo," 167–68).
6. Neumann, *Origins*, 87. For other references in this paragraph, see *Origins*, 82, 85, 95, and *Great Mother*, 222. Neumann's primary source is Herman Kees, *Der Götterglaube im alten Aegypten*.
7. The actual Sarah Curran, as opposed to Tommy Moore's romantic languisher, married, three years after Emmet's execution, a young British army officer, Capt. Henry Sturgeon, a nephew of Lord Rockingham. My allusions to Gertrude, King

Hamlet's adulterate queen, are meant to suggest another level of reference, one appropriate to Joyce, whose preoccupation with *Hamlet*, especially the king cuckolded by Gertrude, is shared by Stephen, who holds forth on the subject for an entire chapter, "Scylla and Charybdis."

8. I am quoting Weldon Thornton, whose source is Helen Landreth's *The Pursuit of Robert Emmet*, 352. Synopsizing Landreth, Thornton notes, "The severed head was taken by the artist George Petrie, to make a death mask, and the body was coffined and buried in the public burying ground known as the Hospital Fields, though it was soon removed." In 1903, the centennial of Emmet's death, the *United Irishman* carried a number of stories on the latest in a long series of attempts to locate Emmet's burial place. In 1904, the year in which *Ulysses* is set, the search led to a vault that contained the remains of five bodies, only four of which were registered. "One, enclosed in a thin penal shell, was the headless skeleton of a young man about Emmet's build" (Landreth, *Pursuit*, 353). See Thornton, *Allusions in* Ulysses, 105–6. Thornton is glossing a reference to Emmet's burial in the "Hades" episode.

9. U 9. The Latin is from the "Ordo Commendationis Animae," a prayer to be said by the bedside of the dying "during the death agony." In the Irish Roman Catholic *Ritual* Joyce was familiar with, it was translated: "may the lilied throng of radiant Confessors encompass thee; may the choir of rejoicing Virgins welcome thee." Suzette Henke stresses the devouring aspect of this maternal vampire-ghost associated with Ireland, the sea, and the rituals of Catholicism. In "the womb of mother Ireland, in the lap of the ocean, Stephen is haunted by Mary Dedalus," a "castrating female who evokes 'scrotumtightening' anxiety." In an act of "psychic cannibalism," she wants to "devour her son's life as the lice had fed on his blood." Her ghost "calls him to a eucharistic feast in which he himself will be the sacrificial victim" (*A Moraculous Sindbook*, 20–21).

10. Neumann, *Origins*, 61.

11. Krafft-Ebing, who coined the word *masochism*, notes in *Psychopathia Sexualis* that "this perversion" was, until the publication of *Venus in Furs*, "quite unknown to the scientific world as such" (87).

12. U 352. Such "tusks" are a standard feature of the "loathly ladies" of Arthurian literature and grotesquerie. Gower interrupts the "Tale of Florent" in his *Confessio Amantis* in order to devote a page to the lady's ugliness, and in the contemporary *Wedding of Sir Gawain and Dame Ragnell*, the lady is described as "foulle and horrible," with "two teethe on every side / As boris tuskes," one of which "went up and the other doun; / A mouthe fulle wide and foulle y-grown" with grey hair (547–53).

13. Neumann, *Origins*, 61.

14. Frazer, *The Golden Bough*, 1:297–99.

15. Kenner, "The Look of a Queen," 121.

16. In *Stone Men of Malekula*, John Layard discusses the Terrible Goddess of this Melanesian island. The monster, called Le-hev-hev, is spider, man-devouring ogress, and "'Crab woman' with two immense claws" (730). What Neumann calls "the shears of the crab monster" are in turn "identical with" the "two crescent moons that are everywhere connected with the great dark Goddess of the night," crescents that, like the "boars' tusks of the Gorgons," flank "the terrible gullet of death or the devouring

womb" through which the "devouring female" compels dead men to pass (*Great Mother*, 178 and n 27).

17. Walker, *Woman's Encyclopedia of Myths and Secrets*, 216.

18. Richard Kain and Robert Scholes, eds., *The Workshop of Daedalus*, 44. For Stanislaus Joyce's reference to the dream, see *My Brother's Keeper*, 229-30, and cf. FW 193-94.

19. At this point in that stylistic montage, the "Oxen of the Sun" episode, the drunken medical students are pressing an even drunker Stephen about his sexual exploits. He turns from women to that treacherous woman, Ireland herself, but instead of "a land flowing with milk and money," Stephen describes a mother who has suckled him with "a bitter milk." When, a moment later, he is frightened by a loud thunderclap, solicitous Bloom tries to calm him. That Stephen is still brooding on his remorse regarding his mother, his "agenbite of inwit," is clear from the response given by the Bunyanesque narrator: was Stephen's "fear vanquished by calmer's [Bloom's] words? No, for he had in his bosom a spike named Bitterness which could not by words be done away" (U 322-23).

20. I am reminded of another writer's mother, and of her imaginative projection. Though, in the "Induction" to *The Fall of Hyperion*, Keats is also frightened by the Titaness Moneta, his fear is mitigated by the "benignant light" in her eyes. The emaciated visage of Moneta, "deathwards progressing to no death," is tragic rather than gruesome; but, like the worn face behind the bridal veil in Stephen's vision, the face of Moneta is, as Aileen Ward has said, "the face of death itself in the most beautiful and terrifying aspect in which Keats had met it—the face of his dead mother, shrouded for her coffin. It is the ultimate image of Keats's poetry, that 'one scene, one adventure, one picture' which Yeats called the image of man's secret life, which, 'if he would but brood over it his life long,' would bring him in the end to an understanding of all his experience" (*John Keats: The Making of a Poet*, 340).

21. The phrase "word known to all men" echoes a passage, the longest left out of the previously standard texts, that would seem (though there has been some recent controversy) to definitively establish the "word" as "Love." See Richard Ellmann's introduction to the Gabler edition, xii.

22. Sent by Circe to the underworld to hear the prophecy of Tiresias, which will insure the homecoming to Ithaca, Odysseus first encounters the ghost of his mother, Anticlea. Initially brusque, Odysseus is tender with her after he has transacted the essential business with the prophet (*Odyssey* XI).

23. C. H. Peake, *James Joyce: The Citizen and the Artist*, 274.

24. Cf. the strange "embassy of nimble pleaders into his ears" in *Stephen Hero*. Ostensibly "sent by the church" to persuade Stephen to return to the religion he has broken from, these ambassadors are doubtless his own vestiges of conscience (SH, section XXV, 204-6).

25. When Sieglinde (at the time married to Siegmund's enemy Hunding) asks Siegmund why he is called "Woeful," he addresses her as *Fragende Frau* and says that *Hunger . . . Macht uns alle kaput*. Ironically, his longing is for Sieglinde herself, the lost sister he will eventually elope with. The "air" to which Stephen sings accompanies the "bloodoath" in which a drugged Siegfried pledges to woo Brünnhilde, his

beloved, for another—Gunther, with whom he seals the bloodoath guarded over by his sword, *Nothung*. With that fatal oath is also sealed the eventual doom of the gods.

26. Blake, *A Vision of the Last Judgment* and *The Marriage of Heaven and Hell*. "Blake's wings of excess" fuses two Proverbs of Hell: "The road of excess leads to the palace of wisdom" and "No bird soars too high if he soars with his own wings" (*Marriage*, plate 7).

27. Blake, *Marriage of Heaven and Hell*, plate 14.

28. Blake, letter to William Hayley (*Letters*, 36).

29. See the article by the Polish novelist Jan Parandowski, "Meeting with Joyce," in *Portraits of the Artist in Exile*, ed. Willard Potts, 160. I discuss aspects of the Joyce-Blake relationship in "Time's Ruins and the Mansions of Eternity." In *Travesties*, playwright Tom Stoppard has beautifully caught Joyce's Blakean preference of spiritual to corporeal warfare. See below, note 43 to this chapter.

30. Malcolm Brown, *The Politics of Irish Literature: From Thomas Davis to W. B. Yeats*, 225.

31. From the opening lines of the final stanza of the prefatory poem to Blake's *Milton*: "I will not cease from Mental Fight, / Nor shall my Sword sleep in my hand."

32. William York Tindall, *A Reader's Guide to James Joyce*, 209. Tindall is actually glossing a passage earlier in "Circe" in which Bloom is almost run down by a motorman who yells, "Hey, shitbreeches, are you doing the hattrick?" Bloom "trickleaps to the curbstone" to escape (U 355).

33. Gustave Flaubert, *Madame Bovary*, trans. Gerald Hopkins, 159. The possible allusion was noted by Joseph Prescott, "Notes on Joyce's *Ulysses*," 159.

34. This eighteenth-century song, "The Rogue's Delight in Praise of his Strolling Mort," had run through Stephen's mind repeatedly in "Proteus" (39 especially). The two lines he declaims ecstatically to Cissy are: "White thy fambles, red thy gan, / And thy quarrens dainty is" (white hands, red mouth, and dainty body).

35. Walter Hussey de Burgh, in *Irish Orators and Oratory*, ed. T. M. Kettle, 110.

36. From Joyce's article, "Fenianism," in *Il Piccolo della sera* (1907). There he described Fenianism, still a "separatist movement" though it "no longer uses dynamite," as "a desperate and bloody doctrine" whose time has passed. A gradualist who hoped for a bloodless revolution, one not to be "brought about by violence but gradually" (SH 206), Joyce preferred the nonviolence—passive resistance, economic boycotts—advocated by moderate Sinn Feiners. For the passage cited from "Fenianism," see CW 191. See also Dominic Manganiello, *Joyce's Politics*; John Garvin, *Joyce's Disunited Kingdom and the Irish Dimension*; and Deane, "Joyce and Nationalism."

37. Pope, "The First Satire of the Second Book of Horace Imitated," lines 123–28: "Know, all the distant din that world can keep, / Rolls o'er my grotto, and but soothes my sleep. / There, my retreat the best companions grace, / Chiefs out of War, and statesmen out of place; / There St. John mingles with my friendly Bowl / The Feast of Reason and the flow of Soul." The phrase quoted in the next sentence, "Satire's my weapon," occurs in line 69.

38. For details, see my "Time's Ruins and the Mansions of Eternity," 51.

39. See below, note 43 to this chapter.

40. U 273. Two years later, in *Juno and the Paycock*, Sean O'Casey put in the mouth

of his heroine what seems a fusion of Yeats's "Easter 1916" (Too long a sacrifice / Can make a stone of the heart") and this section of *Ulysses*. "Take away our hearts o' stone," prays Juno, "an' give us hearts of flesh. Take away this murtherin an' give us thine own eternal love!"

41. Edmund L. Epstein, "James Augustine Aloysius Joyce," in *Companion to Joyce Studies*, ed. Bowen and Carens, 26. Epstein's suggestion about the genesis of the *Wake* (referred to later in this paragraph) tallies with Hugh Kenner's, made independently at the International Joyce Symposium in Dublin in 1982.

42. That famous paragraph, beginning "riverrun," was written in response to a 1926 letter from Harriet Weaver jokingly requesting, in *Wake*-language, a "grave account of his esteemed Highness Rhaggerick O'Hoggnor's Hogg Tomb" (LJ 1:247; cf. Ellmann, *James Joyce*, 594ff.).

43. U 482. The damning of death and affirming of life should remind the reader of the allusive levels of Stephen's encounter with "Private Carr." The Blakean allusions that pepper Stephen's discourse are apropos since this episode corresponds, in the first place, with Blake's famous run-in, physical and legal, with Private Scholfield or Schofield (variously spelled) in 1803–1804. Though Stephen's encounter may actually compound two incidents from Joyce's own life (see Frank Delaney, *James Joyce's Odyssey*, 53–54), Carr derives his name from the invalided soldier Henry Carr, a British consular official in Zurich with whom Joyce was embroiled in a ludicrous legal action over the price of a pair of trousers in 1918–1919. In *Travesties*, Tom Stoppard has instinctively caught the Blakean quality of Joyce's vision. The curtain comes down on act 1 of *Travesties* with old Carr telling us his dream about Joyce, now long since dead. He indulges in a wish-fulfilling fantasy of corporeal triumph: "I dreamed about him, dreamed I had him in the witness box, a masterly cross-examination, case practically won, admitted it all, the whole thing, the trousers, everything." But even in his own fantasy the former soldier is upstaged by a perfect squelch, with Stoppard utilizing Joyce's Blakean preference of spiritual to corporeal warfare:

and I *flung* at him—"And what did you do in the Great War?" "I wrote *Ulysses*," he said. "What did you do?"
 Bloody nerve.
 (BLACK OUT)

Notes to Chapter 4: The Cries of the Perishing

1. Coventry Patmore, quoted by Yeats in *Samhain: 1905*, following his denial that *Cathleen ni Houlihan* was written "to affect opinion," and alluded to in the opening poem of *Responsibilities*, in which even the most "turbulent" land is capable of drawing "Delight in Art whose end is peace" (VP 288).

2. In the note, oddly, Yeats forgot about the bees; but his point remains: "One felt an overmastering desire not to grow unhappy or embittered, not to lose all sense of the beauty of nature. A stare (our West of Ireland name for a starling) had built in a

hole beside my window and I made these verses out of the feeling of the moment" (Au 580).

3. For the Black Pig as "bad sign," see *Funk and Wagnall's Standard Dictionary of Folklore, Mythology and Legend*, 869. Steven Putzel has explored the sources of Yeats's Black Pig in Irish folk tradition and literature as well as in comparative mythology, including Hindu mythology. In one Hindu story, Vishnu, "in the shape of the great boar, is both creator and destroyer," suggesting a resemblance to Kali herself. "The Black Pig: Yeats's Early Apocalyptic Beast," 99.

4. In this sense the poem seems a Celtic and occult variation on the crucial change in Wordsworth: conversion from attraction to overt political or military action ("farewell to the Warrior's schemes," he announces in *Home at Grasmere*) to concentration on the internal realm of spirit and imagination. Take, as example, the famous description of the crossing of the Simplon Pass. At first disappointed by the gap between his infinite "hope" and the finite height of the Alpine pass (a palpable allegory of the discrepancy between the limitless hope and subsequent disappointment evoked by the French Revolution), Wordsworth recognizes, in retrospect, the glory of Imagination, which finds its consolation and recompense by converting external physical defeat into an internal spiritual triumph:

Under such banners militant, the soul
Seeks for no trophies, struggles for no spoils
That may attest her prowess, blest in thoughts
That are their own perfection and reward.
  (*The Prelude* 6.609–12)

"The militancy of overt political action has been transformed," wrote M. H. Abrams, "into the paradox of spiritual quietism: under such militant banners is no march, but a wise passiveness" (Abrams, "English Romanticism: The Spirit of the Age," in his *The Correspondent Breeze: Essays on English Romanticism*, 65). While Wordsworthian beatitude requires no bowing down to an occult Master, Abrams's synopsis remains applicable to "The Valley of the Black Pig," which begins with banners literally militant and ends in, precisely, "the paradox of spiritual quietism" and a passivity that seems wise and is certainly apolitical. As Phillip L. Marcus has observed of the poem: "The sound patterns, the repetitions, the high percentage of monosyllabic words are designed to push audiences not to the barricades but rather to the quiet, awesome shores of trance" ("The Celtic Revival," in *The Irish World: The Art and Culture of the Irish People*, ed. Brian de Breffny, 218).

5. Rufus M. Jones, *The Eternal Gospel*, 5. In his various references to the mythology underlying his understanding of what the Black Pig symbolizes, Yeats is close to Rhys, Frazer, and—though he does not mention him by name—Max Müller: "I look upon the sunrise and sunset, on the daily return of day and night, on the battle between light and darkness, on the whole solar drama in all its details that is acted every day, every month, every year, in heaven and on earth, as the principal subject of early mythology" (*Lectures on the Science of Language, Second Series*, 537).

6. Allen Grossman, *Poetic Knowledge in the Early Yeats: A Study of* The Wind Among the Reeds, 96.

7. William Sharp, "A Group of Celtic Writers," 36. In his own poetry, Sharp also makes use of symbolism drawn from the Order of the Golden Dawn. He may have been attracted to Yeats's "flaming door" because of his own interest in the gate of Eden, as in his poem "Secret Gate."

8. For an interesting comment on Yeats's amalgamation of occultism and Irish folklore, see Deane, "Joyce and Nationalism," 143.

9. Quoted by F. X. Martin, "Eoin MacNeill on the 1916 Rising," 236, 239.

10. Sean O'Casey, *Autobiographies*, 2:149ff.

11. For the drafts of "The Black Tower," see Jon Stallworthy, *Between the Lines: Yeats's Poetry in the Making*, 227. The "dike" associated with the Black Pig is discussed by Steven Putzel in "The Black Pig."

12. Suzette Henke and Elaine Unkeless, Introduction to *Women in Joyce*, xiv.

13. Here, as in the marvelous final movement of "Lapis Lazuli," Yeats adapts Keats's subtle use of "or" in the penultimate stanza of the "Ode on a Grecian Urn."

14. Neumann, *Great Mother*, 149.

15. I am paraphrasing Seamus Deane on Joyce ("Joyce and Nationalism," 172), who adds (173) that Yeats had a similarly ambitious cultural vision but "gave it up for the theme of individuality."

16. "Among School Children." The other poems alluded to in this paragraph include "The Circus Animals' Desertion," "Friends," "The Stare's Nest by My Window," "A Prayer for My Daughter," "A Bronze Head," and "In Memory of Eva Gore-Booth and Con Markiewicz."

17. Joseph Ignatius Constantine Clarke, *Robert Emmet: A Tragedy of Irish History*, 52. The speaker is a Michael Dwyer.

18. David Blake Knox, "Ideological Factors in Yeats's Early Drama," 89. "Sixteen Dead Men" and "The Rose Tree," coda-poems to "Easter 1916," were first published in *The Dial* in November 1920. Pearse is, of course, the perfect spokesman for this position. He was elected to the Supreme Council of the IRB within two months of his celebrated speech at the graveside of O'Donovan Rossa (1 August 1915), a panegyric in which he declared, "Life springs from death, and from the graves of patriot men and women spring living nations" (*Political Writings and Speeches*, 136–37).

19. Conor Cruise O'Brien, *States of Ireland*, 295 n. 12, 70.

20. Ibid., 303, 313.

21. Seamus Heaney, *Preoccupations: Selected Prose 1968–1978*, 56–57. See also James Lafferty, "Gifts from the Goddess: Heaney's 'Bog People,' " 128.

22. *North*, 45. See Lafferty, "Gifts from the Goddess," 136: "Here Heaney shows Ireland's kinship with the 'man-killing parishes' of Jutland, where once Nerthus fed on her people, as Kathleen Ni Houlihan feeds on her faithful now."

23. *We Irish*, 8–9. See my review, "A Balanced Stance," 180.

24. Unpublished letter from Yeats to Lady Gregory, 12 January 1922; quoted in Cullingford, *Yeats, Ireland and Fascism*, 112.

Notes to Epilogue

1. Seamus Heaney, from "Exposure," the final poem in *North*, 73. *North* indicates, incidentally, that Heaney read *States of Ireland*; he alludes to O'Brien's borrowing of Burke's phrase "little platoon" (*North*, 58; *States of Ireland*, 315).
2. "Gas from a Burner" (CW 243).
3. Heaney, "Station Island," XII; in *Station Island* (92–94).

Works Cited

References to the standard texts of Yeats and Joyce are abbreviated and included parenthetically in my text. For those citations, see Abbreviations, p. viii. Yeats's short story "Kathleen-ny-Houlihan" appeared in *The National Observer* (1894). I also quote from a volume edited by Yeats: *Fairy and Folk Tales of the Irish Peasantry* (London: Walter Scott, 1888).

Other Books and Articles Cited

Abrams, M. H. "English Romanticism: The Spirit of the Age." In Abrams's *The Correspondent Breeze: Essays on English Romanticism*. New York: Norton, 1984.

Andersen, Jørgen. *The Witch on the Wall: Medieval Erotic Sculpture in the British Isles*. Copenhagen: Rosenkilde and Bagger; London: George Allen & Unwin, 1977.

Anderson, Chester G. "Baby Tuckoo: Joyce's 'Features of Infancy.'" In *Approaches to Joyce's "Portrait": Ten Essays*, edited by Thomas F. Staley and Bernard Benstock. Pittsburgh: University of Pittsburgh Press, 1976.

Andreach, Robert J. *Studies in Structure: The Stages of the Spiritual Life*. New York: Fordham University Press, 1964.

Banim, John. "Soggarth Aroon." In *The Dublin Book of Irish Verse, 1728–1909*, edited by John Cooke, 101–3. Dublin: Hodges, Figgis & Co.; London: Oxford University Press, 1913.

Berrow, Hilary. "Eight Nights in the Abbey." In *J. M. Synge: Centenary Papers 1971*, edited by Maurice Harmon. Dublin: Dolmen Press, 1972.

Blake, William. *The Complete Poetry and Prose of William Blake*. Edited by David V. Erdman, commentary by Harold Bloom. Berkeley and Los Angeles: University of California Press, 1981.

———. *The Letters of William Blake*, edited by Geoffrey Keynes. Cambridge: Harvard University Press, 1970.

Bloom, Harold. *Yeats*. London, Oxford, New York: Oxford University Press, 1970.

Bolt, Sydney. *A Preface to James Joyce*. London and New York: Longmans, 1981.

Bordo, Susan. "Anorexia Nervosa: Psychopathology as the Crystallization of Culture." *The Philosophical Forum* 17 (1985–1986): 73–104.

Works Cited

Bowen, Zack, and James F. Carens, eds. *A Companion to Joyce Studies.* Westport, Conn.: Greenwood Press, 1984.
Brennan, Robert. *Allegiance.* Dublin: Browne and Nolan, 1950.
Brown, C. Mackenzie. "Kali, the Mad Mother." In *The Book of the Goddess, Past and Present: An Introduction to Her Religion,* edited by Carl Olson. New York: Crossroad, 1983.
Brown, Malcolm. *The Politics of Irish Literature: From Thomas Davis to W. B. Yeats.* Seattle: University of Washington Press, 1972.
Budge, Sir E. A. Wallis, trans. *The Book of the Dead.* 2d ed. rev. London, 1949.
Burgh, Walter Hussey de. Speech in Irish Parliament (1779). In *Irish Orators and Oratory,* edited by T. M. Kettle. Dublin: Talbot Press, Frederick Stokes, n.d.
Cardozo, Nancy. *Lucky Eyes and a High Heart: The Life of Maud Gonne.* Indianapolis and New York: Bobbs-Merrill, 1978.
Cixous, Hélène. *The Exile of James Joyce.* Translated by Sally A. J. Purcell. New York: David Lewis, 1972.
Clarke, Joseph Ignatius Constantine. *Robert Emmet: A Tragedy of Irish History.* New York: Putnam's Sons, 1881.
Coleridge, Samuel Taylor. *The Complete Poetical Works of Samuel Taylor Coleridge.* 2 vols. Edited by E. H. Coleridge. Oxford: Clarendon Press, 1912.
Collins, Ben L. "Joyce's Use of Yeats and of Irish History: A Reading of 'A Mother.'" *Éire-Ireland* 5 (1970): 45–66.
Comini, Allesandra. "Posters from the War Against Women." *New York Times Book Review* (1 February 1987): 13–14.
Cooke, John, ed. *The Dublin Book of Irish Verse, 1728–1909.* Dublin: Hodges, Figgis & Co.; London: Oxford University Press, 1913.
Coxhead, Elizabeth. *Lady Gregory: A Literary Portrait.* 2d ed. London: Secker and Warburg, 1966 [1961].
Cullingford, Elizabeth. *Yeats, Ireland and Fascism.* New York: New York University Press, 1981.
Deane, Seamus. "Joyce and Nationalism." In *James Joyce: New Perspectives,* edited by Colin MacCabe. Sussex: Harvester Press; Bloomington: Indiana University Press, 1982.
Delaney, Frank. *James Joyce's Odyssey.* New York: Holt, Rinehart, Winston, 1982.
Dijkstra, Bram. *Idols of Perversity: Fantasies of Feminine Evil in Fin de Siècle Culture.* New York: Oxford University Press, 1986.
Dinnerstein, Dorothy. *The Mermaid and the Minotaur.* New York: Harper and Row, 1977.
Donoghue, Denis. *We Irish: Essays on Irish Literature and Society.* New York: Knopf, 1986.
Eliot, T. S. *The Complete Poems and Plays 1909–1950.* New York: Harcourt, Brace, 1962.
Ellmann, Richard. *The Identity of Yeats.* 2d ed. New York: Oxford University Press, 1964 [1953].
———. *James Joyce.* New and Revised Edition. New York, Oxford, Toronto: Oxford University Press, 1982.
Epstein, Edmund L. "James Augustine Aloysius Joyce." In *A Companion to Joyce Stud-*

ies, edited by Zack Bowen and James F. Carens. Westport, Conn.: Greenwood Press, 1984.

Fass, Barbara. *La Belle Dame sans Merci and the Aesthetics of Romanticism.* Detroit: Wayne State University Press, 1974.

Finneran, Richard J., ed. *W. B. Yeats, The Poems: A New Edition.* New York: Macmillan, 1983.

Flanagan, Thomas. "The Quaking Bog." *The New York Review of Books* 35 (31 March 1988): 46–48.

Flaubert, Gustave. *Madame Bovary.* Translated by Gerald Hopkins. New York: Oxford University Press, 1949.

Fletcher, Ian. "Yeats and Lissadell." In *W. B. Yeats, 1865-1965: Centenary Essays on the Art of W. B. Yeats,* edited by D. E. S. Maxwell and S. B. Bushrui. Ibadan, Nigeria: Ibadan University Press, 1965.

Frazer, Sir George. *The Golden Bough.* 2 vols. London: Macmillan, 1890.

Funk and Wagnall's Standard Dictionary of Folklore, Mythology and Legend. New York: Funk and Wagnall, 1972.

Gallagher, S. F. ed. *Woman in Irish Legend, Literature and Life.* Gerrards Cross: Colin Smythe; Totowa, N.J.: Barnes and Noble, 1983.

Garvin, John. *Joyce's Disunited Kingdom and the Irish Dimension.* Dublin: Gill and Macmillan, 1976.

Gay, Peter. *The Bourgeois Experience.* Vol. 1, *The Education of the Senses.* New York: Oxford University Press, 1984.

Gonne, Maud. *Dawn, A Play in One Act and Three Tableaux* (1904). In *Lost Plays of the Irish Renaissance,* edited by Robert Hogan and James Kilroy. Gerrards Cross: Proscenium Press, 1970.

———. *A Servant of the Queen.* Woodbridge, Suffolk: The Boydell Press, 1983 [1938].

———. "Yeats and Ireland." In *Scattering Branches: Tributes to W. B. Yeats,* edited by Stephen Gwynn. New York: Macmillan, 1940.

Graves, Robert. *The Greek Myths.* 2 vols. in 1. New York: George Braziller, 1959.

———. *The White Goddess.* New York: Farrar, Straus, Giroux, n.d. (first published, 1948).

Gregory, Lady Augusta. *Lady Gregory's Journals 1916–1930.* Edited by Lennox Robinson. London: Macmillan, 1947.

———. *Seventy Years.* New York: Macmillan, 1976.

———. *Our Irish Theatre.* New York: Capricorn Books, 1965 [1913].

Griffith, Arthur. "All Ireland." *The United Irishman* (12 April 1902, 17 October 1903).

Grossman, Allen. *Poetic Knowledge in the Early Yeats: A Study of* The Wind Among the Reeds. Charlottesville: University of Virginia Press, 1969.

Guest, Edith M. "Irish Sheela-na-Gigs in 1935." *Journal of the Royal Society of Antiquities of Ireland* 66 (1936): 107–29.

Gwynn, Stephen. *Irish Literature and Drama.* New York: Thomas Nelson and Sons, 1936.

Gwynn, Stephen, ed. *Scattering Branches: Tributes to W. B. Yeats.* New York: Macmillan, 1940.

Heaney, Seamus. *North.* London: Faber and Faber, 1975.

———. *Preoccupations: Selected Prose 1968–1978*. New York: Farrar, Straus, Giroux, 1980.
———. *Station Island*. New York: Farrar, Straus, Giroux, 1985.
Henke, Suzette. *Joyce's Moraculous Sindbook: A Study of Ulysses*. Columbus: Ohio State University Press, 1978.
———. "Stephen Dedalus and Women: A Portrait of the Artist as a Young Misogynist." In *Women in Joyce*, edited by Suzette Henke and Elaine Unkeless. Urbana, Chicago, London: University of Illinois Press, 1982.
Hickey, Helen. *Images of Stone: Figure Sculpture of the Lough Erne Basin*. Belfast: Blackstaff Press, 1976.
Hone, Joseph. *W. B. Yeats, 1865–1939*. 2d ed. New York: St. Martin's Press, 1962 [1942].
Howarth, Herbert. *The Irish Writers: Literature and Nationalism, 1880–1940*. New York: Hill and Wang, 1959.
Jones, Rufus M. *The Eternal Gospel*. New York: Macmillan, 1938.
Joyce, Stanislaus. *My Brother's Keeper*. New York: McGraw-Hill, 1964.
Jung, Carl Gustav. *The Collected Works of Carl G. Jung*. 20 vols. Translated by R. F. C. Hull. Princeton: Princeton University Press, Bollingen Series, 1970–1978.
Kain, Richard, and Robert Scholes. *The Workshop of Daedalus*. Evanston: Northwestern University Press, 1965.
Keane, Patrick J. "A Balanced Stance." *Salmagundi* 73 (1987): 177–86.
———. "Time's Ruins and the Mansions of Eternity." *Bulletin of Research in the Humanities* 86 (1983): 33–66.
———. *A Wild Civility: Interactions in the Poetry and Thought of Robert Graves*. Columbia: University of Missouri Press, 1980.
———. *Yeats's Interactions with Tradition*. Columbia: University of Missouri Press, 1987.
Keane, Patrick J., ed. *William Butler Yeats: A Collection of Criticism*. New York: McGraw-Hill, 1973.
Keats, John. *The Poems of John Keats*. Edited by Jack Stillinger. Cambridge: The Belknap Press of Harvard University Press, 1978.
Kees, Herman. *Der Götterglaube im alten Aegypten*. Mitteilungen der Vorderasiatisch-Agyptischen Gesselschaft, vol. XLV. Leipzig, 1941.
Kenner, Hugh. *A Colder Eye: The Modern Irish Writers*. New York: Penguin, 1983.
———. *Dublin's Joyce*. London: Chatto and Windus, 1955.
———. "The Look of a Queen." In *Woman in Irish Legend, Literature and Life*, edited by S. F. Gallagher. Gerrards Cross: Colin Smythe; Totowa, N.J.: Barnes and Noble, 1983.
Kinsley, David R. "The Hindu Goddess." In *The Encyclopedia of Religion*. 15 vols. Edited by Mircea Eliade. New York: Macmillan, 1987.
———. *The Sword and the Flute: Kali and Krsna, Dark Visions of the Terrible and Sublime in Hindu Mythology*. Berkeley and Los Angeles: University of California Press, 1975.
Knox, David Blake. "Ideological Factors in Yeats's Early Drama." *Anglo-Irish Studies* 5 (1957).
Kolodny, Annette. "Dancing through the Minefield: Some Observations on the Theory, Practice and Politics of Feminist Criticism." *Feminist Studies* 6 (1980): 1–25.
———. "Some Notes on Defining a 'Feminist Literary Criticism.'" *Critical Inquiry* 2 (1975): 75–92.

Krafft-Ebing, Richard von. *Psychopathia Sexualis*. New York: Stein and Day, 1965.
Krause, Wolfgang. *Die Kelten*. Tübingen, 1929.
Lafferty, James J. "Gifts from the Goddess: Heaney's 'Bog People.'" *Eire-Ireland* 17 (1982): 127-36.
Landreth, Helen. *The Pursuit of Robert Emmet*. New York, 1948.
Lasch, Christopher. *The Culture of Narcissism*. New York: Warner Books, 1979.
Layard, John. *Stone Men of Malekula*. London, 1942.
Loomis, Roger Sherman. *Arthurian Tradition and Chrétien de Troyes*. New York: Columbia University Press, 1949.
Lyons, F. S. L. "The Parnell Theme in Literature." In *Place, Personality and the Irish Writer*, edited by Andrew Carpenter. New York: Barnes and Noble, 1977.
MacBride, Maud Gonne. See Gonne, Maud.
MacNeice, Louis. *Autumn Journal: A Poem*. New York: Random House, 1939.
Maddox, Brenda. "Wakers of the World, Unite! You Have Nothing to Lose But Your Theory." *New York Times Book Review* (16 August 1987): 20.
Mahaffey, Vicki. "Giacomo Joyce." In *A Companion to Joyce Studies*, edited by Zack Bowen and James F. Carens. Westport, Conn.: Greenwood Press, 1984.
Mangan, James Clarence. "Kathaleen-ny-Houlahan." In *The Dublin Book of Irish Verse, 1728-1909*, edited by John Cooke, 136-38. Dublin: Hodges, Figgis & Co.; London: Oxford University Press, 1913.
Manganiello, Dominic. *Joyce's Politics*. London, Boston, Henley: Routledge and Kegan Paul, 1980.
Marcus, Phillip L. "The Celtic Revival." In *The Irish World: The Art and Culture of the Irish People*, edited by Brian de Breffny. New York: Harrison House/Harry N. Abrams, 1986.
Markiewicz, Constance. *Prison Letters of Countess Markiewicz*. London: Longmans, Green, 1934.
Martin, F. X. "Eoin MacNeill on the 1916 Rising." *Irish Historical Studies* 12 (1961): 226-71.
Maxwell, D. E. S., and S. B. Bushrui, eds. *W. B. Yeats, 1865-1965: Centenary Essays on the Art of W. B. Yeats*. Ibadan, Nigeria: Ibadan University Press, 1965.
Mercier, Vivian. *The Irish Comic Tradition*. London, Oxford, New York: Oxford University Press, 1969, 1962.
Moi, Toril. *Sexual/Textual Politics*. London: Methuen, 1985.
Moore, John Rees. *Masks of Love and Death: Yeats as Dramatist*. Ithaca and London: Cornell University Press, 1971.
Müller, Max. *Lectures on the Science of Language, Second Series*. London and New York, 1869.
Nathan, Leonard E. *The Tragic Drama of William Butler Yeats: Figures in a Dance*. New York and London: Columbia University Press, 1965.
Neumann, Erich. *The Great Mother: An Analysis of the Archetype*. Translated by Ralph Mannheim. 2d ed. Princeton: Princeton University Press, Bollingen Series XLVII, 1963.
———. *The Origins and History of Consciousness*. Princeton: Princeton University Press, Bollingen Series XLII, 1954.

O'Brien, Conor Cruise. *States of Ireland*. New York: Vintage, 1972.
O'Brien, Darcy. *The Consciousness of James Joyce*. Princeton: Princeton University Press, 1968.
———. "Some Determinants of Molly Bloom." In *Approaches to "Ulysses,"* edited by Thomas F. Staley and Bernard Benstock. Pittsburgh: University of Pittsburgh Press, 1970.
O'Brien, Maire Cruise. "The Female Principle in Gaelic Poetry." In *Woman in Irish Legend, Literature and Life*, edited by S. F. Gallagher. Gerrards Cross: Colin Smythe; Totowa, N.J.: Barnes and Noble, 1983.
O'Casey, Sean. *Autobiographies*. 2 vols. London: Macmillan, 1963.
———. *Drums Under the Window*. London: Macmillan, 1945.
———. *Inishfallen, Fare Thee Well*. London: Macmillan, 1949.
Olson, Carl, ed. *The Book of the Goddess, Past and Present: An Introduction to Her Religion*. New York: Crossroad, 1983.
Parandowski, Jan. "Meeting with Joyce." In *Portraits of the Artist in Exile*, edited by Willard Potts. Seattle: University of Washington Press, 1979.
Parkin, Andrew. *The Dramatic Imagination of W. B. Yeats*. New York: Barnes and Noble, 1978.
Peake, C. H. *James Joyce: The Citizen and the Artist*. Stanford: Stanford University Press, 1977.
Pearse, Padraic. "By Way of Comment." Introduction to the Christmas 1910 number of *An Macaomh* 2 (1910): 14.
———. *Collected Works of Padraic Pearse: Political Writings and Speeches*. Dublin: Phoenix Publishing Co., n.d.
Praz, Mario. *The Romantic Agony*. Translated by Angus Davidson. 2d ed. London, New York, Toronto: Oxford University Press, 1951 [1933].
Prescott, Joseph. "Notes on Joyce's *Ulysses*." *Modern Language Quarterly* 13 (1952): 149–62.
Putzel, Steven D. "The Black Pig: Yeats's Early Apocalyptic Beast." *Éire-Ireland* 17 (1982): 86–102.
Revard, Stella. "Yeats, Mallarmé, and the Archetypal Feminine." *Papers on Language and Literature* 8, supplement (1972): 112-27.
Reynolds, Lorna. "Women in Irish, Legend, Life and Literature." In *Woman in Irish Legend, Literature and Life*, edited by S. F. Gallagher. Gerrards Cross: Colin Smythe; Totowa, N.J.: Barnes and Noble, 1983.
Ross, Anne. "The Divine Hag of the Pagan Celts." In *The Witch Figure: Essays in Honour of Katharine M. Briggs*, 139–64. London: Methuen, 1973.
———. *Pagan Celtic Britain: Studies in Iconography and Tradition*. London: Routledge and Kegan Paul, 1967.
Rothenstein, Sir William. *Since Fifty: Men and Memories, 1922- 1938*. New York: Macmillan, 1940.
Russell, George (AE). *Letters from AE*. Edited by Alan Denson. London, New York, Toronto: Abelard-Schuman, 1961.
Sacher-Masoch, Leopold von. *Venus in Furs*. New York: G. Braziller, 1971.
Safire, William. "On Language." *New York Times Magazine*, 3 May 1987.

Salzman, M. Renee. "Magna Mater: Great Mother of the Roman Empire." In *The Book of the Goddess, Past and Present: An Introduction to Her Religion*, edited by Carl Olson. New York: Crossroad, 1983.
Scott, Bonnie Kime. *Joyce and Feminism*. Bloomington: Indiana University Press; Sussex: Harvester Press, 1984.
———. "The Woman in the Black Straw Hat: A Transitional Priestess in *Stephen Hero*." In *James Joyce Quarterly* 16 (1979): 407–16.
Scott, G. R. *Phallic Worship*. Westport, Conn.: Associated Booksellers, n.d.
Shakespeare, William. *The Complete Pelican Shakespeare*. General Editor, Alfred Harbage. Baltimore: Penguin, 1969.
Sharkey, John. *Celtic Mysteries: The Ancient Religion*. London: Thames and Hudson, 1975.
Sharp, William. "A Group of Celtic Writers." Unsigned review of Yeats's *The Wind Among the Reeds. Fortnightly Review* 65 (1899): 36–48.
Shaw, George Bernard. *John Bull's Other Island* (1904). In *Complete Plays, with Prefaces*. 6 vols. New York: Dodd, Mead, 1962.
Shiublaigh, Máire nic. *First Annual Report of Inghinidhe na hEireann*. Dublin: O'Brien and Ards, 1901.
Shiublaigh, Máire nic, and Edward Kenny. *The Splendid Years*. Dublin: James Duffy, 1955.
Sjoestedt, Marie-Louise. *Gods and Heroes of the Celts*. London, 1949.
Stalker, John. *The Stalker Affair: One Man's Battle with Power and Politics in Northern Ireland*. New York: Viking, 1988.
Stallworthy, Jon. *Between the Lines: Yeats's Poetry in the Making*. Oxford: Clarendon Press, 1963.
Stoppard, Tom. *Travesties*. New York: Grove Press, 1975.
Strong, L. A. G. "William Butler Yeats." In *Scattering Branches: Tributes to W. B. Yeats*, edited by Stephen Gwynn. New York: Macmillan, 1940.
Swinburne, Algernon Charles. *The Poems of Algernon Charles Swinburne*. 6 vols. New York and London: Harper and Brothers, 1904.
Thompson, William Irwin. *The Imagination of an Insurrection: Dublin, Easter 1916*. New York: Oxford University Press, 1967.
Thornton, Weldon. *Allusions in* Ulysses. Chapel Hill: University of North Carolina Press, 1961.
Tindall, William York. *A Reader's Guide to James Joyce*. New York: Noonday, 1959.
Tynan, Katherine. *Twenty Five Years: Reminiscences*. New York: Devin Adair, 1913.
Vendler, Helen. *Yeats's* Vision *and the Later Plays*. Cambridge: Harvard University Press, 1963.
Wagner, Richard. *The Ring of the Nibelung*. Translated by Andrew Porter. New York and London: Norton, 1977.
Walker, Barbara G. *The Woman's Encyclopedia of Myths and Secrets*. San Francisco: Harper and Row, 1983.
Ward, Aileen. *John Keats: The Making of a Poet*. New York: Viking Press, 1963.
Webster, Brenda. *Yeats: A Psychoanalytic Study*. Stanford: Stanford University Press, 1973.

Wilde, Oscar. *Salome*. Boston: Salem House, 1987.
Wilson, F. A. C. "Yeats's 'A Bronze Head': A Freudian Investigation." *Literature and Psychology* 22 (1972): 5–12.
Zimmer, Heinrich. "The Indian World Mother." In *The Mystic Vision*. Princeton and London: Princeton University Press, Bollingen Series XXX, 1968.

Index

AE. *See* Russell, George
"Agenbite of inwit," 44, 58, 66, 69, 126n19
Amor matris, 58, 65
Anderson, Chester G., 44, 123n35, 124n5
Anna Livia Plurabelle, xv, 34, 37, 116n7, 122n24
Attis, 27, 61

Banim, John: "*Soggarth Aroon*," 75-76
Bella (Bloom's dominatrix in *Ulysses*), 59-61, 67
Beo (Celtic sow-goddess), 51
Blake, William, 18, 20, 23-24, 41, 69-70, 71, 77, 78-79, 86, 94, 128n43; "And Did Those Feet," 72, 79, 127n31; "Auguries of Innocence," 77; *Letters*, 120n2; *The Marriage of Heaven and Hell*, 127n26, 127n27; "The Mental Traveller," 18, 42-43
Bloom, Leopold: opposed to violence, ii, 52-53, 79-80, 99; subservient to Molly, xi, 55, 56, 60, 123n36; subservient to Bella, 20, 59-61, 67; helps Stephen, 63, 68, 77, 78; and the Eucharist, 123-24n37
Bloom, Molly: as Devourer, xi, 113n1, 114n8; as life-figure, 37, 56, 122n24; dominates husband, 55, 60, 120n53, 123n36; male-projected character, 114n8; mentioned, 52
Bordo, Susan, ix, xiv, 19-20, 120n49
Brown, Malcolm, 70-71, 127n50
Burch, Vacher, 41, 42
Byron, Lord: "Darkness," 72; Byronic hero, 120n50

Carr, Private: Stephen's antagonist, 71, 73, 75, 77-79, 81; in Stoppard's *Travesties*, 128n43
Carrion crow, x, xi, 10, 44, 73, 74, 76, 77, 79, 81, 82. *See also* Morrigu
Casey, Mr. (defender of Parnell in *Portrait*), 43, 44-47
Cathleen ni Houlihan (Yeats), ix, x, xiv, xvi, 2-17, 21, 27, 33, 34, 43, 52, 56-57, 83, 84, 87-88, 89, 90, 93, 94, 95, 96, 97, 99, 118n28; Yeats's comments on, 5, 8, 9, 12-13, 116-17n11, 117n17; Yeats's ambivalence or misgivings regarding, xiv, 4, 8-10, 97; Lady Gregory and, 116-17n11, 118n34; G. B. Shaw's reaction to, 118n34; text of play, 103-12. *See also* Joyce, James: parodies *Cathleen ni Houlihan*
Cathleen ni Houlihan, v, ix-x, xii, xiii, xvi-xvii, 1-2, 3, 5-17, 19, 49-50, 56-57, 66, 67, 72-81, 83, 89, 90, 91, 92, 94, 95, 96, 98, 101, 116n7, 118-19n41, 124n2. *See also Cathleen ni Houlihan*; Gonne, Maud; Joyce, James: parodies *Cathleen ni Houlihan*
Catholicism, Irish; Catholic Church: associated by Joyce with the Terrible Mother, xv, 4, 21, 34, 35, 36, 37, 50, 58, 66-67, 72, 81, 122n22; opposition to Parnell, 38, 42, 44-48, 123-24n37
Celtic war goddess. *See* Morrigu
Circe, 59-61
Citizen, the: Irish chauvinist, 14, 52-53, 74, 78, 79-80
Civil War, Irish, v, 40, 80-81, 82-83, 99. *See also* "Troubles"
Cixous, Hélène, 47, 123-24n37
Clery, Emma, 34-35
Cohen, Bella. *See* Bella
Coleridge, S. T.: *Christabel*, 15; "Kubla Khan" and prefatory note, 23-24, 120n1
Collins, Ben L., 2-3, 116n6
Conroy, Gretta, 3, 34
Corpsechewer, xi, 37, 55, 59, 63, 66, 67, 81
Crab woman, vi, 63, 64, 125-26n16
Cuchulain, x, 8-9, 29-30, 86, 91, 92, 93, 117n20. *See also* Yeats: "Cuchulain Comforted" and *The Death of Cuchulain*
Cullingford, Elizabeth, 7, 117n19, 130n24
Curran, Sarah, 53, 54, 55, 124n7. *See also* Emmet, Robert
Cybele, 27, 61, 127n8

Dante. *See* Riordan, Mrs.
Davin (Nationalist friend of Stephen in *Portrait*), 12, 50, 51, 54, 57, 80, 124n4
Deane, Seamus, 99, 101, 122n29, 130n15
Dedalus, May (Stephen's mother): as ghoulish Terrible Mother, xi, 37, 51, 56, 58-59, 61-67, 68, 69, 73, 74, 75, 81, 94, 125n9; and Catholic Church, 34, 35, 36, 72; in Christmas dinner scene, 45, 47; as nourishing mother, 123n35
Dedalus, Simon (Stephen's father): in Christmas dinner scene, 43, 44-48

Index

Dedalus, Stephen: Joyce's alter ego, ix, xiv; confrontation with his mother's ghost, xi, 36, 37, 51, 56, 58–59, 61–69, 74, 81, 94; guilt regarding mother, 34, 58, 66, 67, 69, 123n35, 126n19; opposed to Nationalism, 34–35, 50–51, 57–58, 85; rebellion against Church, 34–35, 50, 66–67, 72; threatened by female figures, 44, 123n35, 124n5; in Christmas dinner scene, 45, 47; opposed to violence, 69–79, 81, 92, 94; as artist, 123n35, 123n37

Devouring Female, v, x–xiv, 14, 16–21, 33, 36–37, 41, 42, 43, 44, 47–48, 50–51, 52, 55–56, 61–69, 72, 73, 76–77, 79, 80–81, 84, 93, 95–96, 98–99, 101–2, 124n5; Cathleen ni Houlihan as, ix–x, xiv, 4, 7, 8, 14, 15, 16–17, 95, 118–19n41. *See also* Carrion crow; Corpsechewer; Crab woman; Morrigu; Sheela-na-gig; Spider; Terrible Mother

Dijkstra, Bram: *Idols of Perversity*, 20, 35, 115n12, 121n14

Donoghue, Denis, xvi, 3–4, 99, 101, 115n17

Easter Rising, 7, 8, 9, 13, 39, 40, 89, 91. *See also* "Troubles"

Egan, Kevin: Fenian dynamitard, 70–71

Eliot, T. S., xxi; "Little Gidding," 101; "The Love Song of J. Alfred Prufrock," 120n4

Emmet, Robert: Irish rebel, 52, 54, 90; execution of, 55, 124n7, 125n8; execution parodied by Joyce, 52, 53; in "Parnell's Funeral," 42; play *Robert Emmet*, 96, 130n17

Fenians, 43, 52, 55, 70–71, 76, 80, 84, 95, 127n36
Fin de siècle, xii, xiv, xv, 20, 21, 22, 36
Fitzgerald, Lord Edward, 5, 42, 90
Frazer, Sir James G., 41, 61; *The Golden Bough*, xii, 27, 61, 84, 125n14
Freud, Sigmund, 116n7; *Totem and Taboo*, 43, 47

Gay, Peter, 20, 120n49
Gillane, Michael (hero lured by Cathleen in Yeats's play), 5–7, 15–16, 80, 90, 104–12
Gonne, Maud: Yeats's composite beloved, muse, and femme fatale, x, xii, xiv, 4, 8, 17, 21, 27, 28, 33, 35, 118n38, 121n10; embodiment of Cathleen ni Houlihan, xii, xiv, 4, 71; plays title role in Yeats's play, xii, xiv, 4, 5, 11–12, 13, 15–16, 33, 58, 95, 96, 97; Irish revolutionary, xiii, 9, 13, 117n12, 118n38; Yeats offers his genius to, xiv, 4, 8, 13, 27, 94; and the Daughters of Erin, 4; and the 1798 centennial, 5; contrasted with Yeats, 10; Arthur Griffith infatuated with, 11, 118n28; prefers a propagandistic art, 12, 115n13, 117n25; her "mysterious eye," 15, 33, 95; as type of the Morrigu, 31, 33, 95, 123n36; *Dawn*, 117–18n25; in MacNeice's *Autumn Journal*, 49; in Joyce's *Ulysses*, 70–71; *A Servant of the Queen*, ii, 15, 118n37

—In Yeats's poetry: "No Second Troy," xii, 33; "He Wishes for the Cloths of Heaven," xiii, 57; "The Cap and Bells," 13–14, 21, 26, 27; "A Bronze Head," 21, 28, 31–34, 35, 37, 123n36; "Friends," 26, 35; "Among School Children," 31, 32, 33, 95–96; "The Secret Rose," 86

Gore-Booth, Eva, 13
Graves, Robert, x, 20–21, 28, 29; *The White Goddess*, 20–21, 28, 120n52; *The Greek Myths*, 121n11
Great Mother (positive aspects), x, 56, 58, 65, 77, 94, 119n47, 126n20; in the work of Yeats, x, xv, 18; in Joyce, xv, 18, 34, 116n7. *See also* Terrible Mother
Gregory, Lady Augusta, x, 4, 6, 13, 116–17n11, 118n35; *The Deliverer*, 38, 41
Griffith, Arthur, 10–11, 12, 117n12
Gwynn, Stephen, 9, 11–12, 15, 117n21

Hag of Beare, 17, 19, 119n44
Heaney, Seamus: "Sheelagh na Gig," ix, x, 20, 114n1; "Feeling into Words" (1974 lecture), 98, 99; "Kinship," 98; "Station Island," 100–101; "Exposure," 100, 131n1
Henke, Suzette, xv, 44, 46, 114n8, 115n14, 123n35, 125n9, 130n12
Homer, 14, 58, 59, 61, 64, 66
Howarth, Herbert, 39, 45, 122n28

Joyce, James, ii, v, ix, xi, xiv, xv, 18, 34–81, 100–101; and Parnell, ix, 17, 21, 38, 41, 43, 44–48; and Yeats, x, xii, 2, 20, 21, 22, 83, 85, 92, 94, 96; parodies *Cathleen ni Houlihan*, x, xiv, 2–4, 21–22, 56–57, 61, 66, 72–81, 116n7; and images of the Female, xi, xii, xv, 34, 35–37, 43–48, 51, 52–56, 56–69, 70–71, 113–14n1, 114n8, 115n14, 116n7, 120n53,

122n21, 122n22, 122n24, 123n35, 123n36, 124n5, 125n9, 126n19; and Irish Nationalism, ix, xiv, 3-4, 14, 34, 45-48, 50-81, 127n36; influenced by Blake, 18, 20, 69-71, 78-79, 128n43; opposed to violence, 4, 55, 78-79, 92, 127n36; as a ghost in Heaney's "Station Island," 100-101
Works
—Play: *Exiles*, 34
—Poetry: "The Death of Parnell" (in "Ivy Day in the Committee Room"), 38-45; "Gas from a Burner," 38-39, 122n27; "The Holy Office," 4, 41, 118n26; "Et Tu, Healy," 38
—Prose: "The Day of the Rabblement," 2; "The Dead," 2, 34, 116n7, 122n21; *Dubliners*, xiv, 2, 122n21, 122n27, 124n3; *Finnegans Wake*, xv, 3, 4, 18, 34, 53, 67, 79, 80-81; *Giacomo Joyce*, xii, 34, 35-37, 65, 122n23, 122n24; "Ivy Day in the Committee Room," 38, 45; "A Mother," 2-3, 4, 71, 116n6, 122n21; "A Portrait of the Artist," 41; *A Portrait of the Artist as a Young Man*, ix, xv, 12, 14, 18, 21, 35, 37, 43-48, 50-51, 57, 58, 67, 80, 94, 123n37; "The Shade of Parnell," 38-40; "The Sisters," 122n21; *Stephen Hero*, 34-35, 36, 41, 122n22, 126n24; "Two Gallants," 2, 57, 122n21. *See also* Ulysses
Joyce, May (Joyce's mother), 36, 65, 66. *See also* Dedalus, May
Jung, Carl Gustav, xi, xv, 18

Kali, x, xiii, 17, 19, 20, 29, 30, 92, 113n1, 119n44, 119n47. *See also* Terrible Mother; Zimmer, Heinrich
Kate Strong (parody of Cathleen ni Houlihan in *Finnegans Wake*), 3, 75
Kathleen (in Joyce's "A Mother"), 2, 4
Kathleen ni Hoolihan, Kathleen ni Houlihan. *See* Cathleen ni Houlihan
Keats, John: "Ode on Melancholy," xiv, 26; "La Belle Dame sans Merci," 17, 24, 119n41; "Lamia," 37; "Ode on a Grecian Urn," 43, 93, 130n13
Kenner, Hugh, 3, 4, 61-62, 80, 114n8, 116n6, 116n7, 118n33, 128n41
King Billy (pantomime William of Orange), v, xvii, 97, 98, 99, 102
Kinsley, David R., 17, 19, 119n44, 119n47

Kolodny, Annette, xv-xvi, 115n16

Lasch, Christopher, 19, 120n49
Leanhaun Shee (Gaelic Muse), x, xii, xiv, 8, 15, 20, 26, 28. *See also* Terrible Mother
Lyons, F. S. L., 39, 40, 122n29, 122n30

MacNeice, Louis: *Autumn Journal*, 3, 49-50
MacNeill, Eoin, 1, 90-91, 130n9
Maeve, xiv, 29-30
Mahaffey, Vicki, 37, 122n24
Mallarmé, Stéphane: *Hérodiade*, 20, 29, 115n10, 121n13
Mangan, James Clarence: "Kathaleen-ny-Houlahan," 11, 15, 115n13, 118n28
Markiewicz, Countess Constance, ix-x, 13, 95-96, 118n34
Mathers, MacGregor, 87-88
Mercier, Vivian, 113-14n1, 114n5
Moore, Thomas: "She Is Far from the Land," 52, 53; "Where Is the Slave?," 53
Morrigu, the (Celtic war goddess), x-xi, xii, 8, 10, 14, 15, 28, 30, 31, 33, 76-77, 79, 80, 91, 95, 114n5, 121n16, 123n36
Mulligan, Buck (in *Ulysses*), 56-57, 59, 62, 64, 66, 75, 77, 79

Neumann, Erich, x, xv, 18-19, 27, 37, 51, 93; *The Great Mother*, 18-19, 114n2, 114n5, 114n6, 119n45, 124n6, 130n14; *Origin and History of Consciousness*, 18, 27, 119n45, 121n9, 124n6
Nietzsche, Friedrich, 69, 87, 121n17
Northern Ireland, v, xvi-xvii, 33, 79, 98, 99, 100, 102, 115n18. *See also* "Troubles"
Nothung (Wagnerian sword), 37, 64, 67-69, 72, 79, 126-27n25

O'Brien, Conor Cruise, xvi, 40, 97, 99, 100, 101; *States of Ireland*, 100, 123n32, 130n19, 131n1
O'Brien, Darcy, xi, 114n8
O'Brien, Maire Cruise, 1-2, 19, 116n3, 119n44, 119n48
O'Casey, Sean, 16, 91, 118n28, 127-28n40, 137n40
O'Connor, Rory, 80-81

Old Gummy Granny (pantomime Cath-

leen ni Houlihan in *Ulysses*), 50, 51, 64, 66, 68, 72–81, 124n2
Old milkwoman (parody of Cathleen ni Houlihan in *Ulysses*), 56–58, 64, 72–73
"Old sow that eats her farrow," ix, xi, 18, 41, 44, 50, 51, 72, 73, 76–77, 81, 85–86, 95, 121n7, 124n3, 124n5. *See also* Sow image
Orpheus, xiii, 28, 121n11
O'Shea, Katherine, 40, 42, 46
O'Shea, William, 40–41

Parnell, Charles Stewart, v, 37–48; central figure in Irish political mythology, ix, 17, 38–40; scapegoat hero, ix, 38, 55, 59, 96; "hounded" to his grave, 40, 41, 45, 48, 59, 91; and Yeats, ix, 17, 38, 39–40; and Joyce, ix, 17, 21, 38, 41; in "Parnell's Funeral," 41–43; in the Christmas dinner scene in *Portrait*, 43, 44–48, 59, 61, 67
Pearse, Padraic: and the cult of blood sacrifice, ii, 7, 9, 90, 96, 130n18; Irish patriot, 7, 14–15; and the cult of Cuchulain, 8–9; in "The Statues," 9; in "Three Songs to the One Burden," 9; in "The Rose Tree," 96
Pope, Alexander: "The First Satire of the Second Book of Horace Imitated," 79, 127n37
Popper, Amalia, 35
Pound, Ezra, 28, 35

Riordan, Mrs. (Dante): destructive woman of *Portrait*, 37, 43, 44–48, 50; opposed to Parnell, 43, 44–48, 124n38; spokeswoman of church, 45–48; pious crone in *Ulysses*, 52–53
Roman Catholicism. *See* Catholicism
"Romantic Ireland," xvi, 3, 71, 90
Rowan, Bertha (in *Exiles*), 34, 122n24
Ross, Anne, 28, 114n5, 118n28, 121n12
Russell, George (AE), 2, 116n4

Salome. See Wilde, Oscar
Salome, xii, xiii, 20, 26, 29, 92, 101, 114n10, 120n4
Scott, Bonnie Kime, xv, 115n15, 116n7, 122n22, 123n35, 124n5
Shakespeare, William: *Hamlet*, 32, 50, 73, 121n18, 124–25n7; *King Lear*, 32, 121n19; *Macbeth*, 78; Sonnets, 26, 32, 82, 98
Shan Van Vocht, 1, 7, 57, 78, 80, 90–91

Shaw, George Bernard, 13; *John Bull's Other Island*, 1, 116n2, 118n35
Sheela-na-gig, x, xi, xii, 19, 55, 95, 113–14n1, 114n5. *See also* Devouring Female; Terrible Mother
Sheila, my own (in *Ulysses*), 51, 54–56, 57, 77
Shiublaigh, Máire nic, 4, 117n12, 118n35
Sinn Fein: movement, 10, 117n12; exclamation, 53
Social Democratic Labour party, v
Sow-goddess. *See* Sow image
Sow image, 51, 59–61, 84, 85–86, 87. *See also* "Old sow that eats her farrow"
Spider (aspect of Devouring Female), xi
Stalker, John, 115n18
Strong, L. A. G., 16, 118n39
Swinburne, Algernon Charles, 59, 64; "The Oblation," 57
Synge, John Millington, 10, 11, 12, 91; *The Playboy of the Western World*, 10, 11; *The Shadow of the Glen*, 11, 12, 118n25

Terrible Mother (negative aspect of the Great Mother), v, ix, x–xiii, 4, 15–21, 26–30, 33, 34, 36–37, 41, 42, 44, 45, 46, 48, 58–69, 71–72, 73, 76, 77, 80, 81, 84–85, 93–94, 95–96, 98–99, 101–2. *See also* Circe, Devouring Female, Kali, Leanhaun Shee, Sheela-na-gig
Tone, Wolfe, 5, 15, 90; in "Parnell's Funeral," 42; in *Portrait*, 50, 55; in *Ulysses*, 52, 73
"Troubles," Irish, 13, 16, 17, 39, 40, 80–81, 91, 101, 102. *See also* Civil War, Irish; Easter Rising; Northern Ireland

Ulysses, ii, ix, xi, xiv, xv, 3, 14, 18, 34, 37, 44, 80, 81, 83, 113n1, 114n8, 120n53, 123n35
—Individual episodes: "Calypso," 123n36; "Circe," 20, 36, 37, 50, 51, 56, 59–69, 71–79, 123n36, 125n8; "Cyclops," ii, 14, 52–56, 64, 74, 79–80; "Eumaeus," 80; "Lotus-Eaters," 124n37; "Nestor," 69–70; "Oxen of the Sun," 64–65, 77; "Penelope," xi, xv, 37; "Proteus," 58, 70–71; "Scylla and Charybdis," 73, 125n7; "Telemachus," 51, 56–59, 64, 72, 100

Wagner, Richard, 37, 72, 87; *The Ring of the Nibelung*, 68–69, 126–27n25. *See also* Nothung

Watts, Isaac, 44, 123n34
Webster, Brenda, 26, 120n5
White Goddess, x, xii, 20–21, 120n53
Wilde, Oscar, v, 20, 115n10; *Salome*, xii, xiii, 28, 36
Wordsworth, William, 85, 129n4

Yeats, William Butler; poet-muse relationship to Maud Gonne, v, xiv, xii-xiv, 4, 8, 13, 27, 28, 94; and Irish political violence, v, xiv, 14, 22, 79, 80, 82–83, 84, 86–89, 91–97, 99, 101–2; and Parnell, ix, 17, 38, 39–40, 41–43; ambivalence toward *Cathleen ni Houlihan*, x, xiv, 4, 8–10, 97; images of the Female, xi, xiii, 20–21, 23–33, 101–2; meeting with Joyce, 2; comments on *Cathleen ni Houlihan*, 5, 8, 9, 12–13, 14, 116–17n11; influenced by Blake, 18, 20, 42–43, 69; comments on "The Cap and Bells," 23–24, 27; comments on Christmas dinner scene in *Portrait*, 43; as ghost in Eliot's "Little Gidding," 101

Works

—Plays: *The Death of Cuchulain*, x, 17, 21, 29–30, 33; *A Full Moon in March*, xii, 17, 21, 28–29; *The King of the Great Clock Tower*, xii, 17, 21, 28–29; *The Land of Heart's Desire*, 117n17; *Purgatory*, 121n17; *The Shadowy Waters*, 121n13. See also *Cathleen ni Houlihan*

—Poems: "Among School Children," 31–33, 37, 96, 121n17; "The Black Tower," 92, 130n11; "A Bronze Head," 21, 28, 31–33, 34, 35, 95, 122n20, 123n36; "The Cap and Bells," xiii-xiv, 13–14, 21, 22, 23–28, 60, 83, 94, 115n11; "Church and State," 47; "The Circus Animals' Desertion," 3, 95, 116n9; "Coole Park, 1929," 92; Crazy Jane sequence, xv; "Cuchulain Comforted," 30, 83, 92, 93, 101; "The Death of the Hare," 93; "A Dialogue of Self and Soul," 121n17; "Easter 1916," ii, 7, 8, 13, 89–90; "Friends," 26, 35, 95; "He Gives his Beloved certain Rhymes," xiii; "He Mourns for the Change that has come upon Him and his Beloved, and longs for the End of the World," 85; "He Wishes for the Cloths of Heaven," xiii, 57, 60, 115n11; "Her Vision in the Wood," 85; "His Dream," 14, 27; *The Island of Statues*, 21; "I am of Ireland," 91; "In Memory of Eva Gore-Booth and Con Markiewicz," 13, 95–96; "Lapis Lazuli," 121n19; "Leda and the Swan," 121n14; "The Man and the Echo," xiv, 9, 10, 13, 82, 92–93; *A Man Young and Old*, 93; *Meditations in Time of Civil War*, 82–83, 95, 98, 99; "Mourn—and then Onward!," 38; "Nineteen Hundred and Nineteen," 82, 101–2; "No Second Troy," 33; "On a Political Prisoner," 118n34; "Parnell's Funeral," 17, 38, 41–43, 123n33; "The People," 10, 117n24; "A Prayer for My Daughter," 32, 95; "Red Hanrahan's Song about Ireland," xiv, 115n13; "Remorse for Intemperate Speech," 96; "The Rose Tree," 96; "The Secret Rose," 86; "The Seeker," 21; "September 1913," xvi, 7, 90; "Sixteen Dead Men," 97; "Solomon and the Witch," xi; "The Song of Wandering Aengus," 35; "Three Songs to the One Burden," 9; "The Statues," 9, 117n20; "To a Shade," 38; "To Ireland in the Coming Times," 10–11; "Two Songs from a Play," 81, 82; "The Two Titans," 21; "Vacillation," 61; "The Valley of the Black Pig," xi, 10, 22, 83–89, 92, 93, 94, 129n3, 129n4; "Who Goes with Fergus?," 58, 66; *The Wind Among the Reeds*, xii-xiii, 22, 23, 84–86, 88, 92, 121n7; *A Woman Young and Old*, xv

—Prose: "The Adoration of the Magi," 34; "The Binding of the Hair," xiii; *The Celtic Twilight*, 87; *Fairy and Folk Tales of the Irish Peasantry*, x; "Irish Fairies, Ghosts, Witches, etc.," 114n4; "Kathleen-ny-Houlihan," xii, xiii; *On the Boiler*, 10; *Samhain* articles, 2, 4, 8, 12, 13, 14; *The Secret Rose*, xii, xiii; "The Stirring of the Bones," v; *A Vision*, 10, 42

Zimmer, Heinrich, 19, 26, 120n47, 121n14

Permissions

I would like, once again, to thank A. P. Watt Ltd. on behalf of Anne Yeats and Michael B. Yeats, Macmillan Publishing Company, Inc., New York, and Macmillan London Ltd. for permission to quote from the following works of William Butler Yeats: *Autobiographies,* © 1963, renewed by Bertha Georgie Yeats; *Essays and Introductions,* © 1961 by Mrs. W. B. Yeats; *Explorations,* © 1962 by Mrs. W. B. Yeats; *The Letters of W. B. Yeats,* edited by Allan Wade, © 1954 by Anne Butler Yeats; *Mythologies,* © Mrs. W. B. Yeats; *A Vision,* © renewed 1965 by Bertha Georgie Yeats and Anne Butler Yeats; *The Variorum Edition of the Poems of W. B. Yeats,* edited by Peter Allt and Russell K. Alspach, © 1957; and *The Variorum Edition of the Plays of W. B. Yeats,* edited by Russell K. Alspach and Bertha Georgie Yeats, copyright © 1965 Macmillan & Co. Ltd.

For permission to quote from *Memoirs,* edited by Denis Donoghue, © 1972 by Michael B. Yeats and Anne Yeats, I am grateful to A. P. Watt Ltd.

Grateful acknowledgment is given for permission to use the following copyright material of James Joyce:

From *The Critical Writings of James Joyce,* edited by Ellsworth Mason and Richard Ellmann. Copyright © by Harriet Weaver and F. Lionel Monro, administrators of the Estate of James Joyce. Copyright renewed © 1987 by F. Lionel Monro. All rights reserved. Reprinted by permission of Viking Penguin, Inc., Faber and Faber Ltd., and The Society of Authors as the literary representative of the Estate of James Joyce.

From *Dubliners* by James Joyce. Copyright 1916 by B. W. Huebsch. Definitive text Copyright © 1967 by the Estate of James Joyce. All rights reserved. Reprinted by permission of Viking Penguin, Inc., the Executors of the James Joyce Estate, Jonathan Cape Ltd., and The Society of Authors as the literary representative of the Estate of James Joyce.

From *Finnegans Wake* by James Joyce. Copyright 1939 by James Joyce. Copyright renewed © 1967 by George Joyce and Lucia Joyce. All rights reserved. Reprinted by permission of Viking Penguin, Inc., and The Society of Authors as the literary representative of the Estate of James Joyce.

From *Giacomo Joyce* by James Joyce. Copyright © 1959, 1967, 1968 by F. Lionel Monro, Administrator of the Estate of James Joyce. All rights reserved. Reprinted by permission of Viking Penguin, Inc., and The Society of Authors as the literary representative of the Estate of James Joyce.

From *Letters of James Joyce,* Volumes II and III, edited by Richard Ellmann. Copyright © 1966 by F. Lionel Monro, Administrator of the Estate of James Joyce. All rights reserved. Reprinted by permission of Viking Penguin, Inc., Faber and Faber Ltd., and The Society of Authors as the literary representative of the Estate of James Joyce.

From *A Portrait of the Artist as a Young Man* by James Joyce. Copyright 1916 by B. W. Huebsch. Copyright renewed 1944 by Nora Joyce. Definitive text Copyright © 1964 by the Estate of James Joyce. All rights reserved. Reprinted by permission of Viking Penguin, Inc., the Executors of the James Joyce Estate, Jonathan Cape Ltd., and The Society of Authors as the literary representative of the Estate of James Joyce.

From *Stephen Hero* by James Joyce. Reprinted by permission of the Executors of the James Joyce Estate, Jonathan Cape Ltd., and The Society of Authors as the literary representative of the Estate of James Joyce.

From *Ulysses: The Corrected Text* by James Joyce. Copyright © 1986 by Random House, Inc. All rights reserved. Reprinted by permission of Random House, Inc., The Bodley Head Ltd., and the Society of Authors as the literary representative of the Estate of James Joyce.

PR 8755
.K 43
1988   Keane

TERRIBLE BEAUTY

D'Youville College Library
320 Porter Avenue
Buffalo, New York   14201